Understanding Society through Popular Music

"*Understanding Society through Popular Music* deserves a sociological 'high five' for a job well done. This revised edition connects the importance of sociology to 'everyday life' even further by focusing on a subject important to us all—music! By applying a sociological lens to popular forms of music at the individual and group level, this book delivers up important theories in our discipline but does so with an engaging and delightful writing style. From our individual experience and cultural understanding of music to studies of music scenes, subcultures, and institutions, students will see how music influences and is influenced by key sociological concepts such as: *social identity*, *deviance*, *race*, *class*, *gender*, *technology*, *institutions* (e.g., *family and religion*), *globalization*, *power,* and *politics*. An excellent teaching tool, this book doesn't just explain the significance of music in our lives, it reminds us of the importance of sociology for all areas of social life. This book is an excellent text or supplemental text for undergraduates and a research primer for those who study music from a variety of other disciplines."

—*Lori Holyfield, Sociology and Criminal Justice, University of Arkansas*

Written for Introductory Sociology and Sociology of Popular Music courses, the second edition of *Understanding Society through Popular Music* uses popular music to illustrate fundamental social institutions, theories, sociological concepts, and processes. The authors use music, a social phenomenon of great interest, to draw students in and bring life to their study of sociology. The new edition has been updated with cutting-edge thinking on, and current examples of, subcultures, politics, and technology.

Joseph A. Kotarba is Professor of Sociology and Director of the Center for Social Inquiry at Texas State University-San Marcos. He received his doctorate from the University of California at San Diego. Dr. Kotarba's scholarly focus is the sociology of everyday life, and he works primarily in the areas of culture, health, qualitative methods, and existential social theory. Dr. Kotarba is the author or editor of eight books, and 95 articles and book chapters. His most recent book is *Baby Boomer Rock'n'Roll Fans: The Music Never Ends* (Scarecrow Press, 2013).

Bryce Merrill currently works at the Western States Arts Federation, a research, technology, and cultural policy organization, and has been instrumental in developing the nation's first performing arts grant program for independent musicians, the Independent Music on Tour (IMTour) program. His applied research now examines the working lives of touring independent musicians in the Western United States. He is also a fellow at the Center for Social Inquiry at Texas State University-San Marcos.

J. Patrick Williams is a sociologist who has studied and taught various aspects of media culture, pop culture, and subculture, with a particular focus on how they relate to young people. He is the author of *Subcultural Theory: Traditions and Concepts* (Polity, 2011) and the editor of *Authenticity in Culture, Self and Society* (Ashgate, 2009), *The Players' Realm: Studies on the Culture of Video Games and Gaming* (McFarland, 2007), and *Gaming as Culture: Essays in Social Reality, Identity and Experience in Fantasy Games* (McFarland, 2006). He works at Nanyang Technological University in Singapore.

Phillip Vannini is Professor of Communication & Culture at Royal Roads University in Victoria, BC, and Canada Research Chair in Innovative Learning and Public Ethnography. He is author/editor of nine books, including the recent *Ferry Tales: Mobility, Place, and Time on Canada's West Coast* and *The Senses in Self, Society, and Culture*. He is also editor of the Routledge series in innovative ethnographies.

Understanding Society through Popular Music

Second Edition

Joseph A. Kotarba
Bryce Merrill
J. Patrick Williams
Phillip Vannini

 Routledge
Taylor & Francis Group

NEW YORK AND LONDON

Please visit the book's companion website at
www.routledge.com/cw/kotarba

This edition published 2013
by Routledge
711 Third Avenue, New York, NY 10017

Simultaneously published in the UK
by Routledge
2 Park Square, Milton Park, Abingdon, Oxon OX14 4RN

Routledge is an imprint of the Taylor & Francis Group, an informa business

First edition published 2008 by Routledge

Library of Congress Cataloging in Publication Data
Kotarba, Joseph A.
Understanding society through popular music / Joseph A. Kotarba, Bryce Merrill, J. Patrick
Williams, Phillip Vannini. — 2nd ed.
  p. cm.
  Includes bibliographical references and index.
  1. Popular music—Social aspects. I. Merrill, Bryce. II. Williams, J. Patrick, 1970- III. Vannini,
Phillip. IV. Title.
  ML3918.P67K67 2013
  306.4'8424—dc23
  2012030134

ISBN: 978–0–415–64194–4 (hbk)
ISBN: 978–0–415–64195–1 (pbk)
ISBN: 978–0–203–07681–1 (ebk)

Typeset in Adobe Caslon and Copperplate
by RefineCatch Limited, Bungay, Suffolk

Printed and bound in the United States of America
by Edwards Brothers, Inc.

CONTENTS

ACKNOWLEDGMENTS

We would like to thank the following reviewers for their helpful feedback:

Tammy Anderson, University of Delaware
Victor P. Corona, Columbia University
Mark Pedelty, University of Minnesota
John Siqueiros, University of Texas, El Paso
Scott Weiss, St. Francis College

PREFACE

When we began thinking and talking about revising our successful textbook *Understanding Society through Popular Music*, Phillip and I were quite aware of the main lesson we learned from the first edition: the materials and examples we culled from the world of popular music became out-of-date very quickly. To some degree, this is an unavoidable problem. Unlike the majority of textbooks in the field that take an historical perspective on popular music, we felt the classic sociological obligation to write about current trends and events. Well, our students were our greatest critics in this regard. I recall lecturing in class one day about gender issues in popular music when the topic of Avril Lavigne came up. I thought I was on top of things when I smugly questioned whether getting married would shatter Avril's in-your-face punk image, when a number of students in unison laughed and said that Avril was not only divorced but on the verge of getting her own scent and designer clothing line. Does this mean I must regularly consult *Entertainment Tonight* to stay on top of events in the world of popular music?

I guess the next logical question is: What has changed and what has remained the same in the world of popular music since our first edition was published in 2009? Well, as one would expect, many things are new in popular music, but sometimes it seems like little has changed. Digital music and earbuds are pandemic, as we increasingly listen to recorded and radio music alone. Yet concert attendance, especially performed by older, established groups, continues to grow. The varieties of dance and hip-hop styles continue to expand—dubstep, for example—yet Jay-Z and Beyoncé are clearly the (conservative) first family of pop music. We now archive our personal music collections in the clouds, but the music per se does not seem all that different. We have Lady Gaga, Katy Perry, and Nicki Minaj—are they that much different from Madonna and Mary J. Blige?

What has changed, and continues to change, is the audience for all this music. There seems to always be a market for a Taylor Swift or a Justin Bieber; as we continue to replenish the population, we will have a constant influx of pre-adolescent kids who are anxious to learn about themselves, others, relationships, and feelings. So that, as is convenient for we sociologists, there is constant social change impacting the world of popular music. Baby boomers have not changed their tastes in music much from the 1960s and 1970s, but their ability and desire to keep purchasing music in various formats has not slowed down much over the years.

Popular music is ubiquitous; it truly serves as the soundtrack of our everyday lives. Indeed, it seems as if a tune is always accompanying our daily rhythms: from the wake-up call through our alarm radio and our favorite morning tunes on the ride to work and school, to the beats of campus life or office cubicle culture, and from the gas pumps to the supermarket and health club—not to mention music television, ubiquitous MP3 players, movie scores, and the very sounds and melodies of the spaces that surround us, from the chirping of sparrows to the crashing of waves. Music is everywhere. There is a sonorous dimension for everything—for every purpose, every group of listeners, every mood, and every occasion. And, everywhere we listen, music comes to us (or from us) as a product: the product of technological relations which resulted in its creation and distribution; the product of geographic dimensions which shape trends, availability, and connection to space and place; the product of historical periods which shape fashions, costs, expectations, and considerations on what is appropriate or not appropriate; the product of social classes, genders, age groups, and ethnicities, each with their relation to preferred forms of musical styles; as well as the product of familial, religious, and biographic particulars which influence the tunes that strike a chord with our heart and our sense of self. Indeed, ask yourself what you did when we asked you to turn some music on. Did you look for your iTunes library? Scrambled to dig out your latest favorite CD? Rolled the dial to find your favorite radio station? Turned on MTV, VH1, CMT, or BET? Whatever you did, and whatever we all do, music is not just the product of harmony, melody, and rhythm relations, but perhaps more importantly a *social* product. Many people are involved with creation of our musical experiences, as well as our music per se.

Our purpose and approach mark an important difference between our book and other texts. This concise textbook is organized in terms of conventional sociological topics and is oriented to the needs of two precisely defined audiences. The first audience is made up of undergraduate students of introductory sociology, for which the textbook is meant as a supplemental text. Each chapter is tied to a traditional topic in introductory sociology. We use popular music to illustrate fundamental social institutions, theories, sociological concepts, and processes, and we are the first in doing so in the hope of drawing our readers into the fascinating and ever-relevant world of sociology. We write with confidence that reading and thinking about popular music will open up class discussions, debate, and reflection on the power of sociological study and the importance of a sociological imagination. The second audience is made up of students of courses in the sociology of popular music. The uniqueness of our book for that audience comes from our placing popular music within the complex and ever-changing context of everyday life. We help students *see* popular music through a distinctively sociological lens. We hope that both audiences benefit from our accessible language, our use of diverse and contemporary data from the world of popular music and popular culture, and our personable tone.

Popular music provides the soundtrack for everyday life for many people, while providing practical meanings for making sense of everyday life. Accordingly, the textbook is organized to accomplish two instructional objectives. First, we show how popular music affects all major social institutions. Second, we show how popular music can be used to illustrate fundamental sociological theories and concepts. In other words, we are using a social phenomenon of great interest to students to draw them in, to bring life to their/your study of sociology.

This textbook is derived both from our personal interests in music, as well as our teaching and scholarly research on popular music.

The present text evolved from a previous collaboration. In 2006, Phillip and I co-edited a special issue of the sociological journal *Symbolic Interaction*. The topic was popular music, and the contributions reflected both the enthusiasm and the sophistication of the study of popular music through an interactionist perspective. Papers included discussions of the jazz music scene; grotesque rock music, such as the Marilyn Manson phenomenon; and the work of the hip-hop DJ. This work produced the idea—leading to the design of this text—that the sociology of popular music had evolved to the point where it could, and should, make an impact on the ways we understand and teach sociology in general. For the revised edition of our text, Phillip and I decided to enlist the assistance of two scholars of everyday life, Patrick and Bryce. They have enriched and enlivened the text with cutting-edge thinking on, and current examples of, subcultures, politics, and technology.

I have taught undergraduate and graduate courses in the sociology of popular music at the University of Houston for 20 years, and currently at Texas State University-San Marcos. I am a scholar in the field of the sociology of everyday life and popular music. I have recently established and continue to curate an online community for the interactionist study of music and society, which can be accessed at www.symbolicinteraction.org. I have conducted research and published essays on popular music topics including the postmodernization of rock music, as exemplified by the popularity of Metallica, and punk, heavy metal, and Christian heavy metal club scenes. I recently collaborated on a team project, funded by the U.S. National Institute on Drug Abuse, examining the multi-faceted use of Internet-based support groups by rave party, designer drug users. While serving as Chair at the University of Houston, I organized a team of graduate students to conduct a comprehensive ethnographic study of the various Latino music scenes in Houston, funded by the Joseph Werlin Foundation. My most recent book on popular music is *Baby Boomer Rock'n'Roll Fans: The Music Never Ends*, published by Scarecrow Press in 2013a. As founder of the Center for Social Inquiry at Texas State University, I am directing research on the role rap music is playing in the North African and Middle Eastern *check this out.*

resistance movements, and Americana music, among other topics. I enjoy all styles of popular music, new and old: music I share with my children (e.g., Chopin and Radiohead), and music I share with my wife, Polly (e.g., Sting and Paul McCartney).

One summer in the mid-1990s, Bryce Merrill rode in the back of a pick-up truck with four other band mates from Pensacola, Florida, to New Orleans to play a punk show. Upon arrival, the club owner looked at the band and asked, "You boys have your own sound, right?" Bryce and his band responded, "Hell yeah, we do. Nobody sounds like us!" But the club owner wasn't asking if Bryce's band had a novel sound. He wanted to know if they'd brought a PA with them, because the club didn't have one. They stayed at the club about as long as Bryce's career as an aspiring musician lasted, which is to say not long at all. A failed musician, he was reborn many years later as a sociologist. (Sociology has been famously derided as being obsessed with "nuts, sluts, and perverts," so the transition from punk to sociologist always made a lot of sense to Bryce.) He has since published on topics ranging from home music recording to music's relationship to the brain. Bryce currently works at the Western States Arts Federation, a research, technology, and cultural policy organization, and has been instrumental in developing the nation's first performing arts grant program for independent musicians, the Independent Music on Tour (IMTour) program. His applied research now examines the working lives of touring independent musicians in the Western United States. He is also a fellow at the Center for Social Inquiry at Texas State University-San Marcos.

Him too

Patrick Williams teaches and conducts research in culture and media. In addition, he works in the area of youth culture and is particularly interested in the experiences of participating in youth subcultures, many of which are rooted in music. Ironically, Patrick's work has partly functioned as a critique of the assumptions many people make about the significance of music in subcultural experience. Studying the straight-edge subculture in the early 2000s, he found that music was only one of several different media channels through which young people were attracted to music subcultures. Nevertheless, his work has not rejected the importance of music, but rather sought to clarify its relevance versus other media. Patrick's interest in straight edge came

youth subcultures

"If somebody likes it, it's good"

out of his own participation in the subculture, having been introduced to it via punk bands like Minor Threat and Seven Seconds in the mid-1980s. By the end of the decade he had begun an amateur career as a drummer and crossed over from hardcore punk and straight-edge music to extreme metal in the early 1990s. For a decade he played in death metal bands and in general has long been a fan of "unpopular" music. We put the word "unpopular" in quotations to let the reader know that we do not easily buy into categories such as popular and unpopular. As we will discuss in the Introduction, such categories are useful for people, though not real in an objective sense. One of the ways Patrick has attempted to expand students' experiences with various music genres is through study-abroad trips during the summer months, in which he has led groups to various music festivals across Europe, from world-class jazz festivals in Switzerland and heavy metal concerts in Romania to tiny, multi-ethnic folk festivals in Serbia—with lots of stops in between.

Like Patrick, Phillip Vannini teaches popular music in relation to cultural theory, media, and cultural studies. A sociologist by training and a communication and cultural studies scholar by vocation, he has examined a range of cultural phenomena, ranging from the value of authenticity in music, to cultural representations of the popular self and youth culture. His theoretical focus in terms of popular music is on developing models for the practical ways people use music in everyday life. One of his most recent pieces is the application of the logic of music to understanding the logic of social interaction. He has also published essays on Avril Lavigne, Britney Spears, the indie-rock produced by Constellation Records, and the genre of teen pop. Phillip is very picky about his music. He loves progressive hardcore punk, space rock, grunge (yes, still), and music with roots in his local beloved environment of Vancouver Island, British Columbia.

Although we work within our own particular theoretical styles, ranging from symbolic interactionism to social constructivism, we are all students of what we call *everyday life*. That means that we study, teach, and write about the ways people deal with practical problems in very practical ways. The "stuff" that we observe and use as data are *social meanings* (Kotarba 2002b; Vannini 2008); that is, the rules, values, *like this phrase*

rituals, customs, understandings, and experiences that people use on a daily basis to make sense of the world in which they live. Therefore, the topics we choose to examine in our work and to discuss in this text are topics that are important to the people for whom popular music is a key source of meaning for their lives.

The term "ethnographic tourism" (Kotarba 2013a) pretty much summarizes the way we study popular music in everyday life. Our work is ethnographic to the degree that it attempts to describe popular music in terms of the natural situations in which it occurs, and in terms of the language, feelings, and perceptions of the individuals who experience it. When the researcher assumes that the phenomenon in question is everywhere, then he or she should act like—pretend to be—a stranger or tourist in a foreign land. Indeed the researcher should act like a foreigner in one's own land in order to *observe* the phenomenon that was previously ignored or taken for granted by both researchers and members of the culture at large. The world of everyday life and popular music fits this scenario well. Our primary research strategy involves observation of ordinary, everyday life activities of ordinary people, musical performances, personas, texts, rituals, and music-related objects. And we hope to have some fun while doing this, too, not unlike a tourist would.

Cool

In assembling the second edition, we have kept what we believe, and the reviewers and our students have told us, are the most valuable and sociologically interesting features of the first edition. We have updated that material, and have added new topics to reflect the increasingly complex world of popular music, but also to reflect areas of intellectual growth in the sociology of popular music. Briefly, our Introduction and nine chapters are as follows.

The Introduction presents a brief discussion of the four major theoretical paradigms in sociology, with examples of how each approaches the study of popular music. In addition, the varieties of the sociologies of everyday life—symbolic interactionism, dramaturgy, phenomenology/ethnomethodology, social constructivism, existential sociology, and postmodernism—are presented, the theoretical perspectives used by the authors of this text in their own research.

Chapter 1, on interaction, is new to our book. Social interaction is the fundamental feature of social life, especially as seen by everyday life *is popular music represent a social problem*

sociologists. We present two contrasting examples of interaction to illustrate its importance. The first is a discussion of internal interaction, specifically, the phenomenological-existential process by which we experience "catchy" pop songs. The second is a discussion of group-level interaction, specifically the importance of the *scene* in the experience of popular music.

Good!

Chapter 2, on families, focuses on the impact popular music has on this venerable social institution. We examine the way certain moral entrepreneurs have tried to define popular music, rock'n'roll in particular, as a social problem. After conceptualizing popular music as a feature of children's culture, we present a recent example of the social construction of (music) evil: the banning of Katy Perry from *Sesame Street*.

Chapter 3, on self and the life course, now contains an enhanced discussion of the key concept of the *self* in everyday life sociology, including the relationship and contrast between *self* and *identity*. Popular music supports a range of adult self-experiences we conceptualize as the *e-self, self as lover, self as parent-self,* and, increasingly among baby boomers, the *self as grandparent*. Popular music provides the opportunity for growth during middle age and beyond.

Awesome!

Chapter 4 is a complete rewriting and expansion of the discussion of deviance in the first edition. We go into greater detail on the labeling perspective on deviance—a cornerstone of the constructivist perspective on deviance—and the specific process by which some music comes to be defined as (un)popular, immoral, and so forth. The concept of *sub-culture* is a powerful tool to examine political resistance among youth.

Chapter 5, on religion, is new. We discuss the complex relationship between popular music and religion, especially in terms of how, increasingly, religious music reflects the musical styles and marketing strategies of secular popular music. We explore five different ways popular music and religion relate in everyday life.

Chapter 6, on politics, explores some of the key sociological concepts in the area, with a bit of a critical take. We present a more developed discussion of Constellation Records as an example of a progressive, albeit small, force in the record industry. Our best example of the unfortunate use of popular music to gain unfair political ends is the recently resolved case of the "West Memphis Three."

Chapter 7, on gender, race, and class, explores these three key variables in sociological analysis of music. Additions to this chapter include an extended discussion of the social construction of gender in popular music, not only among female stars but also among male performers, such as everyone's favorite—Justin Bieber.

Chapter 8, on technology, is a new, exciting, and timely addition to our book. We examine the intricate ways in which music and technology make each other possible. We use the term "technoculture" to explain the complex interconnections between technology as things, symbols, and practices. All sorts of activities that involve music—from bike riding to memory making and Christmas shopping—are influenced by technology.

Chapter 9 describe the process of globalization and social change taking place throughout the world. Globalization refers to the multidirectional networking of culture(s) that allows for, and in fact encourages, creative cultural experiences around the world. We present examples from Phillip's visit to Nepal, my research in Poland, and other ways popular music serves as a medium for that networking.

We did not work alone on this book. We enlisted the assistance of students in our undergraduate and graduate courses in the sociology of popular music, as well as courses in mass media and popular culture studies. These students not only help us learn about other people's musical experiences, share their rich musical experiences with us, and to further reflect on our tastes and ideas, but also help us stay abreast of changing styles, artists, music performance activities, and technology. We also make good use of data or information derived from observations and reflections on our musical experiences as well as those of our families—all rock'n'roll fans. We also benefited from the gracious help of our editor at Routledge, Steve Rutter, and our reviewers, who helped us to clarify our ideas, stay on task, and organize our thoughts. Just like music, a book, too, is a collective social product.

Joe Kotarba
San Marcos, Texas
November 7, 2012

INTRODUCTION

THE SOCIOLOGY OF POPULAR MUSIC

In March 2010, Joe Kotarba's daughter, Jessie, got married in New Orleans, LA. It was a beautiful wedding on a beautiful day. The actual ceremony took place in Audubon Park in the historic Garden District. The reception was also in the park, hosted down the candlelit path in the elegant Tea Room.

Among all the neat things taking place that day, Joe can recall the important role music played in the festivities. Perhaps that is because he loves music, or because he studies music as a sociologist, or because everything about his only and favorite daughter's wedding was unforgettable. In any event, the memories are clear. The string quartet performed the instrumental "Hope on Board" by Tom Petty and the Heartbreakers as the guests were escorted to their seats. As the wedding party and family made their entrances the quartet performed the traditional Bach "Air on G String" and "Arioso." As Joe escorted Jessie down the aisle, the quartet played Schubert's classical version of the "Ave Maria." (Joe was in tears at this point.) The quartet performed "Hymne" by Vangelis during the flower exchange honoring the mothers. At the conclusion of the ceremony, the quartet played Taylor Swift's "Love Story" for the recessional as the bride and groom walked back down the aisle to the applause of the loving crowd. The quartet ended the ceremony with "Music for a Found Harmonium" for the postlude while guests made their way to the reception. During cocktails just before dinner, the peaceful air was permeated by Carla—Joe's son Andrew's friend—playing classic standards on the harp. After dinner, the DJ

1

played all sorts of requests, ranging from The Lettermen's "The Way You Look Tonight" as the soundtrack for the father-daughter dance, to "Hava Nagila" as requested and appreciated by the groom, Stan's, Jewish family. Other songs included the Black Eyed Peas' "I Gotta Feeling" to open the dance floor; Beyoncé's "Single Ladies" for the bouquet toss; Johnny Cash/Joaquin Phoenix's "Ring of Fire" for the cutting of the cake; "When the Saints Go Marching In" for the second line; and Israel Kamakawiwo'ole's "Somewhere Over the Rainbow/What a Wonderful World" for the last song.

Music is not just an important part of weddings; it is one of the most important aspects of our culture and thus the way we live our everyday lives. Music helps us order our life experiences and make sense of them. It helps us enjoy the good times as well as the bad, becoming the soundtrack for life. As Tia DeNora (2000: 16–17), one of the most insightful sociologists of music, put it:

> Music is not merely a "meaningful" or "communicative" medium . . . At the level of daily life, music has power. It is implicated in the very dimension of social agency . . . Music may influence how people compose their bodies, how they conduct themselves, how they experience the passage of time, how they feel—in terms of energy and emotion—about themselves, about others, and about situations.

Music defines so many of the activities we engage in, especially those things that escape words or for which words are inadequate by themselves, to create the present and prepare for memories in the future. During the wedding, the string quartet itself provided a dimension of elegance through the application of a classical motif. The "Ave Maria" accomplished the same end, but also positioned Jessie's parents and guests into the scene, demonstrating respect for Jessie's parents by adding a Catholic theme to the otherwise fairly secular wedding. It also served to welcome Jessie's family and guests by painting the wedding as familiar, sacred, and comfortable. Taylor Swift's song reminded everyone that love is new, the string quartet established the moment to dissolve the wedding into the reception, while the aural harp music created a

creating Mood
(Tahey)

center of pleasant attention during cocktails. All the different kinds of music played after dinner—loud and soft, modern and old—reminded everyone of the inseparable link between music and dance. The Lettermen provided the soundtrack for a loving yet ominously terminal waltz between a proud dad and his princess daughter; the "Hava Nagila" provided the soundtrack for family pride and fun. When Joe jumped around playfully during "Hava Nagila," it marked the true melding of two families.

How can we include all the different styles of music performed at such a wedding as popular music, as we do in this book? A traditional distinction in the study of music is that between popular music and classical music. Theodor Adorno (1949) argued that classical music has a liberating effect on its audiences insofar as it creates a healthy dialectic between a representation of the world as fact and a presentation of possible, perhaps even utopian, visions of society. Beethoven was his hero in this regard. Popular music, on the other hand, precluded open discourse between the objective and the subjective and instead presented a vision of reality that is whole, unchanging, unproblematic. Put simply, classical music supported democracy, whereas popular music supported the rigid world-view that ends up in fascism.

Adorno's insights are powerful, yet they unfortunately parallel over-simplified thinking that says that popular music is inferior because the audiences attracted to it are somehow inferior. The distinction between fine art/classical music and popular art/popular music ends up an elitist theory. As sociologists we must remain skeptical of all classifications. As sociologists of everyday life, we want to focus on the practices people use to make music an integral part of their lives.

In the present text, we argue that classical music is really a sub-category of popular music, for two reasons. First, if we agree that the word "popular" more or less means "of the people," then popular music is the music preferred by the people (that is, a good number of them). Following this argument, if many people today—and therefore not only and not anymore a hyper-privileged, "cultured," upper-class and aristocratic-like minority—enjoy classical music, is classical music not popular music as well? The answer would have to be an absolute "Yes." In fact, many more people across social classes enjoy classical music today than ever before. Attendance at the many productions around the world of *The Nutcracker* during the Christmas season increases every year. Second, the industry that produces, records, promotes, and establishes performances of classical music is the same industry that creates popular music. For example, classical music has a "star" system that places celebrity performers on international tours as well as *The Letterman Show* on TV as guests. Think of Joshua Bell, Yo-Yo Ma, Sarah Brightman, and Placido Domingo.

At this point, some of you may feel a degree of satisfaction knowing that distinctions—such as those between "high-status" musical styles like opera and "low-status" musical styles like rap or rock—are arbitrary, politically motivated *social constructions*. You might even be thinking about Facebooking that high-school classical music teacher who looked down on your mohawk, to remind him/her of that. On the other hand, some of you may recognize that, despite the arbitrariness of any objective or universal hierarchy of values between musical expressions, some differences among them do indeed exist. After all, you can't just show up for a night at the opera theater with a surfboard, for example. And your typical opera-goer, no matter how "local" he/she claims to be, wouldn't be allowed to surf your waves and share your surf rock on the beach in his/her sharply pressed tuxedo. In fact, while distinctions are always more or less ideological, in practice they do work. Another way of saying this is that reality may be a matter of conventions and ideas, but those conventions and ideas are really meaningful in their consequences. Such is one of the basic ideas behind the paradigm, or worldview, known as the sociology of everyday life, the very starting point of our introduction to this book.

The Sociology of Everyday Life and the Sociology of Popular Music

Introduction to sociology textbooks generally survey three bodies of sociological theory: functionalist, conflict, and interactionist theories. Functionalist theory was very important in the beginning of the sociology of popular music right after the end of World War II. Talcott Parsons (1949) and James Coleman (1961) were interested in understanding the way society would manage the great bulge in the American population today known as the baby boomer generation.

Bobyboom *safety valve* *Theory*

Both saw the emerging "youth culture" as a mechanism that society was establishing to do this. Parsons argued that the youth culture functioned as a *safety valve* to help manage and release all the energy (sexual and otherwise) and leisure time that adolescence was producing. For example, rock'n'roll sock hops were controlled events, chaperoned by adults, at which kids could meet each other, dance, and have fun in a safe way. Coleman studied high-school culture and found that the varieties of popular music available to teenagers helped organize them by social class and to prepare them for adulthood. Working-class kids liked rockabilly, whereas middle-class kids liked pop performers such as The Four Freshmen. Coleman was particularly interested in the way the rapid increase in the number of high schools to not only accommodate—warehouse?—all the teenagers, but to accommodate teenagers who find themselves the object of compulsory attendance rules that were becoming fashionable after the war. Functionalism is not the most popular approach in the sociology of music. Much of functionalist research examines the relationship between social class membership and the arts/music (e.g., Dimaggio and Mukhtar 2004).

Conflict theory sees society as an ongoing confrontation between social classes, genders, or races/ethnicities (Ritzer 2011). One group tries to exert control over the other in order to profit materially, or to have one's beliefs or world-view be dominant over others. Conflict theorists thus see popular music—again, rock'n'roll in particular—as either a tool of the dominant group to keep others in economic or political submission (e.g., music as a way to divert the masses' attention away from significant issues) or as a tool for political resistance to the dominant group (e.g., anti-war and protest music). The focus on economic and political conflict tends to ignore certain topics near and dear to humanistic scholars, who prefer to explore the sociological significance of music as a source of meaning for everyday life, for who we are, and as a mechanism for group solidarity.

Symbolic Interactionism is a theoretical perspective in sociology "that places meaning, interaction, and human agency at the center of understanding social life" (Sandstrom, Martin, and Fine 2006). People interact or communicate with each other to achieve practical meanings for situations and objects in the world. The most important object we

Question: what is the purpose of pop music? what role does it serve?

what does the song mean to you?

work hard to define is the *self*, the experience of individuality that makes humans distinctive among all forms of life. Symbolic interactionist work in popular music is among the most creative of all sociological takes. The annual series *Studies in Symbolic Interaction* has a special issue dedicated to popular music, to which three of the four authors of this text—Joe Kotarba, Bryce Merrill, and Patrick Williams—contribute.

Now, symbolic interactionism is perhaps the most important, yet only one, branch of the more general theoretical perspective we call the sociology of everyday life (EDL) that we will use in this text. As Douglas (1976) notes, the sociolog(ies) of everyday life consist of those theories that see society as the product of people communicating, interacting and working hard to establish the semblance—if not at least the appearance—of social order and the meaningfulness of life. Everyday life refers to the actual situations in which people live, face problems, seek meaning for those problems, and apply practical solutions to those problems. Symbolic interactionist theory is the primary analytical framework in EDL, and the other theories all result from or are closely related to interactionism. Ethnomethodology, for example, sees talk or conversation as the essence of social life, not simply as a way of describing social life (Mehan and Wood 1975). Dramaturgy sees everyday life as if it were a theater. People perform with and for each other by following scripts provided by their cultures (Goffman 1959). Phenomenology locates the essence of social life in consciousness; social life is a reflection of the ways our minds construct the image of social order (Psathas 1973).

The two most recent varieties of EDL sociology are existential sociology and postmodernism. Existential sociology argues, like symbolic interactionism does, that the primary goal of social interaction is developing, nurturing, safeguarding, and preserving the self: the sense of who you are. Existential sociology differs, however, in the emphasis it places on the contemporary social situation in which the self is constantly changing and adapting to a constantly changing social and cultural landscape. Existential sociology also sees the experience of individuality as value- and feeling-based as well as a cognitive or conscious experience. Joe Kotarba's recent book (2013a) on baby boomer rock'n'roll fans discusses the many and varied experiences of self by and through which aging rockers continue to use music to make sense of themselves and the ever-changing world around them. Postmodernism is perhaps the most radical of the sociologies of everyday life in the way it argues that society is not simply regulated by culture, as the functionalists maintain, but is culture per se. Our values, ideas, and morals emanate increasingly from the mass media. Churches, schools, civics classes, and newspapers are being replaced by the Internet, YouTube, iPads, and, of course, television (Kotarba and Johnson 2002).

A melding of EDL perspectives with conflict theory produces a style of EDL sociology that is very influential in our text and our work in popular music: social constructionism (SC). SC prefers to study popular music as a meaningful set of practices, performances, and texts in the social world. In doing so, it focuses on what people do together with music and with one another. The analytical attention is on "doing," that is, on practice, action, conduct, behavior, rituals, work, and in the consequences of ideas, values, roles, scripts, language, and norms. People make social realities by acting in accord with (and often in spite of) one another. In the case of music, constructionism explains, for example, *How* how genres take shape; how people shape, follow, and abandon the *genres* musical fashions they have created; how people construct a sense of *take* identity, individual and collective, around music; and so forth (Kotarba *shape* and Vannini 2006).

What makes constructivism unique and very useful for the study of cultural phenomena like music is the way it generally blends well with critical theory. Now, critical theory is not synonymous with conflict theory, yet critical theory has emerged from conflict theory. Conflict theory was born out of the writings of Karl Marx and his immediate and more orthodox followers. Critical theory is instead more closely associated with the Frankfurt School of Critical Theory first, and then with the (British) University of Birmingham's Centre for Contemporary Cultural Studies (henceforth, CCCS). It is especially the latter institution that, in the late 1970s and 1980s, renewed sociological and interdisciplinary interest in critical theory, in popular culture and popular music studies, and in the potential of a uniquely constructionist and critical agenda. It did so by downplaying the role of the economy in society. For Marx, capital-based relations accounted for the entire structure of social organization. But, for his critical followers of the Frankfurt School, the economy, while a strong force, was not the only social force to be reckoned with, and certainly was not omnipotent, as Marx envisioned it. Thus, while they maintained their critical stance toward social inequality, they toned down their emphasis on how fixed those inequalities are. People do exercise the ability to make sense of and impact their situation in life, as social constructionism maintains. This blending of critical theory's emphasis on the economic power exercised by groups that manipulate, if not control, the culture industries with social constructionism's emphasis on human agency is demonstrated in the research on popular music conducted within the CCCS tradition (Hall and Jefferson 1977). For example, Dick Hebdige (1979) examined the way politically disenfranchised youth in England co-opted upper-class *style* in clothing and entertainment as a form of symbolic resistance to the ruling class in Britain.

Now, a lot of theory consumed all at once can give anyone a stomach-ache, so let us step back a bit for a second and go back to popular music. Let us imagine a character, a guy or girl like many others. Let's give this character a name: Cameron. Cameron lives in Seattle. Not just any Seattle, but the Seattle of the early 1990s. Yeah, the grungey one! Cameron looks like many youths around town: jeans, a Mudhoney T-shirt and a hooded sweatshirt, disheveled look, mellow attitude, yet politically aware and more or less involved in environmental issues and other social causes. Cameron has a particular taste in music and is a huge music buff: grunge, indie rock, anything heavy with the exception of glam, butt-rock-type guitar music. Cameron is also growing up. Maybe wondering a bit about the future and worrying about paying bills and eventually having to settle down with a ballooning student loan debt. Cameron works odd days at Kinko's, takes classes at Seattle Central Community College, drives his beat-up Nissan every other weekend to catch some good shows down in Olympia—and occasionally plays bass guitar with some Evergreen State College friends—and every now and then parties downtown at the Crocodile. A pretty normal life, right? So, why does Cameron matter to us?

Cameron matters to us as sociologists of popular music because his identity (among other things) cannot be understood without a comprehension of the role that music plays in his life. Only by focusing on the meanings that Cameron attributes to music, by paying attention to how that music allows Cameron to cement social ties with friends, to understand the politics of the world, to express emotionality and so forth, can we hope to understand Cameron a bit better. To do this, we need to put ourselves in Cameron's shoes. We need to do this in order to understand how he makes his world, and how he attributes meaning to it. In other words, we need to become ethnographic tourists in Cameron's life. We need to hang out with Cameron, listen to his stories, and see life from his perspective. This is what, generally, a constructionist does. A constructionist follows *interpretive* approaches to studying the world, approaches that allow for a thick description of Cameron's (and others') social world, approaches that rely on the use of qualitative and humanist data. Yet, a full understanding of Cameron's life with music might require something else.

To put Cameron's life in perspective, we might need to understand his social position. As a grunge fan, Cameron has already engaged in a bit of social positioning of his own, whether he is aware of this or not. In its early stages grunge emerged as a form of protest music: protest against the growing standardization of youth culture, against the superficiality of popular culture, against both the consumerism and excessive hedonism of the music of the 1980s, and against the idealistic and utopian values of the hippie generation that preceded it. Cameron's musical identity might then very well be understood as a battle cry born out of social angst: angst toward his biographical particulars (such as growing up in a quickly expanding and increasingly wealthy city) and angst toward the general political marginalization of youth culture and youth issues by the political system. And this is what a critical approach to social/musical issues does: it attempts to understand the meanings of musical choices, discourses, and practices by critically reflecting on social positions and on the stratification of social positions. It focuses on those particular historical and political discourses, musical (and other) texts, and practices through which social positions can be created and expressed, and through which hierarchies and inequalities can be highlighted and critiqued.

Together, the everyday life approach and the critical approach in sociology make for a very thorough understanding of the social dimensions of everyday life. Without pretending to speak for others—without having first undertaken to see the world from their eyes—a sociology of popular music that is grounded in an everyday life approach speaks about others and the self of the writer as well. And it does so with a very keen focus on matters of culture. Indeed, one might say that the scope of such a sociological analysis is similar to the work of a cultural interpreter insofar as we learn about the culture of a social world (like that of Cameron's life) and write about that culture for another culture altogether: the culture of sociologists, students of sociology, and any reader interested in social issues. Given the importance of a firm understanding of culture, let us work toward a clarification of that idea.

Music and Culture

Culture is a way of life. Despite the fact that some people refer to culture as an ensemble of artistic practices, folk customs, and educational background, sociologists and other social scientists view culture differently: as a system of symbolic meanings and a variety of processes of formation, exchange, and use of those meanings. When we understand culture as a way of life we become sensitized to seeing the presence of culture everywhere. This is why, as sociologists of everyday life, we feel particularly keen on attempting to understand and explain the most taken-for-granted and minute cultural expressions. Rather than explaining the concept of culture further by providing additional definitions, let us try to capture the uniqueness of the culture of our times by returning to our earlier example.

To anyone who has lived their life much earlier in the 20th century, Cameron's life would seem full of choices. Cameron didn't have to take a job at Kinko's, to choose to drive an old and beat-up Nissan, or to go to school to Seattle Central Community College. As a matter of fact, Cameron—being from North Bend, outside of Seattle—didn't have to move to the city. Music, too, is a choice. And the choice for Cameron is endless. Any shelves of any music store offer a vast choice of musical styles: country, heavy metal, R&B, rap, classical, industrial, etc.

why choose the music that for chose?

—choice -

Cameron's choice to abandon religion in his early teens is also a choice. Clothing style is also a choice. We could continue on and on, but you get the point that we are making: if there is one distinguishing characteristic of the way of life of our times, it is that we have an unprecedented amount of choice. Ask your grandparents, if you can, about their choices when they were your age—like how many recordings they could choose from at the "music store." You'll get a different picture. And they'll get a good laugh out of your question. They'll laugh *with* you, of course.

Musical choices are cultural choices. After all, music is part of the *Good* way we choose to live our life. And if it is a culture of choice that we speak of, then perhaps we need to wonder what the deeper consequences of choosing are. Sociologist Anthony Giddens (1991) writes that never before has Western culture been so receptive to the power of choice. Indeed, who we ourselves are, as individuals, is a matter of choice. Our self is a project of sorts. Cameron, in fact, could very well decide to trade in his grunge-rock CD collection for some rap music, sell back his clothes at Value Village and buy Hammer-style parachute pants, and move to Los Angeles, too. The following month, or year, Cameron could start over, with another identity of choice. You could, too. We could, too. The reason why we don't change all the time is because change, and the very possibility of change, provokes some anxiety in all of us. Anxiety, doubt, and fearing the loss of any sort of grounding or safety net are the necessary counterparts of a culture rich in choices and in the power of choosing. Cameron's angst comes in part from being a member of a generation that—perhaps more than any other generation before—has felt the freedom to choose. Angst, thus, comes in Cameron's case from the absence of firm traditions: the traditions that your grandparents and especially great-grandparents will tell you about if you ask them about their choices.

Some sociologists have decided to assign a moniker, which we have already discussed, to the culture we have described: *postmodern*. By postmodern culture, they mean a culture in which one's way of life is less grounded in traditions and more in choices, less grounded in certainties and more in doubts (Baudrillard 1983). A postmodern culture is marked by the seemingly endless availability of choice: fragmented musical

postmodern culture

styles, endless stimulation from multiple mass media of communication, the explosion of consumption and consumerism, the increased interconnectedness of the globe. Many more characteristics could be mentioned and many discussions could be opened. Yet, for the sake of brevity, simply understand this: Cameron's sense of self and identity, and Cameron's way of life, has the quality of an open project in a way that is more distinctly so than in any other time in modern history. Sociologists who believe in the truth of this statement are known as postmodernists. Elements of postmodern theory, which have great impact on everyday life sociology, and references to postmodern culture, occasionally ooze all over our insights throughout this book, and hopefully now you will know what we mean by that ever-contentious expression: "postmodernism."

limits of choice

To conclude this section, let us reflect on an element of our example that we have . . . er . . . chosen to neglect: the limitations and costs of choices. Let us return to our example. Cameron's choice to become a grunge-rock fan may seem arbitrary and inconsequential at first, but it is in actuality quite the opposite. Choices are hardly ever random. So if we spoke to Cameron we might learn that he was never intending to become who he is. Yet, lack of educational opportunities in his hometown made it more or less necessary to move to Seattle. Some of his high-school friends were in the same position, so moving to a city was not only a necessity in relation to education but also represented the opportunity to maintain social networks. Cameron might also tell us that the choice for a college was more or less forced by limited opportunities. Many of Cameron's friends' parents were able to fund study at Evergreen State College for their children. Cameron instead had to take a job at Kinko's to help pay for tuition. That took time away from playing in a rock band. It also made Cameron resentful, politically motivated, and particularly sensitive to the appeal of lyrics like those of "Hunger Strike" by Temple of the Dog: "I don't mind stealing bread from the mouths of decadence."

Sociologists of everyday life such as us, as critical constructionists and postmodernists, might then suggest that choice exists, but it is *structured* or limited by several characteristics of the very social structures that enable ways of life and the amount of choice therein. Music, and musical cultures, are then serious sociological business, business which allows us to understand a great deal about society and social theory in general—the very scope of this book. Even though by now it seems obvious to you that studying popular music is a very useful and smart way of understanding social relations, this was not always the case. In the next section we briefly review the recent history of the study of music within sociology and a little bit of the history of sociology itself.

A Very Brief History of the Study of Popular Music in Sociology

Since we have more or less erased the boundaries between popular music and classical music for the sake of subjecting both to sociological analysis, let us demarcate our territory—that is, the precise field that we explore in this book—by choosing an expression that captures the identity of the diverse types of music on which we focus here. Let us choose the expression "popular music." Popular music is then intended to refer here to all types of music that are processed through, and share the logic of, the mass media.

Please note: we use several terms or labels for musical styles that, hopefully, are not too confusing. *Popular music* is the most general category we will analyze. Pop music refers to all styles of music that is mass-produced, mass-marketed, and in general treated as a commodity in our North American societies. *Rock'n'roll* refers to that style of popular music that emerged after World War II as a distinct feature of youth culture. Rock'n'roll is loud, fast, guitar-driven, typically amplified, very danceable, and oriented toward young—i.e., teenage—audiences (Kotarba 1987). *Rock* refers to more contemporary versions of rock'n'roll. *Jazz, rap, dance, noise*, etc. are other styles of popular music.

We can ordinarily think of popular music as emerging during the early 20th century, when music became an economic commodity in our society, to be produced and marketed like any other consumable goods. There were two technological events that fueled this phenomenon. First, the advent of radio in the 1920s brought music into the homes of millions of North Americans. Perhaps the major impact of radio on music was its ability to present new and different styles of music beyond the classical, family, church, and community-based music to which people were accustomed previously. Second, the advent of recorded

Differences 'tween rock 'n' roll + rock

music, in a period that critical theorist Walter Benjamin (1969) referred to as the *age of mechanical reproduction*, turned music into a personal possession—with a price tag—that could be experienced and enjoyed at will, that could be distributed widely, and that could make music a lucrative business for producer, composer, and musician alike.

Much of the early scholarly work on popular music, including that of the Frankfurt School, was written from a critical, if not elitist, perspective. Theodor Adorno (1949), for example, frowned on jazz (his expression for what we call "pop music") as a low-status form of music that elicited non-rational, animalistic responses from its fans, in contrast to classical music, which supposedly elevated one's mind and spirit. In addition, early critical thinkers like Adorno felt that capitalists marketed popular music to anesthetize the working class politically and to increasingly subjugate them economically.

In recent years, cultural scholars, including sociologists, have been much friendlier toward popular music. These writers were largely baby boomers themselves, who were raised not only on pop music, but on rock'n'roll music specifically. To them, popular music is a fundamental force in North American and—increasingly global—culture, to be appreciated as well as understood. Later generations of scholars who went through their youth in the late 1960s, 1970s, and 1980s felt very similar to their baby boomer predecessors. The sociology of music then became overwhelmingly the sociology of popular music. We argue that there have been four moments in the sociological analysis of popular music that closely parallel the historical development of pop itself in Western society over the past 50 years. We will briefly describe these four moments in order to understand the evolution of both social phenomena. The key theme that we emphasize in the next paragraphs is that the sociology of popular music has generally focused in its earlier years on rock'n'roll. With the growing diversification of rock and multiplication of styles that originate in but deviate from rock, the sociology of pop music has become more diversified as well.

The first moment of rock'n'roll occurred during the 1950s, when youth culture as we know it was born. We are acknowledging, of course, the fact that the cultural and musicological roots of rock'n'roll can be traced back at least several decades before that (Friedlander 1996). It was during the 1950s, however, that rock'n'roll received its name and dramatically entered North American everyday life and parlance. Interestingly, early sociological views on youth culture in general and rock'n'roll specifically were quite positive and supportive of this cultural movement. As we mentioned earlier, James Coleman (1961) conceptualized rock'n'roll as *youth culture*. He observed, through his massive study of American high schools, that early rock'n'rollers like Elvis Presley and Buddy Holly provided a mechanism for helping the community manage the burgeoning population of teenagers resulting from the success of the emerging middle-class family (1950s and 1960s). The growing varieties of popular music in the 1950s helped socialize young people into their "appropriate" social classes. Coleman saw rock'n'roll as the soundtrack for working-class youth. In many ways, early scholarly writing on rock'n'roll discovered this music as it was already understood and experienced by its fans.

The second moment of rock'n'roll occurred during the late 1960s and 1970s. Rock'n'roll music grew to become a cultural entity much greater than the beat for sock hops or the drive-in. It took on broader political implications through its links to the civil rights and anti-war movements. In the second moment, sociologists like Simon Frith (1981) and George Lewis (1983) conceptualized rock'n'roll as *popular culture*. They focused on rock'n'roll music as the product of the popular culture industry in capitalistic society. They also acknowledged the fact that the rock'n'roll audience was much more diverse than the notion of "youth" implies. Experientially, there were white, black, gay, men's and women's rock'n'roll(s) and, subsequently, markets.

The third moment occurred in the 1970s and 1980s when rock'n'roll lost some of its critical appeal and became increasingly entrenched in and controlled by the entertainment industry. The ensuing revolt against corporate rock'n'roll, especially in terms of the new wave and punk movements in England, led British scholars such as Dick Hebdige and others writing from the Birmingham School to conceptualize rock'n'roll as *subculture*. They examined the political nature of rock and other styles as subversive voices of working-class teenagers, especially in Great Britain. These scholars advanced the methodologies used to study rock'n'roll from classic survey research to semiotics. This approach fit the objective of understanding how audiences define and integrate music into their already constituted realities (i.e., social class memberships). Thus, the working-class punk subculture appropriated elements of upper-class culture, like dress, and used them to ridicule and criticize the life of the rich and powerful.

In the fourth moment of the 1980s and 1990s, sociologists joined other scholarly observers to conceptualize rock'n'roll as *culture*. They saw rock'n'roll as simply one feature of a postindustrial or postmodern culture undergoing radical transformation. The generational boundaries that so obviously delineated youth from their parents were cracking. Lawrence Grossberg (1992a), for example, proclaimed the death of rock'n'roll insofar as it no longer functions to empower teenagers by differentiating them from their parents and other adults. By the time we entered the 1990s, cross-generational pop music that could be enjoyed by everyone had started to supplant rock'n'roll as the dominant soundtrack in American culture. Rap music has taken over much of rock'n'roll's political role. Yet rock'n'roll has not simply died. In the spirit of the postmodern era in which we live, rock'n'roll has dissolved into the pastiche of popular music that results in white rappers like Eminem, rock and rapper groups Linkin Park, and pop acts ranging from Britney Spears and Justin Bieber to Nicki Minaj and John Legend. MTV and VH1 in the United States, and Much Music and Much More Music in Canada, have been major media forces in creating this cultural gumbo. As E. Ann Kaplan (1987) has noted, MTV is a reflection of the pervasiveness of the visual dimension of postmodern culture, as rock'n'roll has been absorbed by the overwhelming power of the television medium on which teenagers have been raised.

Therefore, rock'n'roll is no longer synonymous with popular music, but should be seen as one facet of the increasingly complex musical and cultural phenomenon known as popular music. Popular music of all styles has taken on many of the attributes and values of the world of rock'n'roll—volume, fast pace, sensuality, amplification, and so forth . . . Just think of the ongoing controversy in country music. Are Keith Urban and The Band Perry rock'n'roll or country? It's hard to say when the back-up bands are rock bands with, on occasion, a pedal guitar or fiddle thrown in.

Age is another factor in this growing complexity. Amid all these changes taking place in popular music and the entertainment industry's search for new audiences and ways to provide music to them, we witness numerous ways in which adults are increasingly present in and relevant to rock'n'roll and popular music. Beatles CD compilations have been among the highest selling music at Christmas for many years. Middle-aged fans pay hundreds of dollars to sit in the "Gold Circle" seats at Eagles and Who concerts, where they sip white wine instead of the Boone's Farm of their college days many years ago. The summer concert "shed" scene would be very thin without sold-out Aerosmith, Chicago, Kansas, Paul Simon, James Taylor, Crosby, Stills and Nash, Sting/ *good* Police, and REO Speedwagon stops. Why have so many adults not *?* outgrown rock'n'roll? Why do innumerable teenagers angrily shout to their parents to "turn that noise down" when mom and dad are grooving to an old Rolling Stones CD? Why do so many adults continue to operationalize "popular music" in terms of the rock'n'roll idiom with which they grew up?

In a very postmodern way, the continuing fourth moment of rock'n'roll will continue to defy earlier patterns of performance, consumption, and style. We can safely say that we are in fact moving into a fifth moment of pop music and pop music studies within sociology. The fifth moment is a typically postmodern one, marked by extreme diversification of both musical offer and sociological offer, by increasing doubt over the authenticity of pop music, by a loss of musical tradition (like rock'n'roll), accompanied by a nostalgic and pastiche-like recovery of the past, and by the increasing global fusion of styles and blurring of differences. Sociologically, this translates in a coming-together of theoretical perspectives on the study of popular music, and an explosion in the sociological interest in popular culture. Indeed, as culture industries try to appeal to consumers by listening to their needs for diversity, so do the "sociological industries." And indeed our book also attempts to answer the introductory student's need for diversity in pedagogical scope!

We will close with the following illustrative observation. On July 7, 2007, "Live Earth: The Concerts for a Climate in Crisis" consisted of ten concerts in eight countries that played to the largest music benefit crowd ever. There were numerous new artists that one might expect to

Are we in a 5th moment?

be attractive to the youngest audience members, such as Wolfmother and Ludacris. Yet, perennial favorites Madonna, the Police, Bon Jovi, and Melissa Etheridge—artists whom the parents of the youngest audience members made famous years ago—were presented as headliners. Their performances were, in fact, among the most spirited of all 257 performances on July 7, 2007. Old-school rock'n'roll as the new youth culture? Go figure.

Conclusion: Cultivating a Musical and Sociological Imagination

If we wish to understand the meanings of pop music and be critical of those cultural practices and values that result in the formation or re-creation of cultural injustices, we need to follow an approach to the study of our subject matter which is interpretive and critical at the same time. In doing so, we privilege methods and data that allow us to take the role and perspective of the people we intend to understand, that allow us to focus on the construction of meaning through language and language use, and that allow us to interpret the significance of music-related practices in a precise historical, political, geographical, and economic context. In our Preface we discussed our approach to the study of all this. We called it ethnographic tourism, and explained how it constitutes an example of the sociological study of everyday life. In this Introduction, we have discussed our constructionist and critical perspective, explained how and why this perspective is best followed via the use of qualitative data, and how important it is to maintain a healthy skepticism toward all social facts. Much of what we have done constitutes an example of sociological imagination.

Critical and interpretive sociologist C. Wright Mills (1959) coined the expression "sociological imagination" to refer to the ability to connect, by way of reflection, seemingly unconnected individual and social forces, and in particular biographical and historical issues. Sociology attempts to foster a sociological imagination in all its publics—both students and stakeholders—by getting them to reflect on the greater relevance of personal problems as social issues. Our focus on the study of pop music has precisely that objective in mind, as well. Because few things matter to students as much as music does, we believe that, by allowing students to reflect on the structuring of music as a social product, we can introduce students to sociological theory and research. In doing so, we wish to focus in particular on three issues (see Mills 1959):

1. What is the structure of a particular musical social scene and how does it differ from and compare to other actual and possible forms of social organization?
2. What are the key features of this musical social scene, and what is its unique position and relation with greater historical processes?
3. What are the defining characteristics of men and women engaged in these musical social scenes, and what goes on in their everyday lives?

By asking such questions, and by searching for answers to them, we can hope to understand how simple behavior like choosing one's music is the result of complex economic factors as well as deeply held and personal tastes and values. By understanding the links between individual biography and social history, we can therefore comprehend the lives of individuals like Cameron and the historical and social contexts in which lives are lived. It is with this goal in mind, and by using music as a lens for doing this, that we write this book.

Could use as a template for a project(s)

1

INTERACTION

Interaction is the essence of all varieties of interactionist sociology, and in fact of everyday life. One of the founders of symbolic interaction, Herbert Blumer (1969), stated unequivocally that society consists of people engaging in symbolic interaction. On a constant, everyday basis, we interact with each other, people in the past, people in the future, and ourselves. Through interaction, we become human, respond pragmatically to social situations, negotiate social meanings, shape our behavior, experience and manage emotions, and shape and refine culture (Sandstrom et al. 2006). Interaction can occur through any number of media: speech, visual symbols, written text, and—of course—music. Interaction is first and foremost the mechanism for generating and sharing meanings.

In terms of music, interaction occurs in any number of ways. We talk over lunch with our friends about the *American Idol* contestants we saw last night on TV. We read about the latest music tours and artists' scandals in *Rolling Stone* magazine. In fact, Joe Kotarba is now pondering the black and white poster of the Rolling Stones perched over his desk as he writes. (I don't care what the critics say: Keith Richards looks really cool smoking his unfiltered cigarette while sporting his sunglasses and funky hat.) We drag our dates to the Katy Perry concert tour documentary, *Part of Me*, to get a glimpse of the latest pink, purple, and polka dot fashions. We turn our smartphones or laptops to YouTube to witness the Tupac Shakur holographic performance at Coachella everyone's talking about—now, that's scary!

the Concept of the pop song

what is a pop song?

Symbolic interaction over music can range from the most personal and intimate to the most public and mass-mediated. In order to illustrate the role interaction plays in our popular music experiences, we will provide two examples from the ends of the continuum. The first is personal interaction with one's self regarding what we will define as a distinctly sociological concept of the *pop song*. The second is the much more public interaction that takes place at *music scenes*.

The Pop Song: Stuck in Your Head

Commonsensically, we all know what a pop song is. Our general cultural and industry definitions include the following typical characteristics—formulaic; melody-driven; short (three minutes or so long); danceable; lyrics deal with love or fun; simple instrumentation; and happy—among other characteristics. Many of us say we hate the kinds of pop songs we are describing for the above reasons, but also because they sound childish or are marketed to (dumb) kids; are bad music; are wimpy and/or bubblegummy; are unsophisticated; are "chick songs"; are commodified product marketed to us incessantly by the capitalistic music industry; are disposable; are mind-numbing, etc. You get the picture.

We all know this, because these are commonsense definitions of pop songs. These definitions are shared by all critics, professional and otherwise. Sociologically, we have a responsibility to look beyond common sense to sculpt a definition of a pop song that unpacks—deconstructs?—taken-for-granted definitions of, and assumptions about, pop songs. Put differently, sociologists of everyday life especially want to explore the actual experience of a pop song to see how meaning is attributed to or derived from a pop song. Furthermore, as constructivists, we are interested in the way people use pop songs to create a sense of self, definitions of situation, relationships, feelings, and other social objects (Mead 1934).

Case in point: Carly Rae Jepsen had the number one hit single "Call Me Maybe" in the summer of 2012. Carly Rae is apparently a bit of a Justin Bieber protégée from Canada. Before her current hit, she was a singer-songwriter perhaps best known for her third-place finish on the 2007 season of *Canadian Idol*. Justin Bieber made her an international star when he tweeted "'Call Me Maybe' by Carly Rae Jepsen is probably

what is catchy? "Call me Maybe"
"Happy" even better

the catchiest song I've ever heard" to his 22 million followers. Soon, celebrities ranging from Justin Bieber and Selena Gomez to Katy Perry and James Franco were uploading YouTube video clip versions they made of Carly Rae's hit (Green 2012).

Sociologically, the questions arise: Why is "Call Me Maybe" so popular? What do we mean when we say that a pop song is "catchy"? How do people experience a catchy song? Within the sociology of everyday life, the phenomenological perspective is a very useful tool for answering these questions. Phenomenology focuses on the way people perceive, organize, make practical sense of and define common, everyday events and social phenomena (Sokolowski 2000). In the summer of 2012, Joe Kotarba conducted a study to answer these questions. He taught an online course, "The Sociology of Popular Music," at Texas State University. The students in this course were juniors and seniors from a wide range of majors. He set up a forum and asked his students to discuss these questions. Their responses were open, honest, well written, and sophisticated. (This is typically the case when students are asked to write about themselves and topics near and dear to them!) He analyzed the threads that resulted in terms of a sociological model of the pop music song. The class determined that there are (at least) 10 common characteristics of pop music songs (Kotarba 2013b).

(1) *A pop song is catchy.* "Catchy" is the key experience in a pop song. Students talked about catchy in terms of the way a song occupies one's consciousness. The mind "plays" the song as if it was an iPod or radio in the mind. However, a song seems to be catchy only after the listener reflects on it to some degree, giving meaning to it. This meaning can be a reflection on the kind of situation the singer is creating with the song. An internal dialogue with the singer ensues that serves to enter the song into retrievable memory:

"Call Me Maybe" is a catchy song. When I heard it the first time all I heard was a girl singing, "here's my number, call me maybe." That sounds a little wishy washy to me. Almost like if the guy doesn't call her, oh well! But let's be honest, if a girl gives you her number, she wants you to call and if you don't she's going to internalize it and wonder what's wrong with her that you don't like! When I listened to the song a second time, really focusing on the lyrics, I heard a girl describe how this guy looks, how he makes her feel, etc. and her response is "Call Me Maybe." When I hear this song I do turn it up, it's got a great beat and is ok to listen to while sitting in five o'clock traffic. I don't sing along to this song, but when my girlfriend is in the car with me she does.

The meaning can be the imagery of a social situation in which the song is initially experienced alone, but triggered or reinforced when experienced with another. Even so, a catchy song can be contagious if there is occasion to experience the song, such as an extra credit course assignment:

When we were assigned this extra credit, I thought, "Hmm. I guess I'll have to listen to it." So I planned on looking on YouTube or something. Instead, one day I was driving home from work, flipped on a Top 40 station, and it was on (imagine that ...). I heard it that day and literally all I could think was "Wow ... this is not a good song." But it was danceable and catchy. By the second chorus, I found myself embarrassingly singing along.

Or, when driving around with a colleague from work:

But, alas, I work at a news station and we all share cars. Got in the car with a reporter on the way to a shoot yesterday and—"HEY I JUST MET YOU ..." —The reporter looked at me and said, "Ugh. They play this too much." But we both started singing it. And maybe dancing a little ... a lot.

Or, even while writing up the course assignment:

Then, all day (with very few hours of sleep, mind you) I was humming it, sometimes mumbling—"so call me maybeeee"—the lyrics to myself . . . I would catch myself, bobbing my head, tapping my fingers . . . and I would stop . . . for about two minutes . . . and there it was again. "Hey I just met you, and this is crazy, but here's my number, so call me maybe" . . . I would just like to add that I've also been singing it in my head the entire time I've been writing this post.

Yet, catchiness can be an unpleasant experience:

As soon as the song went off, I changed the channel. Never wanting to hear it again. Maybe I would have liked it in my younger days . . . the Britney Spears days. I probably would have liked it in high school at some point, and that is who I think likes it the most. High school girls (and boys if they'll admit it). I certainly don't like it . . . because it gets SO stuck in my head.

And it can be out of one's control:

Ear worm

I believe that Call Me Maybe has reached its status as the ≠1 single record in the country because of its catchiness. When I sat down and looked at the title the chorus began playing in my head. There also is no real way to get it out of my head no matter how hard about all I have said so far is that I absolutely dislike this song. If just by mentioning it to me I start singing the chorus in my head I can't imagine for somebody that enjoys this song.

Several students, almost all men or middle-aged women, indicated that the song was not catchy for them, but they were generally able to explain, quite analytically, why they were able to maintain control:

My issue is, I have a lot of other things on my mind. The younger students do not have kids or a husband to worry about. . . . Songs like that talk about things that are relevant to younger kids, like boyfriends, dates, falling in love, stuff like that. Besides that . . . it's the kind of song that goes up and down, emotionally or, well, in terms of feelings. The older you get, the less you really want to vibrate, if you will, like that. I like my music to help me mellow out.

(2) *A general, commonsensical belief is that pop songs are essentially "chick" songs.* We can define "chick" songs as those that are directed toward a specific female audience, often comprised of young women, and that contain simple, if not naive, lyrics about love and romance:

> When I heard this song for the first time I was at the pool with some friends and it was blaring over the radio and I could tell a lot of the girls there liked it because they all started singing or humming to it. I guess I was late hearing this song for the first time because everyone knew it except me. I thought it was catchy but not the type of song I would put on my iPod. Interestingly enough when I went home I YouTubed the song and realized how popular it was and that it even had its own dance. I think about the 5th or 6th time I heard Call Me Maybe it started to grow on me and I can remember singing the lyrics in my head and saying the chorus out loud.

(3) *Listeners who do not like the pop song can generally surmise who might.* Phenomenologically, we can think of these explanations as members' theories. We all have explanations for events that take place in our worlds. In terms of "Call Me Maybe," the students who offered the most developed theories of why others like the song seemed to use their theories to create distance between themselves and the song's fans:

> Ok, so I admit the first time I heard this song was a couple days ago because of this assignment. I Googled it and a YouTube video of the Miami Dolphins cheerleaders lip sync and dance routine to it came up, so I went with it. Later I did see the actual video for it, and it was surprisingly sexual for a song that seemed to have its target audience in its teens. I couldn't help but at least tap my toe to it, but maybe that was the cheerleaders. The fast beat made it easy to dance to, and it will appeal to a very wide demographic of

young people, world-wide. It struck me as the same type of entry to pop music that Britney Spears had, with regard to age, sex, genre and sexuality in the video. Actually, it did remind me of the fact many mid-twenties and thirties women will totally rock out to this song even though they know that it is intended for a younger audience. Maybe because it takes them back to the times when they were in high school and rocking out to new pop songs. On the surface the song feels like something teenage girls are sure to listen to as an anthem for their early crushes in life. It's sure to make the middle school dances in the fall.

(4) *The pop song not only engages the listener, but draws the listener in.* There is a bit of a contagion factor with catchy pop songs:

> Well for sure this song is very catchy. I find it very annoying and I am unsure how it became popular. But every time I hear it on the radio, I somehow sing along and know the words. I don't know how or why I know it. The melody is so easy to hum along to it. It is one of those songs that just finds you and you know the song the second time you hear it. The first time I heard it I was confused and thought it was a parody of a real song, and then I heard it again and somehow was singing along. Yet I still find the song very annoying and I don't like it. I don't know who would like it and why, but I think that it's not that people like it, it's one of those songs that you can't get a rid of and plays on the radio every hour so you just deal with it. It's like that song that won't leave you alone.

The song seems to seep into one's consciousness when there is space for it, such as during episodes of boredom:

> When I'm at work, I get really bored sometimes. I could do my job blindfolded and asleep . . . You know, when your mind is not paying attention, you can get bad thoughts . . . boyfriend problems, something you forgot to do—lots of stuff like that. Now, that's when a song like that is fun. It fills your mind with good feelings, good things to enjoy.

(5) *The pop song's lyrics are either not a factor in catchiness or sufficiently open-ended to allow for catchiness to the music per se.*

The first time I heard this song was at work. I was writing up a marketing plan and found that I had begun humming and moving along to a song which in turn made me start to actually listen to the song and I had no problems catching on to the tune and by the end of the song I already knew most of the lyrics . . . Listening to the actual words made me really dislike the "song." The beat is in fact catchy, thinking about it or even hearing someone mention the title and my head becomes filled with the tune and the most irritating part about it is I would have enjoyed the song as an adolescent.

And . . .

This song is so simple, catchy, and almost meaningless. It fits perfectly the definition of a pop music song! . . . Now I will have this song in my head for the rest of the night. I don't think the song is great but it's not bad either. It's just your typical teen bubblegum pop trying to make it big. It seems like the lyrics are very easy to parody.

(6) *When the pop song is experienced alone, the effects of the song are personal and immediately pleasurable.*

The first time I heard this song I thought it was absolutely ridiculous. I thought the lyrics were just plain stupid, and repeated over and over and over again. However dumb I think the song is, I do agree that it is catchy. It is upbeat and has a beat that you can easily tap your fingers or nod your head to. I cannot remember if I was doing this the first time I heard it but I just listened to it again and found myself shaking my head.

The song can even give the listener a sense of empowerment when pondering otherwise difficult situations, like meeting men in clubs:

I have heard the song "Call Me Maybe" multiples of times. After the first time hearing it I would catch myself singing along to the chorus and bobbing my head side to side while driving. It made me feel like I could get any guy in the club, no matter how attractive he was. It gave me confidence yet a little mystery in who I am. I would never truly find myself going up to just some hot guy and handing him a card—you can't do that, no matter what self esteem problems you may have. I have to say I love this song.

(7) *When the pop song is experienced in the presence of others, the shared experience is simple, pleasurable, and fun—play rather than intellectual or artistic meaning-making and sharing.*

I first heard this song going to work at 5:30 in the morning. I'm a morning person to begin with, so when it got into the chorus, I found myself cranking it up and rolling down the windows for everyone to jam out to. I found the beat simple and catchy and I was beating on everything in the car I could find. My brother and sister were not that happy about it though, but when you're the driver you get to make the rules. My fellow co-workers like to put it on as we are doing our morning cleaning duties as lifeguards, because it puts us all in a good mood. We actually sing too loud sometimes and no one can actually hear the song playing, just three obnoxious boys singing at the top of our lungs at 6:30 in the morning. Life Guarding is a pretty dull job, so we have to keep ourselves entertained. I give many thanks to this song for making my mornings.

And at a different kind of work site:

I first heard this song when I was at work about 3 months ago. My co-worker and I were un-boxing projectors and testing them before we put them on the shelf. It was pretty typical for Bridget to play music while we were at work, but this one caught me off guard because she normally listens to country. At first, I was turned off because of the singers high pitch voice. Also, since I am in a relationship I wasn't really into the whole "call me, maybe" line. My co-worker kept replaying it though. So eventually it got stuck in our heads and we sang it the rest of the day. It doesn't surprise me that this is the number one song in the country right now. It is very catchy, it is playful, and it is about something universal—love!

(8) *The pop song is perceived as formulaic, as a replication, or merely as fashionable.* This can be true whether you like a song or not:

first of all, are you kidding me? ... secondly, really, are you kidding me? ... this is the number one single in the country? ... man, I am so fearful of what is to come of the music industry ... this isn't even a song! ... it's one long hook on repeat! ... but it does stand to reason that she would be a Bieber protégé because his "songs" are all constructed the same way ... his mega hit "baby" was produced in the same track ... unfortunately this is what the music industry is producing today and calling them hits ... I think they need to add an "s" to "hits" and then we'd have a more accurate description of this garbage that they're passing off as quality artistic expression ... between these types of songs and the advent of autotune, anyone who has a cute face and can sing in at least one key effectively can be a pop star ... but for real ... ≠1 in the country? ... you gotta be kiddin' me.

And ...

The first time I heard this song was about twenty minutes ago. It is most definitely not my kind of music ... The tune is kind of catchy I hate to say. It almost made me want to tap my feet, or sing along if I knew the words. The sound was interesting, but it sounded like tons of other pop songs I have heard before ... Overall, I would not listen to this song again unless it was what my fiancée was listening to. She really likes this style of music. I have to listen to this type of music sometimes in the interest of compromising. After all, in my truck she has to listen to my music the majority of the time.

(9) *The pop song provides good soundtrack music.* Students do not ordinarily listen to catchy pop songs with perfect attention. They are typically doing something else while the song is playing:

> I first came across "Call Me Maybe" early one Tuesday morning when I was searching iTunes for new music. The song had just been released that same day and I had listened to the "Disney-Bop" sound. Later that week I was at a friend's apartment on a Saturday night getting dressed to go out and she had a playlist blaring from her iHome. As my friend and I were putting the finishing touches on our outfits and standing in the living room "Call Me Maybe" started playing. Instantly my friend began singing and dancing around and I couldn't help but do the same; my dancing could've also stemmed from my intake of alcohol but either way I was enjoying the song and my irritation at the singer's high-pitched voice had subsided. While at first I was unsure about if "Call Me Maybe" was my taste, throughout the night: getting dressed; driving to the bar; going back to my friend's apartment to raid the refrigerator this song was always playing and I knew that my initial thoughts about it had dissipated and I thoroughly liked the song. Now I have "Call Me Maybe" on numerous CDs and playlist and whenever I listen to the song whether in the car or getting dressed I always find myself moving my head even if the slightest amount. When I am driving, especially during a long drive I play it as loud as I can manage without busting my car's speakers and always sing at the top of my lungs, especially if I am with a friend and we both know the song. I enjoy the song and it makes me happy and instantly picks up my mood when I listen to it and that makes me feel good knowing that if I am having a bad day all I have to do is go to a certain song and push play.

(10) *Repetitious play in the mass media reinforces the catchability of the pop song.*

> Dumbest. Song. Ever. But it's so catchy! Annoyingly catchy. In fact, now that I've typed out the lyrics, I'm still singing the song in my

head. I stopped listening to Top 40 radio stations a little over a month ago because of how often they play the same songs, so I was doing a very good job of never having heard this song until extremely recently . . . I had seen the lyrics everywhere. People were posting them on Facebook as wall posts, photo album titles, comments, captions, etc. With as popular as the song was, I REALLY didn't want to hear it . . . I would just like to add that I've also been singing it in my head the entire time I've been writing this post.

The above exercise on "Call Me Maybe" illustrates several key socio-logical features of pop music. Perhaps the most interesting is the way popular music fits in with the other things we do and need to do in everyday life. Unlike classical music, which is a music experience that typically demands one's full attention (e.g., do not let your cell phone go off during Chopin—and no talking, please!), pop music is very accommodating. This may be one of its strengths: it does not require us to change in any significant way.

In a related sense, the soundtrack function of popular music is valu-able yet easily accessible. We all listen to music as we drive. We have our ear buds in place as we walk to the classroom building and take the elevator to the fourth floor. We listen to pop at work, at home, on dates, and just about everywhere else. Do you listen to music during class?

Perhaps the most valuable feature of pop music to our everyday lives is the way it adds *motion* to our routines, activities, thoughts, feelings, and sense of self. By motion, we mean that pop music can change the pace of everyday life, the relevance of time, acceleration of activities, and anticipation of future events. The value of Katy Perry's very popular "Firework" to Joe Kotarba's everyday life is a case in point. The song is a fast-paced dance song, but you do not have to dance to it. Like "Call Me Maybe," you can virtually dance in place to it: tapping your fingers, bobbing your head. "Firework" is very hummable, allowing talent-starved fans like Joe to take part in the performance, whether in the shower or while writing books. The song is complex, insofar as it contains a string element along with electronic accompaniment. The music, in addition to the story in the lyrics, provides spaces in the song to discover things, even after listening to it many times. Like the best pop sings, "Firework" provides a great ringtone. It is a ringtone, however, that Joe can control with a bit of mystery and excitement, disclosing it only to people he wants to hear it, never at a faculty meeting at the university, but among people he wants to impress that he is a Katy Perry fan. During the July 4 celebrations on TV in 2011 and 2012, "Firework" not only provided an appropriate title, but raised the level of excitement and pace for events that can be a bit long and, well, boring after a while.

In a similar vein, Tia DeNora (2000: 157–158) wrote about music in general as a *force*:

> It is in all these locations—from gilded concert hall to mega-mall, from bus terminal to bedroom—that music makes available ways of feeling, being, moving and thinking, that it animates us, that it keeps us "awake." Music, too, is a way of happening, it issues as an audible channel, a series of audible articulated signals. In this sense, music is not "about" anything but is rather a material that happens over time and in particular ways.... indeed, it creates its own time and its own history, cyclical, linear, recursive.

What about *your* favorite pop song?

The Music Scene: Tunes in the Community

We have just looked at some of the most personal, interactional features of the popular music experience. We will now move down the continuum to see how popular music is experienced at the level of community. Sociologically, we think of community in broader terms than commonly thought. A community is a group of people, real or imagined, who offer a sense of belonging to, and a source of meaning for, the individual (see Ferris and Stein 2011). People come together in a community, physically or virtually, on the basis of shared ideas, goals, and/or history. The particular kind of community we will explore is the *music scene*.

The Scene

The social scene is a useful concept for organizing thinking culture in a community setting. John Irwin (1977) wrote about the scene as an inclusive concept that involves everyone related to a cultural phenomenon

what is a scene?

(e.g., artists, audiences, management, vendors, and critics); the ecological location of the phenomenon (e.g., districts, clubs, recording studios, and rehearsal rooms); and the products of this interaction (e.g., advertisements, concerts, recordings, and critical reviews). Scenes generally evolve around entertainment-oriented phenomena, such as music, theater, and dance. People typically enter or join a scene for its expressive and direct gratification, not future gratification. Participation is voluntary, and access is generally available to the public, occasionally for the simple price of admission. Irwin's original formulation of the scene used illustrations from 1960s and 1970s California lifestyles, but we will generalize his concept to include a wide range of music communities.

Barry Shank (1994) applied his notion of scene to the production of live music in Austin, Texas. He describes the "6th Street" phenomenon, near to and nurtured by the University of Texas, in terms of its history, cultural roots, and economic context. His focus is on the effects the production of music scenes has on the identities of their participants—an area of interest in this book as well. Richard Peterson and Andy Bennett (2004) extended these ideas in formulating the following definition of a music scene as the geosocial location that provides a stage on which all of the esthetic, political, social, and cultural features of local music are played out. Of particular relevance to our discussion is Peterson and Bennett's focus on the way participants use local music scenes to differentiate themselves from others.

It should be clear, on the basis of these general definitions, that there can be many different kinds of music scenes. Peterson and Bennett (2004) discuss the following in their book: jazz, blues, rave, karaoke, Britney Spears, salsa, riot grrrls, goth, skatepunk, anarcho-punk, alternative country, and others. We will now discuss a study of a group of Latino music scenes in Houston, Texas. Joe Kotarba conducted this study with the help of a group of graduate students at the University of Houston (Kotarba, Fackler, and Nowotny, 2009; Nowotny, Fackler, Muschi, Wilson, Vargas, and Kotarba 2010). Each student was responsible for a particular Latino music scene. These scenes included: rock en Español, salsa, Tejano, Norteño, gay Latino dance, mariachi, and professional soccer supporters. The study was designed to be an *ethnography* that involved spending considerable time in the field examining the everyday activities of participants in the scene. We will now describe one of the more recent and most exciting of these scenes: rock en Español. This will give us a chance to illustrate some of the most important sociological features of music scenes in general.

Rock en Español

We can define rock en Español as an international movement to create and perform original rock music in Spanish that incorporates themes relevant to the everyday lives of Latino artists and their audiences (Kotarba 1998: 1). Rock en Español is especially important sociologically to study because it is related to other social processes, such as immigration. It illustrates how third-generation Latinos acquire an identity that integrates their Latino heritage, love for the Spanish language, and awareness and concern for current Latino political issues; and it illustrates the postmodern process of globalization that affects culture in general and Latino culture specifically.

Rock en Español is clearly international, with important production and performance centers in Mexico, Central America, South America, Spain, and the United States. The songs are not merely English rock songs translated into Spanish, as was the case not too long ago when many rock en Español bands made a living covering popular rock songs for customers in Latin clubs. Furthermore, the music is not merely the marketing of novelty rock songs sung in Spanish, as was clearly the case with Ritchie Valens' "La Bamba" in the 1950s. And, unlike Valens, who felt it strategic—if not necessary—to shorten his surname from "Valenzuela," *rockeros* feel no need either to disguise their ethnicity or to demean it to make it acceptable to hegemonic Anglo audiences. Instead, *rockeros* celebrate their ethnicity (Kotarba 1998).

Participants in the scene refer to rock en Español as "*el movimiento*," or "the movement." This term denotes the scene as a growing, fashionable trend that is gaining momentum and popularity. This term does not denote a political movement, although politics in the United States and in Mexico are relevant themes in the music. The scene can be found in coffee houses, mainstream rock venues, and even restaurants.

Rock en Español in Houston includes many different styles of rock. Whether indie, alternative, progressive, heavy metal, ska, or others, each particular venue tends to integrate several different styles of Latino music. Politics is pervasive in rock en Español. For instance, the music performed by Molotov from Mexico City, Los Prisioneros from Chile, and Libido from Peru consists almost entirely of songs of liberation, and most rock en Español bands include at least a few political songs in their repertoire. The political themes found in rock en Español represent the social class, ethnic self-definitions, and evolving political orientations of the artists and audience members. There is little if any lyrical discourse on personal disadvantage or discrimination. Put simply, the artists and their audiences, who are largely third-generation Americans, feel they are part of American society. With a sense of confidence in their individual and collective welfare as Americans, they focus their attention on political issues in the lives of *other* Latinos. For instance, it is very fashionable for rock en Español bands to perform songs decrying the plight of undocumented Latinos in the United States.

Perhaps the most eclectic feature of this scene is the DJ's role. Before the bands begin at the Backroom, for example, DJ Raul performs. He operates the expected mixers, turntables, and tape players. This 25-year-old Houston native uses his equipment and DJ skills to display the global context of rock en Español, a globe united more by a common language than perhaps any other feature.

Rock en Español reveals an increasingly fragmented rock'n'roll audience (Barnes 1988). The audience in the Houston scene is interesting because it is not a traditional rock'n'roll audience. Rock en Español fans are generally young adults (in their twenties), either attending college or working at productive jobs. They are overwhelmingly third-generation Mexican Americans who are competently and proudly bilingual. They are upwardly mobile in their careers. There are two visible types of first-generation Americans in the audience. The first group is young, monolingual, working-class men (late teens and early twenties) who are recent arrivals to the United States. They can be seen at venues on the west side of Houston that ordinarily present Tejano or modern Spanish dance music. They attend the occasional rock en Español concert to meet women. The second group is composed of middle-class men and women from Central and South American countries, who attend rock en Español concerts featuring internationally famous artists.

When attending a rock en Español performance, an observer is immediately struck by the importance of the Spanish language. The performers speak fluent and elegant Spanish, at a time in American history when one would expect young, upwardly mobile Latinos to feel great pressure to become predominantly speakers of English.

Overall, rock en Español fans are much like any other rock'n'roll fans. They have even developed ways to type each other. These types allow members to locate others similar to them in musical tastes, interactional styles, and so forth. *Fresas* ("strawberries") are sophisticated fans, largely female, who prefer the lighter/pop versions of rock en Español. They like large crowds and lots of dancing. They can be seen, for example, at the concerts promoted by Edmundo Perez and Vibraciones Alteradas, which attract the widest range of rock en Español audiences. *Greñudos* ("nappy hairs") are working-class fans, largely male, who prefer loud, hard-rock versions of rock en Español.

Scene participants use the scene as a cultural tool in various ways. For instance, although it may appear that rock en Español blocks assimilation through an insistence on Spanish-language use, it in fact functions as an efficient resource for upwardly mobile, third-generation Latinos to become American in the 21st century by creating a music that conforms to the sensibilities of both cultures. Additionally, participation in the rock en Español scene illustrates the current status of Latinos for whom Houston is home, and those for whom Houston is becoming home. Rock en Español functions primarily as a way to become American. The rediscovery of one's heritage through language, culture, politics, and—perhaps most importantly—one's ethnic links with others is a preferred style of people of the third generation coming to grips with the world of their parents and grandparents. Third-generation Jews and Eastern Europeans are now experiencing the same longing for Israel, shtetl, klezmer, and Poland, Chopin, and Catholicism, respectively. Paradoxically, the *rockeros'* rejection of their parents' Tejano and Norteño music in favor of rock'n'roll is not a rejection of their parents, but an effort to share their parents' world on terms that fit with being an American.

Sense of Place

Sense of Place refers to the ways we engage in a reflexive relationship with the places we occupy. We make places as places make us, ourselves, and our identities (Gruenwald 2003). The concept of *sense of place* is important for understanding music scenes in two ways. First, the people involved in producing the music try to create a certain sense of place for the audience, musicians, critics, and others. The coffee houses that offer rock en Español try to meld the intellectual ambience of the coffee house with the particularly bright and colorful aura of Latino culture. Second, Latino music, like other ethnically oriented music styles, has a magical way of creating realities. For rock en Español these realities can include the country of origin, America, or *La Raza* (the mythical land proudly representing the Spanish language and Latino culture). Rock en Español is marked by a contrast between places. Artists and fans alike locate rock en Español on a continuum between cities that are musical, production, and marketing centers—Monterey, Mexico, to Houston is a common link. The Latino experience is marked by movement and a clear sense of distance. The global dimension of rock en Español is reflected in the way DJs commonly sample music from Central American folk musicians as well as South American pop bands.

Rock en Español as Idioculture

The second concept we will discuss is idioculture. Gary Fine (1979: 733) developed the interactionist concept of idioculture in order to stress the importance of studying culture of any kind—including music—in terms of the small groups in which it is lived. For rock en Español, the small groups include the bands, promoters, producers, publicists, fans, and performance venues. Within these groups, fundamental features of rock en Español are worked out—for example, the integration of English and Spanish in composing and performing music favored by all possible audiences. One of the most important and common ways that people use the scene and the idioculture that pervades it is the experience of the *becoming of self*. As Joe Kotarba notes from an existentialist perspective (Kotarba 1984), the self is continuously evolving, changing, and adapting in a continually changing, contemporary social life. The resources for assessing and shaping a sense of self ultimately come from cultural experiences. The becoming of self is analytically noteworthy in our study of Latino music scenes, where many of our respondents are faced with rapidly changing social, political, and cultural environments in which they experience the self. These changes include high mobility (which leaves them with a problematic sense of place), navigation of multiple language communities, and unusual sets of life circumstances that include an ongoing quest for survival among the working class and the development of multiple identities. In light of this, the scene—and the music central to it—becomes an important medium for the "becoming of self," because music is an important cultural resource in Latino communities in general. We can see the ways respondents gravitate toward or even choose styles of Latino music that may vary from the styles with which they grew up or shared with others, as they gravitate toward musical genres that may better fit their many participants.

Conclusion

The argument presented here very likely appears to be self-evident: of course, music takes place in the presence of others. Music is designed to be shared. Nevertheless, sociology goes one step further. The actual experience, feelings, and meaning of music is determined and shaped by the social worlds within which it exists. These worlds can be small, such as the inner world of our bodies and our minds within which we privately enjoy music, not alone but *with ourselves*. Or, these worlds can be large, elaborate, complex, political, cultural, and busily interactive—like a music scene. Isn't music great?

2
FAMILIES

The family is one of the most important institutions in society and one of the most important topics in sociology. The family is what sociologists call a *primary group*, as it is among the groups that are most closely involved in the process of socialization of children to the adult world. We all live in families—whether by birth or by choice, or both—and our family lives are critical determinants of who we are, how we live, how we respond to situations in everyday life, and what our life chances (e.g., careers, health, and incomes) will turn out to be (Williams 1998). Families have cultures of their own, and increasingly borrow from the various cultures available in our contemporary social life to manage their everyday life affairs.

Following Burgess (1926: 5), we can define *family* as a "unity of inter-acting persons." Such a definition escapes, purposefully, criteria of legal or blood ties, and historical and cultural prescriptions. Defining family as a unity of interacting persons also allows us to focus on how families emerge as such unities, as well as on the roles associated with all the persons involved. When we focus on interacting individuals, we also coincidentally zero in on the main focus of this type of interaction: socialization. Formally defined, *socialization* is the "continuous process of negotiated interactions out of which selves are created and re-created" (Gecas 1981: 165). Just like families, socialization never stops, as we are constantly socialized—though at times more than others—into our society by virtue of sheer exposure to norms, values, roles, ideals, beliefs, practices, etc. Families are, however, more central than most other groups to the socialization process because, by virtue of interacting with parental figures, a child acquires early on, and throughout a lifetime, key symbolic resources for the development of a sense of self. More on the self and the life course will be said later.

Not only do family interactions lead to the development of a self-concept, identities, values, beliefs, etc., but family interactions also contribute to nurturance and protection. Yet, even within a family household a child is not immune from external *socialization agents*, like the mass media, and music. Indeed, lay and professional critics have long cast a wary eye to children's culture that has evolved in capitalistic society, largely as a result of the decreasing influence of parental figures, and the growing influence of media as a primary group. We can call these critics *moral entrepreneurs*: individuals who work toward the definition and enforcement of moral values, especially to their liking (Becker 1963). Recently, some of these moral entrepreneurs have been especially critical of materials emanating from the electronic media. These materials include television violence (which allegedly leads to violent behavior among young viewers); music videos (some of which contain sexist or sexually promiscuous messages); and rap music (which is criticized for many reasons, including the promotion of criminal lifestyles and rampant materialism) (see Wilson 1989). Popular music has been critiqued most often and most harshly, being designated as a "social problem" ever since its inception over 50 years ago The purpose of this chapter is to qualify, update, and balance this argument by illustrating the positive as well as potentially negative features of popular music within family settings (Kotarba 1993, 1994b, 2012).

Music as a Social Problem?

Everyday life sociologists do not view social problems as objective conditions. *Social problems* are instead seen as outcomes of negotiations over the meaning and moral value of an event, a state of being, or a situation. Thus, stealing from an early definition by Fuller and Myers (1940: 320), we can say that "social problems are what people think they are and if conditions are not defined as social problems by the people involved in them, they are not problems to those people." To have a social problem, therefore, one needs first to work in concert with others—and perhaps in spite of those with opposing views—toward defining a subject matter as problematic and worthy of concern. That kind of work is known as *social problem work*. Social problem work is the work of moral entrepreneurs. Let us examine the kind of social problem work done by moral entrepreneurs in relation to family and popular music.

Popular music has now fully become an integral feature of North American culture. For three generations, popular music has functioned as a primary source of meaning and leisure time activity for young people. Since its inception in the 1950s, it has been associated with adolescents, and has thus become a medium for both understanding and critiquing the adolescent generation. Some of the earliest socio-logical observers of popular music, namely rock'n'roll, focused on its positive functions for adolescent development.

Another early study, which we mentioned earlier, gives us food for thought on the social problem status of popular music. James Coleman (1961) conducted a now-classic survey of adolescent attitudes and behaviors in various northern Illinois communities in 1955. Coleman was interested in studying both the secondary school experience and adolescent status systems. Coleman found that rock'n'roll was the most popular form of music among both boys and girls. Girls liked to listen to records or the radio more than boys, a phenomenon Coleman explains with the observation that boys had a wider variety of activities available to them. Nevertheless, both boys and girls used rock'n'roll to learn prevailing values for gender roles. Girls used romantic ballads and fan club memberships to learn about boys, dating, and so forth. Boys used "less conventional" stars like Elvis Presley to learn about adventure and masculinity. Overall, Coleman (1961: 236) viewed rock'n'roll positively, since "music and dancing provide a context within which [teenagers] may more easily meet and enjoy the company of the opposite sex." Many teenagers were "passionately devoted" to rock'n'roll (Coleman 1961: 315).

These early sociological observations have, however, been lost in a sea of criticism of the impact of popular music on adolescents (Martin and Segrave 1988). This criticism began in the 1950s with dramatic efforts to eliminate rock'n'roll. Organized burnings of Elvis Presley records because of their alleged association with sinfulness and sexuality were common in fundamentalist communities. In the 1960s, another coalition of moral entrepreneurs argued that rock'n'roll music was unpatriotic, communistic, and the cause of drug abuse. In the 1970s and 1980s, the criticism became organized and sophisticated. Middle-class activist organizations, like the Parents Music Resource Center (PMRC) led by Tipper Gore, opposed much popular music for its alleged deleterious effects on the health of young people. In the 1990s, we find several court cases in which the prosecution and the defense have attempted to legally link popular music, especially heavy metal, goth, and grunge, with suicide and criminal behavior (Hill 1992). Most notably, the infamous Columbine shooting massacre has been linked with the culture of Marilyn Manson fans.

Allan Bloom was among the most influential moral entrepreneurs (1987). He wrote one of the most elegant intellectual attacks on popular music. Bloom, a professor of social thought at the University of Chicago, argued that American universities are in a state of crisis because of their lack of commitment to traditional intellectual standards. Bloom further argued that young people live in a state of intellectual poverty: "Those students do not have books, they most emphatically do have music" (Bloom 1987: 68). Plato, Socrates, and Aristotle all viewed music as a natural mechanism for expressing the passions and preparing the soul for reason. According to Bloom, university students' overwhelming choice in music today, rock music, instead:

> has one appeal only, a barbaric appeal, to sexual desire—not love, not *eros*, but sexual desire undeveloped and untutored . . . young people know that rock has the beat of sexual intercourse . . . Rock music provides premature ecstasy and is like the drug with which it is allied . . . But, as long as they have the Walkman on, they cannot hear what the great tradition has to say. And, after its prolonged use, when they take it off, they find they are deaf.
> (Bloom 1987: 68–81)

In general, many moral entrepreneurs have viewed popular music as either a social problem or a major cause of other social problems.

We wish to propose a contrasting argument. We are not arguing that popular music does not have its shortcomings and undesired effects. Our purpose is to show, however, that listening to rock and pop music has multiple consequences, many of which are positive in light of the role they play in the socialization process and solidifying family relationships. The specific positive consequence to be discussed in this chapter is the many different ways music integrates families and serves as a bridge across generations. This generational bridge allows children, adolescents, and adults to share communication, affect, morality, ethics, and meanings. Later, we will refer to this generation bridge as a kind of role-making.

One major reason critics focus on the dysfunctions of popular music is because they ignore the increasingly obvious fact that rock'n'roll-based popular music is pervasive in North American culture (Kotarba 2002b). We now have three generations who have grown up with popular music and for whom pop music is the preeminent form of music. It serves as the soundtrack for everyday life, providing the context for phenomena such as commercials, patriotic events, high-school graduations, political conventions, and so forth. The positive experiences of pop music simply do not attract the attention of observers, such as journalists and social scientists, whose work is structured around the concept of "the problem." In order to understand the pervasiveness of pop music and its positive as well as negative functions, we propose to somewhat ironically—and courageously!— reconceptualize it as a feature of children's culture.

Pop Music as a Feature of Children's Culture

One of the central foci of interactionist research in relation to the family has to do with the role that family members play in socializing one another, not only to culture, but also to subcultures, like youth culture. And yes, you read correctly: we did say socializing one another. As interactionists we may view socialization as *reciprocal and multi-directional*. In other words, we do not believe that the only kind of socialization is done by parents and guardians unto their children, but also by children unto their parents. Think, for example, of the volume of music listening. How many times have your parents hollered at you to turn the volume down? Well, guess what? The minute you become a parent and you catch your kids listening to music one decibel higher than you're willing to tolerate, you will catch yourself telling them exactly what your parents have told you for years: "Turn it down!!!" Then, chances are, as soon as that sentence escapes your lips, you will catch yourself thinking: "Goodness, I sound like my mom or dad!" In this particular case your children will socialize you to your role and related responsibilities by way of *altercasting* you, that is, by casting you in a role you are supposed to observe. Just like parents socialize children to adult roles, children socialize parents to adult roles! Altercasting is one of the many ways people make roles in everyday life.

Role is a key sociological concept. A *role* can be defined as a part an individual plays within a social setting. A part has rights and duties associated with it, as well as a social status. You can think of a role in a play, for example. Within a play a role is performed by an actor, who plays a script regardless of his/her personality, idiosyncrasies, etc. This happens in everyday social settings as well—as you remember from our loud music example. Also within a play we have minor and starring roles, like we do in society. However, there are some differences between theatrical roles and more mundane ones. Roles in most theatrical productions are strictly enforced by a director, for example, whereas individuals in mundane settings have more power to manipulate their roles and those of others. Within a family we have multiple roles, ranging from parent and relative to child. Roles are also age-graded. A parent is not always just a parent, but the parent of a teenager, or a pre-teen, or a college child, and so forth. Now, with this said, let us return to the music and to how family members socialize one another into specific roles and music-centered age-cultures.

Our thinking posits pop music, especially rock'n'roll styles, as a key element of youth culture. The concept "youth culture," which can be traced at least as far back as the work of Talcott Parsons (1949), is commonly used to denote those everyday practices conducted by adolescents which serve: (1) to identify them as a specific generational cohort, separate from children and adults; (2) as common apparatus for the clarification and resolution of conflict with adults; and (3) to facilitate the process of socialization or transformation into adulthood. Before we go much farther with our argument, let us reflect on the link between music and youth culture.

Conventional thinking isolates certain socio-economic-cultural developments since World War II to construct an explanation for the historically integrated, co-evolution of teenagers and rock and pop (Frith 1981). This theory argues that teenagers were a product of the postwar family. The general cultural portrait of this family is one of middle-class aspiration, if not achievement, suburban orientation, affluence, and consumption. Teenagers in the 1950s comprised not only a demographic bulge in the American population, but also an economic force. Teenagers are viewed as a product of the following formula: allowances + leisure time + energy + parental indulgence. Rock and pop music became an available and useful commodity to sell to teenagers. The music could be readily duplicated, the themes could directly address the angst and adventure of adolescence, and the 45 rpm record could be disposable through the process of the Top 40. As the postwar generation grew into adulthood in the 1960s, they took the previously fun-filled rock'n'roll and turned it into a medium for political dissent and moral/cultural opposition to the generation of their parents. But, as the baby boomers reached full adulthood, they traded in their passion for rock'n'roll for country music and Muzak, leaving succeeding generations of teenagers to consume the hegemonic cultural pablum of formulaic pop and MTV (Grossberg 1992a).

Yet, a powerful cultural experience like growing up with rock'n'roll cannot simply be left behind by movement through the life cycle, that is, by adults' socialization into their new, adult roles. One would reasonably expect to find at least some residual effects of rock'n'roll on adult baby boomers. So, our argument is that if rock'n'roll affected the way they dated, mated, and resisted, then one would reasonably expect rock'n'roll music to shape the way they make their roles, that is, the way they work, parent, construct and service relationships, and in other ways accomplish adulthood. Through our findings and focus, we reveal that, paradoxically, the presence of rock'n'roll in the lives of adults as well as adolescents can be discovered by locating it in the lives and culture of children. How is this possible?

Postmodern theory, which we discussed earlier, is a useful analytical framework for guiding the search for pop music in the nooks and crannies of everyday life. Postmodern theory reminds us that contemporary social life is mass-mediated. Culture is less a reflection of some underlying, formal, firm, structural reality than it is an entity in its own right (Baudrillard 1983). Postmodernism allows the observer to see things not previously visible. For example, postmodernism recently has let us see gender as a critical factor in the process of writing history. Instead of gazing directly at the alleged facts of the past, postmodernism allows historians to focus on the process by which history itself is written. Similarly, postmodern theory lets the sociologist analyze cultural forms like rock'n'roll as free-floating texts with their own styles of production, dissemination, interpretation, and application to everyday life situations. Therefore, at least hypothetically, rock'n'roll is no longer (if it ever was) simply a reflection of the structural positions of adolescents in Western societies, no longer a possession of youth. Rather, cultural items in the postmodern world become available to anyone in society for their individual and subcultural interpretation, modification, and socialization. Rock'n'roll can permeate culture and heavily influence other styles of music and everyday life culture. Another way of saying this is that social roles are less rigid in a postmodern world. We now witness white, middle-class kids listening to and enjoying gangsta rap music. We see Bill Clinton belting out a bluesy groove on his tenor sax, first at his appearance on Arsenio Hall's television program during the presidential campaign and, later, at one of his inaugural parties. To see popular music as a feature of children's culture and a resource for socialization and for role-making within the contemporary postmodern culture helps us to see its presence in all generations in the family, regardless of birth cohort. The concept *children's culture* denotes those everyday practices (1) used by children to interpret and master everyday life; (2) created, acquired, disseminated, and used by adults to construct and define parental relationships with children; and (3) ordinarily associated with children and childhood, yet used by adolescents and adults to interpret, master, or enjoy certain everyday life situations (Kotarba 2012).

What we wish to show and argue in the remainder of this chapter is that pop music serves as a symbolic tool for family members to cross boundaries generally associated with their roles as family members.

In other words, music serves a tool for *role-making* and thus for reciprocal socialization into generational cultures. Thus, for example, children socialize their parents to children's culture through music; parents socialize their children to their own age-specific generational culture. Furthermore, children experience popular music not only as children, but also as a way of learning about their parents' culture, and thus as resource for taking their roles. Similarly, adolescents experience popular music to extend childhood, and adults experience rock'n'roll to relive childhood. We will now provide an inventory of popular music (and in particular rock'n'roll) as a tool for reciprocal socialization, and for blending experiences across generations. We will emphasize those rock'n'roll experiences most taken for granted by professional and lay observers alike, because those experiences function positively as elements of children's culture. We will conclude with a brief discussion of the contribution of this style of analysis to the social scientific literature on rock'n'roll and a reflection on the status of popular music as a social problem.

Adolescents as Children

As mentioned above, standard wisdom on rock'n'roll argues that it has functioned largely to establish adolescence as a distinct stage in the life cycle. Furthermore, rock'n'roll is seen as a weapon in conflicts between adults and adolescents. The mass media contribute to this overstated, over-romanticized view of rock'n'roll and adolescence. The film *Footloose* (Ross 1984), for example, portrays the plausible scenario in which fundamentally conservative, small-town adults view rock'n'roll as an evil influence on their teenagers. Rock'n'roll is portrayed in the film as the gauntlet that forces teenagers to choose between good and evil by choosing their parents or dancing. The rebellious imagery of Elvis Presley portrays a prevailing cultural myth that allies rock'n'roll with youthful rebellion, unbridled sexuality, cross-ethnic intimacy, and a wide range of delinquent activities. The punk and heavy metal imagery has also done this in recent years. These cultural images support an ideological vision of youth culture that overemphasizes the independence, rebellion, and integration of teenagers.

A revisionist or postmodernist reading of this history finds much more diversity within youth culture. For every Elvis Presley fan in the

1950s and 1960s, there was an *American Bandstand* fan. *American Bandstand*, especially in its early days, when it was broadcast live after school from Philadelphia, portrayed rock'n'roll as a form of pop music, in much milder and more acceptable (to adults as well as teenagers) ways. The kids on *American Bandstand* were "all-American" kids. They dressed modestly and neatly. They all chewed Beech-Nut Gum, provided by the sponsor of the program. And, above all, they were extremely well behaved. The boys and girls, especially the "regulars," tended to match up as boyfriends and girlfriends, not as potentially promiscuous dates and mates. *American Bandstand* probably represented most teenagers in American society at that time. And teenagers could not participate in activities like *American Bandstand* without the approval, if not support, of their parents. After all, someone had to drive the kids to the studio or at least give them permission and money to take the bus there, just as someone had to provide the television and permit to watch *American Bandstand* at home.

Parents were, and continue to be, cautious supporters of their children's popular music activities. There is more of a tendency among parents to manage popular music as though their teenagers are children who need to be nurtured and protected, rather than adolescents who must be controlled, sanctioned, and feared. For example, Joe Kotarba's current research on heavy metal and rap music has found the continuation of three generations of ambiguous parental feelings of cautious support toward these styles of pop music. At a Metallica concert in Houston, numerous teenagers indicated that their parents did not approve of heavy metal music for various reasons (e.g., volume, distortion, immorality, and potential affiliation with evil like Satanism). Yet, these same parents carpooled their teenagers and friends to the Astrodome on a school day and, in most cases, bought or provided the money for tickets. One plausible explanation is that, although the parents did not approve of their children's tastes in music, they wanted to do all they could to minimize the risk of anything going wrong that afternoon and to pander, if you will, to their kids. A similar situation exists among African-American and Hispanic parents in terms of the popularity of rap music among their teenagers (Kotarba 1994a). Mass-media-generated images of obstinate if not rebellious youth generally ignore the reflexive relationship between teenagers and their parents. As long as teenagers live at home as legal, financial, and moral dependants—that is, as children—their parents provide the resources for creating musical identities (e.g., allowances, free time, and fashionable hip-hop clothing). Parents then respond to the identities they helped create by controlling, criticizing, sanctioning, and punishing their teenagers for living out their popular music-inspired identities— responding to them as if they were autonomous, responsible adults.

From the teenagers' perspective, popular music is commonly an extension of childhood experiences. The Summer of Love in 1967 is the case in point. Mass-media accounts treat the Monterey Music Festival and Haight-Asbury as benchmarks in the emergence of the youth counterculture. The Summer of Love marked the fulfillment of rock'n'roll as an instrument of adolescent rebellion, within a context of heavy drug use, free love, and political liberation—a clash between young people's values and those of their parents. The media argue that the political events of the late 1960s institutionalized and radicalized the unbridled, individualistic, and existentially youthful rebellion of the 1950s and early 1960s.

A historical and thoughtful reexamination of these events suggests that the innocence of middle-class, postwar, baby boom childhood served as the primary metaphor for these young people. High status was attributed to the "flower child," whom the counterculture posited as the innocent who simply rejected the oppression of the adult establishment. Women in the movement with high status were known as "earth mothers," who nurtured themselves and their peers through natural foods, folk arts, and the ability to roll good joints for the group. Whereas the mass media stress the centrality of Jimi Hendrix and Jim Morrison to the music of this period, more childlike songs like Peter, Paul and Mary's "Puff, the Magic Dragon" and Jefferson Airplane's "White Rabbit" (inspired by *Alice in Wonderland*) were at least as significant. The 1960s generation popularized the use of animation as a format for rock'n'roll (e.g., the Beatles' "Yellow Submarine"). Perhaps the most interesting support for our argument is the way the 1960s generation drifted away from the adult world of commercialized and confined concert halls to the park-like atmosphere of the open-air concert festival, where the audience could play with Frisbees and other toys.

The pervasive mass media increasingly expose young children to popular music. CBS broadcasts "The Doodlebops" on Saturday morning to a very young children's audience. The main characters are Deedee, Rooney, and Moe Doodle—three multi-talented rock stars who are always singing, dancing, and learning from each other. The program emphasizes an appreciation of music and social issues through original songs. Nor does it stop there. Several school supply companies are now marketing math and reading enhancement programs based upon popular music icons and idioms, such as the "Reading, Writing, and Rock'n'roll" curriculum.

Even the darker moments of rock'n'roll have their childlike attributes. Some teenage fans experience heavy metal music as a mechanism for managing lingering, childhood anxieties. Metallica's "Enter Sandman" was a popular video on MTV during 1991–1992. As part of an ethnographic study of homeless teenagers, Joe Kotarba asked these kids to talk about their music. This particular video was very popular with them. He asked them specifically to interpret the very old, scary-looking man in the video. The street kids tended to see the man as a reflection of their own real nightmares, such as physically abusive parents and drug-infested neighborhoods. In a contrasting set of interviews with middle-class kids, Joe commonly heard them say that the man represented nightmares, but only the inconsequential nightmares children have and ultimately outgrow (Kotarba 1994a).

Children as Children

The pervasive mass media increasingly expose young children to popular music. The Teenage Mutant Ninja Turtle rock concert tour and Saturday morning television (e.g., the *M.C. Hammer* cartoon program) all focus on pre-adolescent audiences. Perhaps the best current example is the Hannah Montana phenomenon. Nor does it stop there. Several school supply companies are now marketing math and reading enhancement programs based upon popular music icons and idioms, such as the "Reading, Writing, and Rock'n'roll" curriculum.

But beyond simple marketing, popular music informs our general cultural views of children. *Honey, I Blew Up the Kids* was a popular film comedy in 1992. The storyline had a bumbling, scientist father mistakenly turning his infant into a colossus. As the child innocently marched down a boulevard in Las Vegas, he grabbed the large, neon-lit guitar from a music club and proceeded to pretend to play a rock'n'roll song (a generic, rockabilly song was actually playing in the film's background). The guitar served as a toy for the baby. The imagery suggested the baby as adolescent, an absurdity that helped establish the overall absurdity of the story.

Young children can grasp rock and pop even when it is not intentionally produced for, or marketed to, them. When the pop band Los Lobos covered the 1950s hit "La Bamba," it became a hit among elementary-school-aged children. Like many rock and pop songs, young kids find its simple lyrics silly and its beat fun to dance around to. As country music broadens its appeal by "crossing over" to rock and pop music audiences, it also creates an audience of children. Miley Cyrus's father, country singer Billy Ray Cyrus, had a hit with "Achy Breaky Heart" that has remained a fun song for many children.

An interesting development in children-oriented pop music has been the Gorillaz phenomenon. Gorillaz is an animated rock band that is like a cartoon, except that it is appreciated by adolescents and children alike. Its award-winning videos are animations, and several of its songs have been radio, iTunes and MTV hits. Fans also have access to play figure toys for all the Gorillaz characters.

Adults as Children

Adults who grew up on rock'n'roll may want to relive the fun, excitement, or meaningfulness of their earlier music experiences. This can happen in two ways. First, adults may simply retrieve the past through nostalgia. In many cities, oldies or "classic rock" music stations are the most popular radio stations, catering to audiences approximately 24 to 45 years of age. Rock'n'roll nostalgia also appears in the guise of (roughly) 1950s and 1960s clubs. These clubs are often decorated in postwar diner motif, offering period food such as meatloaf sandwiches and malted milk shakes. Parents and their children dine to piped-in oldies, within an atmosphere resembling that of the *Happy Days* television program.

The baby boomer generation's attempts to maintain the feeling of childhood through rock'n'roll extends into their encounter with adulthood. From the 1980s on, the baby boomer generation has been the strongest supporter of contemporary versions of the rock'n'roll festival. Every large and most medium-sized cities now have what are referred to as "shed venues." These outdoor concert sites, such as Ravinia in Chicago, Wolf Trap in Washington D.C., and the Mitchell Pavilion in Houston, serve as the setting for baby boomers to bring their blankets and their picnic baskets—and often their children and grandchildren— to hear concerts by soft rock and New Age performers. New Age music (e.g., Windham Hill stars such as Yanni and Will Ackerman), by the way, fits our broad definition of rock'n'roll, if not as a genre, at least as a concept. It is simply mellow, electronically amplified music appreciated by adults who want to extend their rock'n'roll experiences, but who for physical or status/cultural reasons choose to give up the volume and anxiety of pure rock'n'roll.

Rock'n'roll nostalgia is interesting because of the types of music chosen by programmers to attract and please their audiences. The music is typically 1950s-style rockabilly or early 1960s pop rock (e.g., the Beach Boys and Motown groups). The primary audience for oldies programming, however, grew up with the somewhat harsher and harder music of the later 1960s (e.g., psychedelia and anti-war music). Most chose to forsake their own music for the easygoing, fun music of their older siblings who grew up in the 1950s. In the language of postmodernism, the oldies culture is a *simulacrum* (see Baudrillard 1983). It never existed in its original state as it is now presented to consumers. Again, adults commonly choose to relive the childlike side of their reconstructed adolescence, not the adult side.

Second, adults may engage in continuous rock'n'roll experiences that are constructed in the present. Many adults, especially males, maintain their original interest in rock'n'roll. They are visible at live concerts of 1960s and 1970s performers who are still "on the road" (e.g., the Rolling Stones, Led Zeppelin, The Who, and the Moody Blues). They continue to buy recorded music, but much less than teenagers do. An intriguing bonding and gift-giving ritual among middle-class and middle-aged adult males is the exchange of tape dubs. One fan will purchase a new recording (preferably on compact disc) and proceed to dub high-quality cassette tape copies for distribution to neighbors, co-workers, business associates, and others with similar tastes. Van Morrison fans are a good example of this trend.

Yet, adults are supported in their pursuit of rock'n'roll by advances in technology and marketing. Adults can listen to their very specific styles of rock'n'roll, without the commercials intended for young people, through satellite radio. They can also purchase their music of choice from the comfort of their home office via amazon.com and iTunes (Kotarba 2012).

Adults may also use rock'n'roll as a medium for rebellion. Practical and proven strategies developed during adolescence to enrage parents and other adults are retrieved to use against current opponents, such as wives. Some men turn up their stereos at home simply to aggravate their wives. In contrast, there are also wives who banish their husbands to the basement or the garage to play their loud music, similar to the shaming banishment of a cigarette-smoking spouse to the backyard (Kotarba 2012).

Adults as Parents

As we have seen, members of all generations use some version of rock'n'roll music in everyday life. The major argument here, however, is that popular music also serves as a bridge across the generations. Rock and pop are shared by children, adolescents, and adults. As one would easily guess, much of this sharing takes place within the family. Yet, contrary to common wisdom, we will argue that much of this sharing is functional and positive: rock and pop help integrate families.

From the early days of Elvis Presley to current issues surrounding rap music, our mass culture has portrayed rock and pop as a source of tension within families (Martin and Segrave 1988). Whether this conflict is over lyrics or volume, or whatever, the fact is that children could not experience music without the implicit, if not explicit, support of their parents (as we have seen in the case of *American Bandstand* and Metallica). The cultural pervasiveness of pop music lets it function in many different ways in the family, much like religion or television have.

We will now present an inventory of these—largely taken-for-granted—positive features of pop and rock music.

Mother and Daughter Bonding

Rock and pop have always served as a special commonality between mothers and daughters. They shared Elvis Presley in the 1950s, Frankie Avalon and the Beatles in the 1960s, and Neil Diamond in the 1970s. In the feminist era of the 1980s and 1990s, however, the object of sharing shifted to other women. Madonna is the case in point.

Madonna represents a popular phenomenon that is attractive to both mothers and daughters. Madonna is a multi-faceted star whose appeal rests upon lifestyle, clothing style, and attitude as well as musical performance. During the Houston stop on the "Like a Virgin" tour, a number of mother–daughter pairs who attended were interviewed. The pairs typically were dressed alike, in outfits such as black bustier and short black skirts, with matching jewelry. During the interviews, they talked about Madonna in similar ways and appeared more like friends than family. In virtually all cases, they noted a distinct lack of true appreciation of Madonna by the men in their lives (e.g., fathers, husbands, brothers, and boyfriends who may look at Madonna and only see a sex object). And, in most cases, the mothers indicated that Madonna served to bring them closer to their daughters.

Gwen Stefani is a pop music phenomenon that is attractive to both mothers and daughters. She is an intriguing singer who makes a fashion statement with an attitude. She is one young, but not too young, performer to whom mothers can relate—unlike marginal artists such as Selena Gomez (to the super-young side) or Ke$ha (to the edge). Molly is a 45-year-old account executive who accompanied her 17-year-old daughter to a recent Gwen Stefani concert: "I like Gwen Stefani because she reminds me a lot of a younger Madonna. She sings with style and dresses with style—although I would never wear some of her outfits."

A currently fashionable style of music shared by mothers and daughters are hip-hop performers like Justin Timberlake and Kanye West. Other female pop performers who fit this category include the recent winners of the *American Idol* television competition, Kelly

Clarkson and Carrie Underwood. Which mother–daughter duo does not like Katy Perry?

Father and Son Bonding

Fathers and sons also use rock and pop music to bond, but in different ways than one might expect. Fathers who learned to play guitar in the 1960s or 1970s teach their sons how to play. Sharing music is difficult, as the younger generation today continues the traditional ideological belief that their music is better than that of their parents. Fathers and sons are considerably more vehement than women in their allegiance to their generation's music. In recent years, musical bonding has been relatively easy in light of the resurgence of 1970s and 1980s reunion bands on tour. In 2012 alone, the Rolling Stones, The Who, Kid Rock, Led Zeppelin, Bruce Springsteen, and the E Street Band, Van Halen, and the Smashing Pumpkins all played the type of loud, guitar-driven rock'n'roll that many dads and sons can share. Also think of how music-centered video games like Guitar Hero bring together kids and parents to rock out over classic and more recent rock anthems.

During Joe Kotarba's study of the evolving rave phenomenon in Houston (Kotarba 1993), he heard one 16-year-old boy exclaim: "I hate my dad's music. He listens to that old shit, like Led Zeppelin." On the other hand, recent trends like rave (i.e., dance parties held in clandestine locations, to the beat of loud synthesized music) display a renaissance in the 1960s counterculture. Psychedelia is "in," for example, with LSD as the drug of choice and lighting provided by mood lamps. Teenagers see rave as a way of retrieving the romance and simplicity of the 1960s. In a way, these kids accept their parents' claim that growing up in the 1960s was special. Another example are Deadhead fathers and their sons sharing the Grateful Dead experience, or current versions of the jam-band phenomenon such as Phish or String Cheese Incident.

In Joe's own family, he had a very special rock'n'roll experience with his oldest son, Chris, when he was 5 years old. They were driving out to a fishing hole in their old pick-up truck, when the local hard rock radio station began playing songs from the Van Halen album *1984*. This is one of Joe's all-time favorite albums and, in a sociological sense, definitive of the state of rock music in the mid-1980s. When the pounding, driving anthem "Panama" came on the radio, it began with the loud rumble of a motorcycle taking off. Chris proceeded to jump around in his seat to the excitement of what he knew as the "motorcycle song." Like any proud baby boomer father, a tear left Joe's eye when he realized that his son was OK: he liked rock'n'roll!

Family Leisure Activities

Rock'n'roll fits well with the burgeoning family leisure and vacation industry. Family theme parks typically have some attraction related to rock'n'roll, such as the complete mock-up of a 1950s small-town main street in the Fiesta Texas theme park in San Antonio. The artists performing at amphitheaters in the Six Flags parks include REO Speedwagon, the Eagles reunion band, and the latest version of the Jefferson Airplane/Starship.

Whereas the concept "family entertainment" in the 1950s, 1960s, and 1970s referred to phenomena such as wholesome television programming, Walt Disney films and home games, it increasingly refers to pop music today. The rock and pop presented usually addresses a common denominator acceptable to both parents and children, such as rockabilly or 1970s power pop groups like Cheap Trick and Aerosmith.

Religious Socialization

Rock'n'roll functions as a mechanism for teaching religious beliefs and values in families, whether or not rock'n'roll is compatible with the particular family's religious orientation. For mainstream Protestant denominations, rock'n'roll increasingly fits the liturgy. For example, when Amy Grant played a concert in Houston several years back as part of her *Angels* album tour, her music was loud and fast (e.g., seven-piece band with double drummers and double lead guitars). Parents accompanying their children to the concert peppered the audience. One father, in his thirties, brought his wife and 10-year-old daughter to the concert (which he learned about at his Lutheran church). When asked about the compatibility of Christian rock music with Christianity, he stated:

> We love Amy Grant. She is married and tours with her husband, which is not the case with regular rock stars. Her songs are full of

Christian messages. Any way you can get the message of Christ to your kids is OK with us.

The variety of Christian rock styles is growing. A particularly intriguing version is Christian heavy metal (Kotarba 2013a). One rock club in Houston routinely books Christian heavy metal bands on Sunday evenings. One evening, they booked a Christian speed metal band, White Cross, that played extremely loud and fast music about Jesus. Joe Kotarba talked to several parents who accompanied their children to the concert. The parents were very polite, clean-cut, middle-class, Southern Baptists surrounded by a sea of punk rockers and headbangers. They very much seemed like the parents of the *American Bandstand* generation discussed above. They created the opportunity for their teenagers to attend the concert by carpooling them and their friends in from the suburbs. They hoped that the message emanating from the long-haired rockers was indeed Christian, but they wanted to see for themselves to make sure that Satan was not infiltrating the event.

Certain Christian denominations view rock'n'roll of any kind as evil, whether under the guise of Christian rock or not. Parents in this faith focus their attention on rock'n'roll as a way of establishing moral boundaries for their children. For example, a very popular video among conservative youth ministers is called *Rock and Roll: A Search for God*. The producer, Eric Holmberg, displays numerous rock album covers to illustrate his argument that rockers, especially heavy metal rockers, advertently or inadvertently proclaim Satanic messages. For fundamentalist parents, rock'n'roll functions as a convenient and accessible way of teaching their children clearly and directly that Satan and evil are present in today's world and can take various attractive forms.

Moral and Historical Socialization

Rock'n'roll functions as a mechanism for articulating general moral rules and values for particular groups. Although the PMRC was broadly based politically, it supported the religious right's concern for the threat rock'n'roll poses to the moral, physical, and psychological health of their children (Weinstein 1991). For middle-class and upwardly mobile African-American parents, rap music clarifies the issue of gender abuse within their community (see Light 1992). In a more institutionalized sense, rap music is becoming the medium of choice among inner-city teachers for transmitting emerging moral messages. For example, rap music is now allowed in the Houston public schools for student talent shows. The local news regularly highlights school programs in which students use rap idioms to convey anti-smoking and anti-drug messages.

Families use rock'n'roll to relay a sense of history to their children. For example, every year on Memorial Day in Houston, various veterans' organizations sponsor a concert and rally at the Miller Outdoor Theater. Most of the veterans present fought in Vietnam, the first war for which rock'n'roll served as the musical soundtrack. Most of the veterans bring their children to the event. Among all the messages and information available to the kids is the type of music popular during the war. A popular band regularly invited to perform is the Guess Who, whose "American Woman" was a major anthem among soldiers. Joe has observed fathers explaining the song to their teenaged and pre-teenaged children, who would otherwise view it as just another of dad's old songs. The fathers explain that the song had different meanings for different men. For some, it reminded them of girlfriends back home who broke up with them during the war. For others, the title was enough to remind them of their faithful girlfriends back home. For still others, the song reminded them of the occasions when they were sitting around camp, smoking pot, and listening to any American rock'n'roll songs available as a way of bridging the many miles between them and home. In Houston, Juneteenth and Cinco de Mayo activities function much the same way for African-American and Latino families, respectively.

The current "green" environmental movement is a current illustration of moral socialization. The audience for "Live Earth" in 2007 was very intergenerational and, ironically, created a situation in which children may have sent environmental messages to parents.

The Social Construction of Evil in Popular Music

As we mentioned above, sociologists of everyday life focus on the social mechanisms by which agents of social control construct or define what is evil and what is not. There are two recent examples of the social construction of evil in popular music in general and rock'n'roll in particular.

The first example is a telephone call made from a group of concerned parents to the editor of the *Houston Chronicle* back in 1993. The leader of the group was concerned about the way rave parties were allowing under-aged teenagers to attend and obtain dance drugs (e.g., ketamine, LSD, and ecstasy). The youngsters would either be able to purchase the drugs on the dance floor or simply be given drugs by older predators in the crowd. The editor called the Texas Commission on Alcohol and Drug Abuse for help, and TCADA called Joe Kotarba, who they knew as a sociologist who studied music and youth subcultures. Joe enlisted the help of a group of graduate students to conduct a study of the emerging rave phenomenon (Kotarba 1993), and soon learned that the parents' "group" that first voiced concerns over rave consisted of one parent, a father from Kingwood, Texas.

The second example occurred in 2010. The producers of *Sesame Street* on PBS broadcast a music video in which Katy Perry and Elmo chased each other around. They were clearly playing a game like tag or Gotcha! Katy Perry was dressed like, well, Katy Perry: Crayola-colored dress, perhaps a bit too short on top and on the bottom, but not otherwise revealing. PBS pulled the video in reaction to objections raised by parents that KP was not a good role model for their very young children. In a conversation with PBS staff in Austin, Texas, Joe was told that there were perhaps two or three parents at most complaining about the KP video.

Discussion and Conclusion

What do we make of the two examples above of social/music control? Were the parents wrong in demonstrating concern for their children's welfare? Probably not—that's what parents are for! Did the parents overreact? In the case of the rave parties, maybe not. Recreational drugs and under-age kids are not a healthy mix. We can commonsensically ask the following rhetorical, if conservative, question: Do the parents have the primary responsibility to make sure their 14-year-old daughters are at home that late in the evening? That moral or even legal judgment is really not within the purview of a sociological analysis. The one, clear sociological observation is that the nature of the "agent of social/music control" in our society has changed. Parents, like the rest of us, have powerful access to the mass media. Parents can communicate their concerns publicly through Facebook, Twitter, and regular email, pin addition to the traditional letter to the editor or mayor. Thus, the extent or pervasiveness of a parental concern over popular music is less clear than would be the case, again, with a traditional medium such as a signed petition.

We have only touched upon the many ways popular music in general and rock'n'roll specifically works positively for people, as a medium of culture and means to family integration. There are obvious limitations to this analysis. The illustrations certainly do not represent all popular music experiences in a systematically sampled way. The generalizations presented here are clearly based primarily upon the experiences of white, middle-class rock'n'roll fans and their families, yet the principles of family culture use discussed here apply across subpopulations in Western societies.

While our empirical focus has been on the family, we have also touched on another important domain of sociological investigation: the study of social problems. The intellectual field of social problems study is predicated on the assumption that social phenomena can be denoted as "problems" because they somehow differ from the norm, the reasonably expected, or simply other phenomena. But when a phenomenon is pervasive throughout or endemic to a group, it is difficult to call it a problem. Rock and pop music are a social problem only if one assumes that it is limited to a portion of the population (teenagers) who use it to harm themselves or others. However, rock and pop "belong" to all portions of the population.

These findings are evidence for the argument that the true "cause" of social problems associated with children and adolescents lies beyond the music they choose to listen to. On the one hand, music simply serves too many positive, integrative functions at the family and individual level for its audiences to be considered a "problem" in its own right. On the other hand, these findings strongly suggest that we look deeper for the roots of children's and adolescents' problems, such as the structure of the family itself. Rock'n'roll is all too often merely a convenient scapegoat for these problems.

3

SELF AND THE LIFE COURSE

Nature vs. Nurture [handwritten]

The notion of *life course* is important to a particularly sociological perspective on people and their behavior. In general, sociologists believe that people are only partially shaped by their biological and genetic capacities. Instead, our self and how we approach social life are constantly shaped by events and experiences that happen all the way through life. We change constantly, if not occasionally dramatically. The concept of life course holds that socialization is a lifelong process (Furstenberg 1991). Accordingly, our appreciation for and use of popular music is a dynamic process that does not end when we become adults.

Social scientists have traditionally focused on popular music experiences among young audiences. The focus has been on pop music specifically as a feature of adolescent culture and, therefore, of teenagers' everyday life experiences. As Simon Frith (1981) noted in his famous sociological text *Sound Effects*, rock music has been fundamental to the experience of growing up ever since the end of World War II. Similarly, sociologists have demonstrated increasing interest over the years in rock and pop music as an indicator of dramatic changes occurring in the social and cultural worlds of teenagers. We can trace this interest at least as far back as David Riesman's (1950) classic examination of the emergence of the *other-directed* personality in post-World War II American society. The new middle class was marked by a weakening of parental control, a preoccupation with consumption, and a shift in the meaning of leisure, resulting in the masses—the lonely crowd—desperately trying to have fun. The time was ripe for the emergence of a youth culture defined by what have come to be known as pop and rock music.

The popular music industry that drives rock and pop continues to expand dramatically—beyond multi-billion-dollar annual sales, globalization, CDs, MP3 technology, and the Internet, and even the resurgence of vinyl! Yet, lay and scholarly observers have generally ignored or underplayed an important element of social and cultural change: rock and pop are no longer limited to, nor solely the possession of, teenagers. The original generation of rock fans— the baby boomers— are now parents and, in some cases, grandparents. The music and musical culture they grew up with has stayed with them, becoming the soundtrack of North American cultures.

The purpose of this chapter is to survey the many ways popular music pervades the everyday lives of adults in North American society. In commonsense terms, we examine what happened to the first, complete generation of rock fans: the baby boomer generation now in late middle age. We argue that rock'n'roll music continues to serve as a critical meaning resource for its adult fans as they continuously experience the becoming of self throughout life. Rock'n'roll evolves into related and contemporary forms of popular music. To better understand how music works throughout the life course, we begin by discussing in some depth the concepts of self, identity, and the life course itself.

Self, Identity, and the Life Course

The self is probably the most important concept for all everyday life sociologists. Yet, it is often used improperly or confused with the concept of identity. Before we proceed to examine the empirical material unique to this chapter, let us discuss in some detail these important ideas. And let us begin with the self. The self, as the word itself suggests, is a reflexive object. Think, for example, of its common use in expressions like "I hurt myself." When you hurt yourself you direct attention (the realization that you are in pain) to you as an object. In doing so you are both a subject (knower and feeler, in this case) of your action and an object (known and felt). You are a subject in the sense that you are the one who is mustering attention and directing focus, and you are an object in the sense that such attention is focused on you. In doing so,

George Herbert Mead (1934) tells us, you are *minding* yourself. It is by minding that, indeed, we create a sense of self. We mind our self into being by, for example, engaging in internal conversations (e.g., thinking about oneself), monitoring our sensations, experiencing feelings about the self, and so forth. The "doing" of all these things is the "doing" of the self. The self, in other words, is a constant process, a way of "self-ing" ourselves into being as a result of our actions as a subject (the "I") and as an object of our actions (the "me").

Song lyrics are great for illustrating the components of the self as identified by Mead. Consider the following made-up (and totally mind-blowing) pop song lyrics:

> I love you girl.
> You mean the world to me.
> You make me feel like a squirrel.
> That's weird and so is me.

In these odd lyrics, the subject part of the self (the "I") is obvious. The subject is the person (ahem, Bryce) writing the lyrics and singing to his fictitious "girl." Think of the "I" part of the self as the lyricist. The second part of the self, the object, is the "me." The lyricist is writing about his self as if it were a thing, something separate from him. In the English language, sometimes we refer to ourselves as "me" and other times as "I." In the lyric above, the use of "me" in line 4 is grammatically incorrect, but it rhymes and, more importantly, that "me" is the "me" part of the self as an object. Of course, the lyrics are crazy, but not the work of a schizophrenic. The sociological view of self is that it is simultaneously a "subject" and an "object," or the lyricist and the lyric. The final part of the self, the one that *minds* the self, is what Mead referred to as the *generalized other*. This term refers to how we think of ourselves from the perspectives of others or, more appropriately, how we imagine others see us. Perhaps these lyrics are weird because the lyricist's generalized other is strange—it has been shaped by life in the Deep South— but they are not entirely unusual in the realm of popular music, as singing about love and girls and even being lyrically silly are generally approved-of ways to write pop songs. The generalized other is the most social part of the self, telling the "I" how to think about the "me" based on how the self imagines the points of views of others. Popular music heavily influences many people's generalized other, and in this way it exerts a sizable influence over our sense of self.

Identity refers to something different from self. An identity is a typification of self, either imposed upon an individual by others (*social identity*) or adopted by self (*personal identity*). For example, if others view Bryce as a punk rocker and treat him as such, his social identity is that, indeed, of a punk rocker. Others could treat him as a punk rocker even in spite of the fact that he carefully distinguishes his identity among available punk styles (and identities) and identifies himself as a hardcore punk rocker (his personal identity). An identity can be more or less stable across social settings. For example, Bryce's youth friends may have always identified him as punk rocker for all his life but, if one evening he were to attend a grindcore concert and enjoy it, he may very well, at least for that evening, identify himself as (and be identified by other concert attendants as) a grindcore fan. We can refer to these momentary identities that we take up and shed on a regular daily basis as *situational identities*. So, for example, despite our more enduring social and personal identities, on any given day we can have situational identities such as bus-rider, grocery-shopper, pedestrian, etc.

The discussion above highlights the processual nature of self and identity. Think of the self as a molecule of water. A molecule of water is made up of two components: hydrogen and oxygen. A self is similarly the result of the combination of two components: the "I" and the "me." A molecule of water is always in flux throughout its life. When suspended amidst clouds and then falling from the sky, it assumes the identity of a raindrop; when frozen up high in the mountains, it has the identity of an ice crystal; when melting and flowing down the mountain, it has the identity of river water; and when merging with the ocean, it assumes the identity of sea water. Now, of course, a molecule of water has no reflexivity (and no personal identity), but from this example you can at least see that its life is a never-ending process and that throughout this process it assumes different identities in light of the settings it inhabits. The same can be said of the self: throughout the life course an individual assumes different social, situational (and also personal) identities as a result of the fluidity of life and the social "pools" with which we come into contact. To the concept of life course we now turn.

A *life course* is a patterned temporal trajectory of individual experiences. Some scholars, notably social psychologists and psychologists, like to identify objective and universal stages typical for all individuals. Interactionists and constructionists are instead less interested in determining fixed stages and more in examining how individuals assign meanings to their progression through life. Their focus is more precisely on "how persons occupying different locations in social space interpret and respond to repeated social messages about the meanings of age" (Clair, Karp, and Yoels 1993: vii). Reflecting on the contribution of these authors, in an influential overview of the concept and research on the life course, sociologists James Holstein and Jay Gubrium (2003: 836) write that "(1) age and life stages, like any temporal categories, can carry multiple meanings; (2) those meanings emerge from social interaction; and (3) the meanings of age and the course of life are refined and reinterpreted in light of the prevailing social definitions of situations that bear on experience through time." As you can obviously see, the life course is therefore about the becoming of self: the fluid process through which we acquire new and diverse roles, social identities, and personal identities. Music, we argue, provides a set of symbolic resources for the definition and reinterpretation of these identities: through music we continuously self ourselves into being. But how, precisely, do we do so?

The Becoming of Self

The existential sociological concept of *the becoming of self* is a useful guide in seeking the sociological answers to this question. Existential social thought is heavily derived from and very close in nature to symbolic interactionism. A difference is that existential sociology views the self "as a unique experience of being within the context of contemporary social conditions, an experience most notably marked by an incessant sense of becoming and an active participation in social change" (Kotarba 1984: 223). The incessant sense of becoming is a reflection of the contemporary need for the individual to be prepared to reshape meanings of self in response to the dictates of a rapidly changing social world. The well-integrated self accepts the reality of change and welcomes new ideas, new experiences, and reformulations of old ideas and experiences that help one adapt to change (Kotarba 1987).

The idea of *becoming* is one of the most important ideas in existentialist thought across disciplines, because it places responsibility for fashioning a self on the individual. Whereas Jean-Paul Sartre (1945) argued dramatically that we are condemned to be free and to choose who we are to become, Maurice Merleau-Ponty (1962) insisted more moderately and sociologically that we must ground our becoming-of-self in the real world in order to cope effectively with it. Thus, an effective strategy for becoming begins with a foundation of personal experience and the constraints of social structure, while evolving in terms of the resources presented by culture. We argue that middle-aged North Americans work with a self that is built to some degree on the meanings provided by the rock'n'roll idiom, and they continue to nurture the self within the ever-present cultural context of rock'n'roll.

Jack Douglas (1984) notes that there are, in fact, two analytically distinct stages of becoming-of-self with which the modern actor contends. The first is *the need to eliminate or control threats to the basic security of self* (e.g., meaninglessness, isolation from others, shame, death). Although existential psychotherapists like Irvin Yalom (1978) argue that chronic insecurity—or neurosis—is pervasive in our society, Douglas argues sociologically that it is more common for the sense of security to vary biographically, situationally, and developmentally. In general, adults try to shape everyday life experiences in order to avoid basic threats to the self. Basic threats to the adult self in our society would include divorce, the loss of a job, the loss of children (e.g., the empty nest syndrome), illness, disability, and poverty. The second stage of becoming-of-self involves *growth of the sense of self*. Growth occurs when the individual seeks new experiences as media for innovative and potentially rewarding meanings for self (Kotarba 1987). It is through growth, or self-actualization as it is often referred to today, that life becomes rich, rewarding, full, and manageable.

As the case of adult rock fans suggests, they nurture their interest in, and experience with, rock'n'roll music for two reasons. On the one hand, keeping up with the music and the culture that were so important to them when growing up helps them maintain *continuity* with the past and thus solidifies the sense of self-security. On the other hand, working hard to keep rock'n'roll current and relevant to their lives helps adults grow as parents, as spiritual beings, and as friends. The process of integrating rock'n'roll into one's continuing life, however, is not always smooth. Joanna Davis (2006) conducted research that reveals how certain members of the punk scene age gracefully, but in other cases an "old punk" is an oxymoron. A critical point about the self is illustrated by her documentation of how the punk "scene" rejects or accepts aging, which is that the self is inherently social. We all require, to a greater or lesser extent, validation and input from others to determine who we are and are allowed to be.

The concept of the *existential self* tells us that the experience of individuality is never complete; the answer to the question "Who am I?" is always tentative. In the postmodern world, the mass media—including popular music—serve as increasingly important audiences to the self. The *self* is situational and mutable (Zurcher 1977). One can be various selves as the fast-paced, ever-changing, uncertain postmodern society requires. In the remainder of this chapter, we provide a working inventory of the various ways adults self themselves into being. These are experiences of self that are common in everyday life, closely related to roles and social and personal identities, and predicated by or embedded in rock'n'roll culture.

The E-Self

As the rock'n'roll fan ages, many of the attractive aspects of the earlier self become increasingly difficult to maintain. There is a tendency for youthfulness, energy, risk-taking, appearance, sensuality, and other aspects of the adolescent or young adult self to become either less available or less desirable. Our culture does, however, provide the resource of an image of social identity that resonates with the affluence of middle age, as well as with the continuing need to establish status/self-esteem. The *e-self* (or electronic self) refers to an experience of individuality in which the affective and philosophical self-resources of rock'n'roll media are displaced or at least supplemented by the increasingly technological and commodified aspects of the media. For the middle-aged fan, what you play your music *on* can be at least as, if not more, important than what you *play*.

Middle age results in less concert attendance and more music experience in the comfort of home, automobile, and, for the energetic, on the jogging trail. A quick reading of *Wired* magazine (October 2004), which is geared toward the affluent and technologically interested middle-aged person, discloses the strategy of marketing rock'n'roll to its audience. There are ads for sophisticated cell phones that allow the consumer to "keep rockin' with your favorite MP3s." The promotion for "THEWIREDAUCTION" on eBay that benefits a children's foundation includes a "limited edition series precision bass guitar signed by Sting" among other high-end music items. The ad for the Bose Music intelligent playback system highlights "its unique ability to listen to the music you play and learn our preferences based on your likes, dislikes, or even your mood at the moment." There are numerous ads for satellite radio systems ands the luxury SUVs that include them as standard equipment.

Such marketing sometimes resonates with the adults it targets. George is a 51-year-old Anglo electrical engineer who has just installed a satellite radio system in his Lexus sedan. He sees two benefits of his musical purchase: "I don't have to mess with CDs or radio anymore. I get to play only the music I like to hear . . . There are stations dedicated just to 80s heavy metal. Cool." George has effectively eliminated the hassles of concert crowds and debates over musical tastes with peers. High technology puts his e-self in control of his musical environment. George can experience his music with the aura of cultural independence that affluent adults seek (Kotarba 2012).

The Self as Lover

A significant aspect of the continuous popularity of rock'n'roll music is its use in helping make sense of others, especially in intimate relationships. Numerous observers have correctly identified the sexist messages present in rock (e.g., McRobbie 1978). A postmodern existentialist view, however, highlights the fact that rock'n'roll music displays an open-ended horizon of meaning for its audiences. What a rock'n'roll music performance means is largely a function of the situation in which it is experienced and the particular self-needs of the audience member (Kotarba 1994a). As time passes, the rock'n'roll audience matures, biographies evolve, men's and women's relationships change, popular music commodities come and go, cultural themes available through the media advance, and we would expect the actual lived experience of popular music to change.

A particular self-need of the mature rock'n'roll fan is to interpret *romantic* phenomena. This can happen in two ways. First, fans can (re) interpret music to fit romantic needs. In Joe Kotarba's autobiographical writing as a rock'n'roll fan (Kotarba 1997) he described the way he used Dion's 1961 classic song "Runaround Sue" to account for the way a girl back in eighth grade rejected his very timid show of affection in favor of that of a more aggressive, older teenaged boy. Like the Sue in the song, Joe's Sue was a *bad* girl and he was merely a victim of her wiles. At a class reunion, 25 years later, he used the same song as the basis for a conversation with the same Sue. They laughed about the silliness of those elementary school days, but Joe's heartbeat jumped a bit when she admitted that she really did like him back then but was too shy to tell him!

Second, fans can gravitate toward music that can be perceived as romantic. Autobiographically, "Smokey" Robinson and the Miracles' "Tracks of My Tears" was a constant play on Joe's 45 rpm record player in 1965, when it put comforting words to yet another heartbreak in his life. He would not have been drawn as much to this new record if he did not have a personal need for its plaintive prose. In general, fans gravitate toward music that fits their everyday life concerns.

The Our Song

Baby boomers use rock'n'roll materials for a range of romantic purposes. They use music (e.g., CDs and DVDs) as birthday and Christmas gifts. They use music to help them appreciate other media, such as films and television. One of the more interesting romantic uses of rock'n'roll music is the *our-song* phenomenon, in which a musical performance serves to define a relationship. Our-songs are clearly not limited to baby boomers. Pre-adolescents, for example, commonly choose songs that remind them of a boy or a girl, but are often too shy to disclose this fact to the other, as we have seen!

For mature rock'n'roll fans, the our-song can function in at least two ways. First, it provides meaning for benchmark events in the relationship. Shirley is a 52-year-old Latina salesperson who is a big Los Lobos fan. She builds anniversary activities around one particular song she and her husband both enjoy:

> We fell in love with "Nadie Quiere Sufrir" at a Los Lobos concert when we were still just dating. It is a very pretty waltz that actually comes from an Edith Piaf song . . . I make sure the CD [with the song] is in the car when we drive to [our anniversary] dinner. He bought me the CD for our anniversary a few years ago . . . Oh, I guess it just makes us feel young again.

Second, the our-song can help the person feel like a lover. As couples age and perhaps find themselves feeling and acting less romantic over time, the our-song can function as a quick emotional fix. Rob is a 58-year-old Anglo executive who has maintained a serious relationship with Tommy, a 47-year-old artist, for about 15 years. Their song is Queen's "Bohemian Rhapsody":

> There will never be another Freddie Mercury. It was really special to have our own gay rock icon . . . I surprise Tommy by playing "Bohemian Rhapsody" now and again. Tommy is still thrilled that I remember it . . . Why? Well, it's one of those songs that make you feel good, to feel that you can be gay and a rocker at the same time . . . I like doing things for Tommy. We are just so busy with our careers, 'makes us feel like an old married couple!

Needless to say, the popular music industry is aware of the market for rock'n'roll goods and services. One of the more recent examples is the advent and growing popularity of rock'n'roll cruises. Carnival Cruise Lines offers the following "Rock'n'Roll Cruise Vacation" in an online ad:

> What could be cooler than a seven-day Caribbean cruise with legendary big-hair 1970s/80s rockers Journey, Styx and REO Speedwagon? Well . . . we'll reserve comment. But, if your idea of

a totally awesome vacation is a seven-day cruise with legendary big-hair 1970s/80s rockers Journey, Styx and REO Speedwagon, you're in luck.

Interactionist sociologists—as you can glean from the above—are not only interested in what individuals experience throughout the life course, but also in "how the life course is interpretively constructed and used by persons to make sense of experience" (Holstein and Gubrium 2003: 841). In order to construct meaning, Holstein and Gubrium tell us, we utilize *narrative resources:* tools for building, shaping and reshaping, and making sense of the becoming of self. Music is a narrative resource. By employing narrative resources and constructing a sense of self endowed with a feeling of continuity and growth, we engage in *biographical work.*

The Self as Parent and Grandparent

As we have shown in Chapter 1, the impact of rock'n'roll on one's self as parent is possibly the most pervasive aspect of the personal rock'n'roll biography. Baby boomers grew up experiencing music as a major medium for communicating with parents. Managing music illustrates one's skill at parenting, as well as one's style of parenting.

There is a greater tendency among parents—apparently across ethnic groups and social classes—to manage rock'n'roll as though their teenagers are children who need to be nurtured and protected rather than as adolescents who must be controlled, sanctioned, and feared. Mass media-generated images of obstinate if not rebellious youth generally ignore the reflexive relationship between teenagers and their parents. Parents then respond to the identities they helped create by controlling, criticizing, sanctioning, and punishing their teenagers for living out their rock'n'roll-inspired identities—responding to them as if they were autonomous, responsible adults.

This *congenial* style of being a parent appears to extend into the next cycle of life: that of grandparent. As Mogelonsky (1996) and other family researchers have noted, grandparents have a tendency to interact with their grandchildren in ways very similar to the ways they interacted with their own children. If pop music was an important feature to them as parents, it will be the same as grandparents. What changes, of course, are styles of music, music technology, and the moral context of pop music. Frank is a 61-year-old retired public school teacher who has two grandchildren: 17-year-old Bobby and 11-year-old Denise. Bobby has been easy to please with musical gifts and experiences. Just as he did with his own son 30 years ago or so, Frank has given Bobby birthday and Christmas gifts of music, but according to current styles: iTune gift cards, an iPod mini, and tickets to a Radiohead concert. However, Frank will not share musical experiences with Bobby because "Bobby listens to a lot of rap, and I just cannot stand that stuff." Denise presented other kinds of difficulties. In addition to a Carrie Underwood CD she wanted for Christmas, she begged Frank for tickets to see Hannah Montana in concert at Reliant Stadium in Houston. Her father told her that the family could not afford tickets, so she strategically asked her doting grandpa. Frank's response was, "How can I tell my little girl no?" but the task of actually getting tickets was monumental:

> I heard that all tickets sold out in about ten minutes. I went online and couldn't get in for almost a half-hour. I actually drove down to the Reliant box office later that morning, and it was the same story. I then went online to eBay and paid $400 for two [nose] bleeds . . . You're old enough to remember when concert tickets were ten bucks at the door. Man, how things have changed, but I promised her.
>
> (Kotarba 2013a)

The Self as Believer

As we have seen, baby boomers' early experiences of rock'n'roll music were complex. They learned to love, play, and dissent through the idiom. They also experienced spirituality (Seay and Neely 1986). In adulthood, the spiritual dimension of rock'n'roll continues to impact the self as believer. The lyrics and mood created by such performers as Van Morrison (*Astral Weeks*) and U2 (*The Joshua Tree*) provide baby boomers with non-sectarian yet religion-friendly soundtracks. New Age music, such as that produced by Windham Hill, functions in the same way.

Rock and pop music has also had direct influence on spirituality by helping shape organized religious ceremonies and rituals to fit the tastes of the adult member. For example, Catholic baby boomers grew up at a time when the Church, largely as a result of Vatican II, encouraged parishes to make use of local musical styles and talent. Witness the emergence of the rock'n'roll mass in the 1970s. Today, the very popular style of praise and worship music, with its electronic keyboard and modern melodies, is infiltrating Catholic liturgy.

An integral segment of the self-as-parent is moral (if not religious or spiritual) socialization. Rock and pop function as mechanisms for teaching religious beliefs and values in many families, whether or not rock is compatible with the particular family's religious orientation. For mainstream Protestant denominations, rock'n'roll increasingly fits with the faith. Take, for example, the success of Jars of Clay—a soft rock Christian band—or Sufjan Stevens, a more "indie" but equally spiritual musical act. In these cases, too, we can see how music functions as a resource selected by fans and made meaningful in their building of a sense of identity.

The Self as Political Actor

Rock'n'roll music serves as a soundtrack for the situations in which baby boomers perceive themselves as political actors. Rock'n'roll can add both atmosphere and meaning to political events. For example, New York punk poet and singer Patti Smith performed a concert in Houston on March 28, 2003—right at the beginning of the war in Iraq. The concert was originally scheduled simply to support an exhibit of her art displayed at the Museum of Contemporary Arts. The audience was overwhelmingly middle-aged people, dressed up in their jeans and long (hippie) skirts. Through conversations with numerous fans after the concert, it was clear that they had *enjoyed* the concert. Patti Smith's poetry and songs (e.g., "People Have the Power") gave them a relevant and identifiable venue for sharing their overwhelmingly negative *feelings* about the war.

Baby boomers grew up utilizing the burgeoning rock music media of the 1960s and 70s as a major source of political ideas for making sense of an increasingly complicated world. Perhaps the most dramatic example of this media influence is *Rolling Stone* (*RS*) magazine. Born in the political and cultural ferment of 1960s San Francisco to its founder,

Jan Wenner, *RS* became the major voice for anti-war, pro-marijuana, anti-establishment thinking. This reporting, of course, complemented *RS*'s coverage of the antics of the Grateful Dead, the Rolling Stones, The Who, and Jefferson Airplane/Starship.

As *RS*'s original readership graduated from college to become businesspeople and college professors, *RS* wisely kept up with the times and has continued to provide a liberal voice for baby boomers not quite ready for membership in the Heritage Foundation. *RS* Issue 1169 (November 8, 2012), for example, published a very flattering cover story on "Obama and the Road Ahead: The *Rolling Stone* Interview," just before the presidential election. The following edition, Issue 1170 (November 22, 2012), published a very warm memorial piece on George McGovern who had recently passed away. McGovern was a favorite of the baby boomers back in the 1960s and 70s who remained involved with mainstream American politics, and who became the heart and soul of the liberal thinking to this day. *RS*'s younger readers were not even born when McGovern developed a strong friendship with gonzo journalist Hunter S. Thompson, who covered the 1972 campaign for *RS*.

Other publications successfully combined rock'n'roll and politics. In fact, *Spin Magazine* published an article in 1992 (July, pp. 60–61) by David Theis on "AIDS." This article highlighted a field research project funded by the National Institute on Drug Abuse and conducted by Joe Kotarba. Kotarba's research team investigated the everyday lives of homeless teenagers in Houston and how their lifestyle put them at risk of AIDS infection. In the midst of hearing sad and often heartbreaking biographies during interviews with these kids, Kotarba and his team were pleased to hear that these kids found great strength and meaning in the popular rock music of the day, in particular Metallica ("Enter Sandman") and Van Halen ("Jump").

Conclusion

We have described several contemporary experiences and manifestations of self to illustrate the ways the rock idiom has remained a major cultural force in the life course of mature fans. There are obviously other experiences. Furthermore, these experiences are not limited to fans. Rock music is also a preeminent aspect of the musician's self who performed rock music many years ago and who continues to perform. These musicians redirect their careers in directions more comfortable, if not more profitable. Kinky Friedman comes to mind. He was a Texas-based bandleader in the 1970s of the infamous Texas Jewboys. He now performs acoustically in small clubs, while managing a very successful line of men's clothing and authoring popular mystery novels. As time passes (Kotarba 2002b), rock'n'roll provides narrative resources for the aging self's biographical work. In interviews, Kotarba routinely hears respondents note how the recent deaths of middle-aged rock'n'roll artists, such as Robert Palmer and George Harrison, are disturbing because these afflictions may be more the result of aging than the excessive lifestyles associated with the premature deaths of artists such as Janis Joplin, Jimi Hendrix, and Jim Morrison. It will be interesting, then, to see the various ways in which baby boomers draw upon the rock idiom as they move beyond middle age. For example, what new meanings will aging boomers attach to the rock idiom? What place will rock have in the grandparent–grandchild relationship? Attending to such questions will highlight the role that music plays in the ongoing becoming-of-self.

4

YOUTH, DEVIANCE, AND SUBCULTURES

Deviance has been a topic of interest in sociology ever since its inception during the industrial revolution. The study of deviance is crucial to the overall goal of sociology for one simple reason: social life is based in large part upon social rules. Macro-sociologists (e.g., the structuralists and functionalists we talked about earlier) usually focus their attention on how social rules such as customs, culture, or laws determine or otherwise shape people's behavior. Everyday life sociologists (e.g., symbolic interactionists and constructionists), on the other hand, emphasize how people actively create, negotiate, reshape, and use social rules to make sense of people's behaviors within situations. But, regardless of theoretical orientation, understanding deviance is the key to a better understanding of social rules, order, and individual and collective behavior.

Deviance seems like an obvious thing . . . you know it when you see it, right? But it's really not so straightforward. A superficial understanding of deviance sees persons, acts, or events as deviations from the norm. For example, while working on this paragraph, Patrick Williams was listening to Psycroptic, a technical death metal band from Tasmania, Australia. If you were to look up the band on myspace or YouTube (or wherever) and listen to the song "Ob(Servant)"—the very song blasting in his ears as he wrote this—you might subsequently define him, the music, or the band as deviant, using words like "terrible" or "senseless noise" or "sick." Or, you might like it and silently thank Patrick for having tipped you off to some new tunes. Either way, simply defining something like death metal music, its musicians, or fans as deviant explains little and instead raises important questions such as who decides which forms of music are normal or deviant. By asking questions like this, the sociological significance of deviance becomes more apparent—focusing on deviance helps make clearer how normal or non-deviant behavior is accomplished. This constructionist approach seems to us much better equipped for understanding deviance and normality than simply assuming that each exists and is objectively real because it emphasizes the meanings shaped by social actors and associated with a sense of order. Again, we are arguing that understanding social rules and order is best accomplished by observing situations in which norms are challenged. Observing challenges, though, means that we understand at least something about norms already. After all, we don't all walk around with rulebooks explaining what we can and cannot say or do. Nor are we born preconditioned to speak a certain language, be attracted to a certain kind of person, or appreciate a certain music genre. Rather, such "normal" things are learned and internalized through participation in everyday life.

This is where the concept of culture becomes very useful. Culture has been an important conceptual tool for scholars studying all aspects of social life for decades to describe how social rules work. Symbolic interactionists see culture as having to do with how people think, feel, and act in concert with others with whom they share understanding. Within social groups, such thoughts, feelings, and actions become patterned and thus shape future thoughts, feelings, and actions. They were around before you were born, but they are also shaped through interaction with your fellows (Becker 1986). Those patterns may change from situation to situation, as would the meanings we attach to them. For example, drinking a beer and feeling giddy while thinking about kissing that cute person across the room may be fine when out with friends on a Friday night, but none of these—the act of drinking alcohol for pleasure, the feeling of giddiness, or sexual thoughts—are acceptable while in a worship service on Sunday morning.

In Chapter 2, we heard questionable claims about whether certain styles of popular music "cause" deviance (e.g., delinquency, suicide) among young people. We explained that as an instance of social problem work. In this chapter, we will broaden the discussion to make sense of the relations among music, patterns of behavior, and deviance. We will not, however, argue that any one of these causes any other. Instead, we want to focus on the cultures of people who prefer music that may be quite normal to them, but who have been labeled more or less as deviant within the context of the larger group culture in which they live. We are therefore not just talking about culture, but specifically about subculture—a culture that differs from the "mainstream" through marginality or opposition (Williams 2011). A subculture emerges around a "bounded (but not closed) network of people who come to share the meaning of specific ideas, material objects, and practices through interaction. Over time, members' interactions develop into a discourse that structures the generation, activation, and diffusion of these ideas, objects, and practices" (Williams and Copes 2005: 70). Whether marginal (labeled as deviant by the mainstream observers or critics) or oppositional (choosing not to conform to mainstream culture), or some combination of the two, there are many subcultures that have emerged around the consumption of music that provide rich and complex patterns of thinking, feeling, and acting through which members share musical experiences.

In what follows, we take an historical look at music subcultures that have emerged in the U.S. and U.K. as we build up a constructionist understanding of deviance. We will rely on concepts from two theories: Howard Becker's (1963) "labeling theory" and Stanley Cohen's (2002) theory of "moral panic." Using their ideas, we will trace the significance of a number of (un)popular music genres, from blues, jazz, and swing in the early 20th century, to hippie, heavy metal, and rap in the latter half of the century. We will close the chapter with some consideration of the role that social media play in subcultural music experience and deviant labels.

What Makes Music (Un)Popular? The Role of Labeling

Some popular music scholars argue that the relationship between music and alternative youth cultures is a product of changes that occurred in the post-World War II political economies of the West, which gave young people more free time and more spending power than they had ever had before (e.g., Bennett 2001; Clarke, Hall, Jefferson, and Roberts 1976). From this perspective, "youth" as a cultural category was a primary driver in the emergence of music cultures. There is certainly good reason to believe such a claim, not the least of which are the "deviant" music cultures that we will describe in this chapter, which emerged since 1945. However, to argue that there were no cultures of popular music before World War II is an oversimplification at best. For thousands of years, groups of people have integrated music into their everyday lives. Further, looking at the early 20th century we can easily find distinct cultures rising around the production and consumption of music. Some of these popular music cultures emerged because musicians and fans created scenes that supported that musical genre. In other cases, people who were not fans of a particular style of music used political and economic resources to label groups of musicians and fans as different or unacceptable. This is not to say that all musicians and their fans are subcultural. Nevertheless, one way to understand this social phenomenon is by referring to how deviant cultures are constructed by both insiders and outsiders of music scenes.

Take, for instance, blues music. Blues music is one of the earliest styles of distinctively American popular music. Blues emerged in the rural U.S. South and river towns in the 1910s and 1920s as a form of folk music (Jones 1963). Referring to the depressed moods (as in "feeling blue") that could characterize everyday life at the very bottom of the social ladder, blues originally signified the experience of working, rural, black poor in the Deep South and developed from a mix of spirituals, work chants, and the reflexive narratives of performers. The distinction between performers and audience members was often blurred, as everyone might take turns singing, playing, and listening to stories relevant to the everyday lives of all those present. Before the technological advances that would enable electrified music decades later—and which would also open up the genre to more white listeners— the lack of financial resources in the blues scene precluded any attempt at developing an organized popular music form per se. Mainstream "WASP" (White Anglo-Saxon Protestant) culture, with its racist tones, as well as the economic problems experienced in the South for decades after the Civil War, resulted in a situation in which blues musicians and their audiences were satisfied to keep their music to themselves. Much of the meaning of the blues was encoded in the lyrics via metaphors and innuendos, and blues remained a subcultural form that few outsiders understood or appreciated.   _JAZZ_

   Jazz music emerged at more or less the same time as the blues, but in different locations (e.g., New Orleans and New York) and developed different scenes (i.e., middle-class urban blacks and whites). Jazz was a popular music genre during the "roaring twenties," brought into the limelight via electricity, radio, and motion pictures, and the immense popularity of dance clubs. While blues was marginal, jazz represented the interaction of (predominantly) black musicians with European musical traditions (Berendt 1982). Jazz itself had many varieties and it became possible to earn a living as a jazz musician in major cities. Rather than the music being part of the everyday culture of the poor, jazz musicians were an amateur and professional lot who chose the lifestyle. Sociologist Howard Becker, who developed "labeling theory," was himself a jazz musician, and several of his published works detail the subcultural lifestyle surrounding jazz. In urban areas, jazz became associated with racial tolerance and women's and gay rights, and recognizable subcultures emerged, such as flappers. Part of the lifestyle involved the use of drugs such as marijuana and heroin, and scene members developed unique "argot"—subcultural slang—to mask the meaning of subcultural communication from straight society:

> Much of the "hip talk" comes directly from the addict's jargon as well as from the musician's. The "secret" bopper's and (later) hipster's language was the essential part of a cult of redefinition, in terms closest to the initiated.
>
> (Jones 1963: 202)

As jazz became a widely recorded style of music, marketed in entertainment centers like New York City, it produced its own cultural media, where jazz music criticism helped convey the jazz vernacular to a wide and appreciative audience via newspapers and magazines dedicated to the genre, further assisting its spread into popular culture.

   As this comparison of early 20th-century blues and jazz suggests, "popular" music is a relative term. Blues was popular among marginal black populations of the rural Deep South, but not in WASP society. Meanwhile jazz, which shared musical roots and similarities with the blues, was popular among a much wider cross-section of the U.S. public, as well as in the U.K. and Europe. And yet, as we will demonstrate in the next section, what is popular to one group of people in one time and place may not be to others in another time or place. This is how deviance itself operates in society; it is a consequence of imbalances among people's definitions of "popular."

In Chapter 2, we discussed the role of the moral entrepreneur. Becker (1963) viewed the work of moral entrepreneurs as a crusade of sorts: "The crusader is not only interested in seeing to it that other people do what he thinks right. He believes that if they do what is right it will be good for them" (p. 148). Sociologically speaking, if a crusade is successful it will result not only in the construction of a social norm, but also in the labeling of those people, events, or objects that stand contrarily. Labeling is thus a very important concept. When we label someone or something as deviant, we exercise moral force. As Becker (1963: 9) put it, by labeling people we make outsiders of them. Deviance, for Becker and other interactionists, is thus a "consequence of the application by others of rules and sanctions to an 'offender.' The deviant is one to whom the label has been successfully applied." In his influential study of outsiders, Becker focused on both the construction and application of social norms, and the consequences of labeling in terms of the identities and social status of those who are labeled. At the time of its publication, and still to this day, Becker's study is insightful. Instead of focusing on the structural consequences of objectively defined deviant acts, or instead of treating deviants as psychologically abnormal, Becker posited deviance as an outcome of social interaction.

Social norms are one of many symbolic and material resources that individuals take into consideration more or less consciously when acting in concert with others. For most of us, most of the time, our knowledge of social norms is rather unconscious and implicit. We see difference and label it as problematic.

Music, Subcultures, and Moral Panics

Along with Howard Becker's work on labeling, Stanley Cohen's (2002) theory of moral panic is important, because it explains the process through which deviance becomes a problem for an entire society. According to Cohen, simply labeling persons, actions, or events as deviant is not enough; society needs to be shown the danger deviance represents in order to legitimate intervention. Going back once more to the pre-World War II period, let us consider the case of swing music in Nazi Germany in the 1930s. Swing music was a form of American big-band jazz that spread across the U.K. and Europe in the 1920s. In Germany, swing was popular among educated, affluent German youths, who were most likely to appreciate music from abroad. Many swing fans were the children of Nazi Party members and thus were expected to be upstanding citizens. In what way could the sons and daughters of the respectable German upper classes pose a threat to the State? According to Wallace and Alt (2001), the threat came from the music they loved. Swing's biggest names were African-American and Jewish and the music came from the English-speaking world. German Swing Kids bought imported records, listened to the latest big-band hits on BBC radio, dressed in English clothing, and engaged the English language through reading and speaking. From the youths' perspective, listening to swing was not intended to be antagonistic toward the dominant cultural order of the day. They were not organized in terms of resistance to the State, yet were labeled as a threat to German society's core value structure, which promoted the racial and cultural superiority of Germany. Over time, swing music became a direct provocation to the National Socialists' ideology of superiority. By 1938, Nazi officials, operating as moral entrepreneurs, had created an exhibition on "Degenerate Music" to inform the German populace about the unacceptability of jazz music, and its consumption was informally banned. From 1939 (when the war started) onwards, listening to the BBC or to Jewish or "Negro" music became illegal activities. The Gestapo and members of the Hitler Youth were tasked with surveiling dance parties and other swing activities, such as listening to the BBC or playing records. Being identified as a repeat offender further increased the likelihood of been labeled as deviant, versus a person caught once, who might be warned to be more careful about how she or he chose to spend their leisure time.

Over time, a nationwide moral panic associated with swing music emerged and reactions became increasingly severe as the war went on. In 1940, swing parties were officially banned and editorials and cartoons began appearing in newspapers that ridiculed the subculture. Parties were raided and attendees arrested and interrogated. Minors could be expelled from high school, thus ruining any chance of a university career, while those who were old enough were sent to the front lines as soldiers, or to penal camps for rehabilitation. Arno Klönne's (1995) archival research demonstrates just how drastic social reaction against Swing Kids became during the war, when a letter was written to S.S. leader Himmler, stating:

> Since the activities of these "Swing Youth" in the home country damages [sic] the strength of the German people, I would recommend that they are brought immediately into a work camp ... I would be very grateful if you could give instructions to the ... authorities to act against these "Swing Youth" with the harshest possible measures.
>
> (cited in Wallace and Alt 2001: 284)

A symbolic interactionist approach to deviance highlights that labeling and reacting are not uniformly managed. In the case of swing, the nature of social reaction depended on the meaning attributed to the individuals involved. Some were sent for rehabilitation; those with Jewish or communist connections were sent to concentration camps; and at least one with "good connections" was released. Nevertheless, to think that listening to popular music could get you thrown into a concentration camp seems drastic. But "drastic" is relative and we must keep in mind that one's definition of "popular" music is not always shared with others.

The Postwar Era: Youth Culture and Deviance on Wholesale

Conservative ideologies are not limited to Nazi Germany. In fact, all societies have moral entrepreneurs who actively work to solidify control of the hearts and minds of fellow citizens. It is against the backdrop of conservativism that oppositional youth subcultures are often discussed—think of hippie, punk, metal, and hip-hop, to name but a few. There are also youth subcultures that oppose liberal thought and politics, such as the "skinheads," who create a musical soundtrack for their activities. These subcultures represent the oppositional (rather than the marginalized) version of deviance. They are the "others" who choose to build their own rules as they break mainstream social norms and orient to a subculture instead. Each of these cultures is known for a number of things, but they all share two common features—music and resistance (Williams 2009). While it would be problematic to conceptualize music as *the* source of inspiration for oppositional subcultures, it also cannot be denied that music is important. But let us not simply romanticize these subcultures, viewing them as heroic stands against culture industries or agents of social control, nor reduce them to the nihilistic actions of disaffected youths. Looking at a series of subcultures in turn, we can instead consider the roles that music and related behaviors have played in communicating resistance to mainstream culture on the one hand, while not ignoring the role of "the system" in creating deviant labels as part of its efforts to control people's behaviors.

To do this seriously, we need a concept that allows us to link music and resistance together in some meaningful way. As we said earlier, there is a correspondence between a particular culture and its internal rules. The concept perhaps best used to interpret the internal structure of a culture is *homology*, which "refers to the relationships among ideology, image, and practice" within a subculture (Williams 2011: 76). Popular music scholar Richard Middleton (1990: 9) further describes homology as "a structural resonance . . . between the different elements making up a socio-cultural whole." Are there certain types of music that go best with specific behaviors? Would the hippie subculture have been the same if its music and drugs had been angrier, or would punk be the same if it had been wrapped only in hope and love? Further, in what ways might music be resistant? These are the kinds of questions that homological studies seek to answer.

Let us jump to the mid-1960s, when the presence of recreational drugs such as marijuana, alcohol, and LSD became widespread among adolescents alongside the mixture of politicized rock and folk music that together characterized what we know today as the hippie counterculture. Besides drugs and music, hippie culture was also known for its collective movements against the war in Vietnam as well as against social inequalities such as racism and sexism. According to some sociologists, hippies typically came from middle-class backgrounds and could afford to react against the strait-laced culture in which they had grown up (Clarke et al. 1976; Willis 1978). Yet, to be sure, the hippies were not all white, not all middle class, and not all interested in radical political change. Instead, many were just youths looking for something fresh and fun, and popular music and drugs were readily available leisure pursuits.

There was a lot of politically oriented popular music during the late 1960s, which was instrumental in disseminating countercultural ideologies among youths across North America and beyond. Hippies' drugs of choice, especially marijuana and LSD, were also significant to hippie music scenes because they enhanced introspective and communal feelings—hallmarks of the counterculture—for musicians and fans alike. Consider Timothy Leary's (1983: 253) famous exhortation for American youths to "turn on, tune in, drop out":

> *Turn on* meant go within to activate your neural and genetic equipment. Become sensitive to the many and various levels of consciousness and the specific triggers that engage them ... *Tune in* meant interact harmoniously with the world around you— externalize, materialize, express your new internal perspectives. *Drop out* suggested an elective, selective, graceful process of detachment from involuntary or unconscious commitments. *Drop out* meant self-reliance, a discovery of one's singularity, a commitment to mobility, choice, and change. Unhappily my explanations of this sequence of personal development were often misinterpreted to mean "Get stoned and abandon all constructive activity."

The implications of Leary's words resonated with countercultural youths who sought alternatives to what was happening in the larger

world (they were the first generation to be able to "consume" the meanings of foreign wars through near-instant television coverage and with the Civil Rights movement still unfolding) and who sought ways to detach themselves from "involuntary or unconscious commitments," refusing to follow rules just because they were there to be followed. According to Stuart Hall (1968: 122), the meaning of Leary's words brought drug use and resistance together.

> "turn on" . . . invites the hippy to switch to the use of mind expanding drugs and to turn on as many members of straight society as he [sic] can reach. But, again, metaphorically, it also means to switch to a more authentic mode of experience, to leave the routes of middle class society . . . "Drop out" . . . means, literally, that the hippy should reject work, power, status, and consumption.

Together with "tune in," which may be interpreted as a call to use available media channels, including music, to stay up-to-date with what was going on in the world, the counterculture of the late 1960s drew together rather clearly the connections among music, drug use, and countercultural ideologies: "It is only through an appreciation of such cultural values, acquired via a total absorption in the hippie lifestyle, that the 'correct' use of drugs and music can be learned and practiced" (Hall 1968: 122).

The 1970s witnessed a decline in the countercultural power of politicized rock music within the context of an increasingly conservative, post-Vietnam era, but the popularization of music-based hedonism continued to grow. Popularly known as "disco" in the 1970s, the phenomenon confronted the conservative, WASP America that had seemingly prevailed against the hippies with newly liberated homo- and heterosexualities as well as equally avid, lifestyle-based drug use (Braunstein 1999). Disco became a dominant form of popular music via what was by then a well-oiled machine of modern music production. Discotheques could be found in almost any city, while the music and style could be found on the radio, spotlighted in television shows, and film. Disco was both "good" and "bad," with the proliferation of cocaine and heroin use coinciding with the popularity of all-night dance parties. Whereas the mellowing drugs among hippies fit homologically with the cultural imperatives of introspection and community-building, disco culture was tied to the use of "uppers" to fuel frenetic music consumption and support a "live for the moment" attitude.

At the same time, rock'n'roll was developing into the heavier and more aggressive forms of punk and heavy metal. Yet heavy metal, with its less overt opposition to the mainstream and superior musicianship versus punk, held more appeal for popular music consumers. Heavy metals acts in the 1970s such as Led Zeppelin, Black Sabbath, and Ted Nugent played shows to tens of thousands in stadiums and sold millions of records, while many punk bands struggled to feed themselves and maintain their equipment at the same time. By the 1980s, metal had developed a new type of relation with mainstream culture. On the one hand, metal contained elements of social disaffection and critique of mainstream cultural values. On the other hand, many bands signed to multinational record labels and earned a considerable profit off their fans' consumptive habits. Consider the following description by Jon Pareles (1988: 26–27), which describes the band Metallica in a way few readers today could imagine:

> The heavy metal rock band Metallica plays loud, high-speed music with lyrics that dwell on dark subjects such as death, madness, nuclear war, and drug abuse. While adhering to heavy metal's basic tenets, the members of Metallica rebel against many of the conventions associated with hard rock music and refuse to package themselves for mass consumption. The band has never made a video for MTV, and, until the advent of all-hard-rock radio formats, Metallica albums were never played on commercial rock radio stations. Nonetheless, the group has attracted an avid following, mainly through tours, heavy metal fan publications, some college radio exposure, and word of mouth.

The "dark subjects" of heavy metal music—visible in album art, attributable to the heavy tones and speed of the music, and audible in the lyrics—became a concern for neo-conservative politicians, religious leaders, and other public interest groups who fueled the fires of moral panic surrounding youth popular music genres. The 1980s in particular witnessed a sustained moral panic around the links between heavy metal music and dangerous activities (drug use, truancy, atheism, occultism), with the Parents' Music Resource Center (PMRC) playing an institutionalized role as moral entrepreneur. Working under the auspices of concerned parenting and "neutral fact-finding," the PMRC was able to create the image of heavy metal fans as subcultural and "to mobilize parental hysteria while avoiding the adult word censorship." The PMRC made it clear that heavy metal was "a threat because it celebrate[d] and legitimate[d] sources of identity and community that [did] not derive from parental models" (Walser 1993: 138). Artists and bands such as Ozzy Osbourne, Judas Priest, and Twisted Sister were vilified as wicked and debase, bent on the entrapment and subjugation of young people's minds. It was claimed that heavy metal records contained hidden messages through "back-masking," instructing listeners in acts of violence and destruction. The PMRC's tactics to control media content and distribution were predicated on making artists appear as deviant and dangerous as possible, framing young fans more as victims than as willfully disobedient kids.

To help the labels stick, social control agencies such as the American Medical Association published warnings about some lyrics being dangerous to its fans:

> The American Medical Association (AMA) and the American Academy of Pediatrics have voiced concerns about certain lyrics used in heavy metal and rap music. The AMA says that messages in these genres may pose a threat to the physical health and emotional well being of particularly vulnerable children and adolescents. The AMA has identified six potentially dangerous music themes: drug and alcohol abuse, suicide, violence, satanic worship, sexual exploitation, and racism. Both the AMA and the Academy of Pediatrics support voluntary regulation and increased social responsibility in the music industry.
>
> (Levine 1991: 16)

Law enforcement officials also performed key roles as moral entrepreneurs in identifying and shaping society's formal and informal definitions of normalcy and its reaction to deviation. In Orange County, California, the local government established a program called "Back In Control" (BIC), which provided parenting workshops for families, especially those with "problem" children. One explicit dimension of the program was to help parents regain control of subcultural minors. In the BIC publication *The Punk and Heavy Metal Handbook*, parents were told that

> punk and heavy metal music oppose the traditional values of those in authority and encourage rebellious and aggressive attitudes and behavior toward parents, educators, law enforcement, and religious leaders. Further... punk and metal generally support behaviors that are violent, immoral, illegal, frequently bizarre and that generally promote drug and alcohol abuse.
>
> (quoted in Rosenbaum and Prinsky 1991: 529)

Police not only gave special talks to high-school student bodies (usually with mandatory attendance policies), but also offered seminars for neighborhood and community groups in which they would outline "warning signs" for parents. These warning signs were stylistic in nature, including T-shirts advertising punk or metal bands, clothing that was black or that had spikes/studs, so-called "punk" jewelry, having more than one piercing in an ear, or wearing dyed or spiked hair. Police talks with parents also focused on heavy metal and punk song lyrics, album artwork, and the lifestyle of rock stars. Court officials were also strategic actors in social reaction against subcultural participants.

Homologically speaking, agents of social control, fans, and scholars have all drawn on the assumed relationship among punk and heavy metal's fast-paced rhythms, spiked and leather-clad appearance, and aggressive lyrics to make sense of the subcultural ideologies that they represent. The skepticism of punk culture toward social institutions may be the reason many punk musicians pride themselves on their *lack* of music training or skill, while the violent lyrics found in heavy metal can be seen to represent the focal concerns of metalheads. What is perhaps most important to draw from this is an understanding of the relation between music, style, deviant behavior, and audience reception. Rather than think in narrow terms about music or lyrics causing people to act in a certain way, we need to think about the larger role these subcultural objects may play in representing aspects of mainstream culture that subculturalists deal with. Themes of war, sexual predation, and anger could be found daily in news, sports, film, and television. Creating music around these themes can logically be said to represent or reflect aspects of mainstream culture rather than to be the autonomously created, sinister message of deviant musicians.

Hip-Hop Subculture and the Commodification of Deviance

Hip-hop, a multi-billion-dollar global culture in the 21st century, emerged out of the African-American ghettos of New York in the 1970s and has since morphed into a multivalent and multiracial phenomenon with a variety of popular cultural and subcultural forms. Rap music stands as the primary creative force within hip-hop culture, while rappers themselves come with diverse biographies and desires. Some rappers are quite political, while others seem to unwittingly promote racialized, group-based violence that propels only the luckiest few out of their marginal position in society. African-American rap artists in the 1970s and early 1980s focused enormous energy on highlighting the black, lower-class experience in modern urban society (and in this way it functions as a modern version of blues music, as previously discussed). As such, rap songs, like those of the other genres we've discussed, "are cultural, ideological inscriptions of meanings conceived, created and constructed, and then projected by performances which suggest that certain ways of being, thinking, looking, and styling are normative, preferable, and validated" (Banfield 2010: 9).

Rap has been approached in terms of the kinds of knowledge and practice that structure its existence and development, with scholars often attempting to decipher it through analyses of lyrical content. Tricia Rose, a noted scholar on the culture of hip-hop, has written about the significance of rap music. Her book *Black Noise* (Rose 1994) began with a discussion of a single word shouted by Flavor Flav, the flamboyant second man in Public Enemy. That word, "Confusion!," from the song "Can't Truss It," complements frontman Chuck D's story about the legacy of slavery and the cultural confusion that contemporary African-American society has experienced as a result. Her overarching question concerns what rap tells us about black Americans' experiences. Her answer is that, in part, rap signifies a "forbidden narrative [and] a symbol of rebellion" (Rose 1994: 5) for millions of fans and consumers around the globe. Rap is part of a broader, "disguised criticism of the powerful [. . . that] produce[s] communal bases of knowledge about social conditions, communal interpretations of them, and quite often serve[s] as the cultural glue that fosters communal resistance" (Rose 1994: 99–100). In short, rap music is seen to collect, mediate, and represent black people's experiences of racial and classed oppressions.

But hip-hop has grown beyond those subcultural roots. One might be tempted to reduce the complexity of rap style today into a few competing types—for example, politically conscious rap that highlights the raced, classed, and often gendered positions of minority groups, versus its apolitical, chauvinistic Top 40 counterpart that glorifies the avoidance of work, the use of recreational drugs, and the control of women's sexuality. This type of distinction could be analytically useful in certain situations, but shouldn't be reified into a "real" division between two separate schools of rap, mainly because there are many examples that defy such simple categories. This is true not only of rap music in the U.S., but throughout the globe (see, e.g., Huq 2006: Ch. 6; Mitchell 2001). In Japan, for example, hip-hop culture is popular, and yet the country lacks the racial divisions and many of the urban problems that fueled its American progenitor. Japanese rappers therefore work to rearticulate the genre's oppositional framework toward "a generational protest against authority figures such as parents and teachers" (Condry 1999, cited in Bennett 2001: 100). In this way, rap continues to morph as artists negotiate and/or recontextualize its significance for local cultures around the world.

Since hip-hop became truly global in the 1990s, it is necessary to study the extent to which the symbols visible/audible in rap today represent the focal concerns of hip-hop subcultural members rather than satisfy the voyeuristic demands of consumer society. Multinational corporations pay millions upon millions of dollars annually to guide the creative process of rap music, while apparel, food, technological, and other types of companies have invested heavily into attracting the fans of hip-hop to their brands, resulting in rap music now being a globally recognized commercial market with its own logics. One of hip-hop's most salient features in popular culture today has to do with the masculine, competitive bias expressed in the style of some of rap's best-known figures. This bias is often expressed by male artists whose lyrics and style are apparently critical of some of society's most basic cultural norms, including a good education, a full-time job, and a loving, cohesive nuclear family for emotional support—cultural norms with a distinctly Anglo-European history. The masculine and racial biases can be seen in rappers' violent resistance to dominant definitions of the role of authority (e.g., N.W.A's "Fuck tha Police" or Ice-T's "Cop Killer," a song he performed with his heavy metal band Body Count), as well as in their objectification of women through an embracement of the "hustler" lifestyle that endorses the forceful treatment of "bitches and hoes" (Copes, Hochstetler, and Williams 2008).

The songs that often get circulated most—whether officially through radio play, or unofficially through illegal markets or peer-to-peer networks—are not necessarily those that critique or reaffirm traditional power lines per se, but rather those where rappers employ innovations in rhythm or rhyme to outshine others in the scene. Rapping and break-dancing, both fundamental parts of early hip-hop subculture, were developed within the contexts of the street corner and other localized gatherings. For members of black urban street society, DJing, and later rapping, afforded individuals the chance to stand out of the crowd. Banfield describes rap music as emerging from exactly this type of circumstance:

> In rap, street poets expressed themselves artistically by claiming to project the most authentic Black style and music. The street corner and the neighborhood party, just as in the past, became the Black performance stage on which community artists reflected their identity and projected their image. The DJ performers had to have "skills" to keep the party going. What made one better than others was his or her ability "to mix it up" between breaks, while changing the record.
>
> (2010: 171)

DJ and rap skills became key measures of status in hip-hop subculture, along with a series of other important distinctions. Over time, as hip-hop became a highly sought-after pop cultural commodity, being a skilled rapper in itself became insufficient for inclusion in hip-hop subculture.

Black artists in particular sought to control access to hip-hop through a rhetorical grounding of hip-hop authenticity. One needed to be black, to be from "the street," to have an "underground" sensibility, and to rap from the heart rather than for the money (McLeod 1999). With skill and the proper credentials comes recognition and status. Yet, some rappers are seen to "sell out" of the subculture by accepting record deals from major labels and moving into middle-class comfort while continuing to rap about the lower-class, urban street culture they've left behind. Since rap's emergence, some of its most popular artists have traveled far: Flavor Flav's "Confusion!" seems less about the legacy of slavery and more about his love life (VH1's *Strange Love* and *Flavor of Love*); Ice-T is better known today as a cop than as a "Cop Killer" (NBC's *Law & Order: Special Victims Unit*); and, despite his claim with Dr. Dre that "Bitches Ain't Shit," Snoop Dogg spends much of his time on reality TV pampering his wife and daughter (E!'s *Snoop Dogg's Father Hood*).

As rap has been transformed into a global commodity, hip-hop artists and fans alike have struggled to negotiate the meaning(s) of rap. Today rap and hip-hop are commodities eagerly consumed by the middle class. Whether in New York, Munich, or Hong Kong, middle-class urban youth preen themselves in the latest "street fashion," throw around mock gang signs, and memorize lyrics to songs that are banned on many airwaves. And no matter how true to life rappers' lyrics may be, the vast portion of record sales are derived from consumers who are totally removed from a life of poverty, drug dealing, and pervasive interpersonal violence. To what extent is the genre today a mode of resistance against "the system," and to what extent has it come to signify a vacuous relationship with pop-cultural economics rooted in middle-class consumption of the cultural "other"?

Music, the Internet, and Deviant Subcultures

Part of the global commodification of hip-hop and other music genres, popular and unpopular alike, has come through the development of social media technologies, which have given industries and consumers unprecedented access to socially driven information about music and music cultures. Throughout history, media technologies, from the earliest recording processes to contemporary digitalization, have shaped and reshaped how individuals and groups experience music culture.

Let us now look at how new media like the Internet have affected the intersections of music, subculture, and deviant identity. To do this, we turn to an Internet forum dedicated to the straight-edge subculture. Straight edge emerged as an offshoot of the hardcore punk subculture in the early 1980s in the United States and now claims worldwide adherents. The term "straight edge" can be traced to a 1981 song entitled "Straight Edge" by the Washington, D.C. band Minor Threat. Its lyrics state:

> I'm a person just like you
> But I've got better things to do
> Than . . .
> Snort white shit up my nose
> Pass out at the shows . . .
> Than sit around and smoke dope
> 'Cause I know I can cope . . .
> Always gonna be in touch
> Never want to use a crutch
> I've got the straight edge
> I've got the straight edge
> I've got the straight edge
> I've got the straight edge
>   (Minor Threat 1981)

Such lyrics were based on "a deep hatred for [the] lifestyle" of mainstream youth as experienced by lead singer Ian MacKaye in the early 1980s (Small and Stuart 1982). Straight edge emerged as a conservative reaction to punk's anarchic orientation; it called on punks to renounce drug use and promiscuity and thereby maintain a "straight edge" over their mainstream peers. The term was taken up by an emerging youth subculture whose members resisted what they saw as consumer-driven and self-indulgent youth cultures, including the nihilism and apathy of many punks. Straight-edge songs, like most hardcore music, are fast-paced, with simple and repetitive power-driven chords. The lyrics, as seen above, stand in stark contrast to mainstream ideologies purveyed in popular radio hits. Straight-edge and other hardcore American punk bands combined the speed and energy of punk music with a mixture of critical and upbeat lyrics. In the 1980s, and still today, straight-edge kids consider themselves deviant and define their values and actions in contrary terms to mainstream culture (Copes and Williams 2007).

Since the late 1990s, the straight-edge subculture has been diffused around the globe through the Internet. This diffusion has taken many forms: personal and official band websites, which may include personal stories of becoming/being straight edge, band biographies, song lyrics, and tattoo galleries; FAQs, listservs, and discussion forums; the trading of straight-edge music via peer-to-peer networks; online stores where fans can buy straight-edge music, shirts, stickers, and so on. As a result of this subcultural diffusion, many individuals discover straight edge in a dislocated form, fractured from its musical roots. Many kids have learned about straight edge online and decided to claim a straight-edge identity. Many of them subsequently join face-to-face straight-edge music scenes, but many others do not (Williams 2006). Those who join face-to-face straight-edge scenes usually come to agree that music is a tie that binds and that participation in a scene is an essential component of being straight edge. Many of these straight edgers argue that the diffusion of straight edge through the Internet has led to a "defusion" of the subculture, a stripping away of its resistant and countercultural heritage as Internet-surfing youths who happen to disapprove of drug use or sexual promiscuity (or who simply have no access to sex and drugs and want to feel good about that) locate and then appropriate the straight-edge identity.

But there are others who identify as straight edge and who rely on the Internet as their sole subcultural resource and means of subcultural interaction. This latter group tends to express the belief that anyone who lives a straight-edge lifestyle—following subcultural "rules" against drug use and promiscuous sex, for example—can be straight edge if they want to be. Such individuals tend to focus on their subcultural affiliation in terms of a personal commitment to a lifestyle rather than to membership in a local music scene. In fact, some straight edgers go so far as to reimagine local music scenes as problems for the subculture. One vocal member of a straight-edge Internet forum argued that people too concerned with music scenes were "blinded because you are doing what is 'cool,' not what you want. You are expressing your views as being, 'you can only be straightedge if you are in the cool crowd.' Well I guess you're cool and I'm not. But I am straightedge because of what I want" (Williams 2006: 190).

However important music might be for oppositional subcultures, there are changes occurring in contemporary societies that require we reassess music's central status in facilitating subcultural participation and identification. Such considerations are important for at least two reasons. First, they suggest that, even when studying music, we can benefit from looking to other media forms to better understand music's relative impact in social life. Second, we can see how important music remains for many young people, especially those who rely on music culture for defining themselves. At stake are young people's subcultural identities and their social-psychological functions, including self-esteem, self-efficacy, and belonging in global subcultural networks.

Conclusion

Traditional societies have had folk music traditions that were by default popular music. In modern societies, however, many different music genres exist alongside one another. Some vie for everyone's attention, while others are happy to remain out of the limelight. Some are produced and marketed by multinational conglomerates and can be found on radio stations around the world, while others are more like traditional folk traditions—relatively small genres that receive relatively little public attention unless they are deemed to deviate in some important way from mainstream norms that demands a reaction. Along with the many changes in norms and tastes over the last century, there have been continual contestations over definitions of what is popular and unpopular music.

These definitions are not natural, but rather are the result of definitions imposed and/or negotiated by social actors. As we have seen in this chapter, music genres that come to be structured alongside behaviors such as drug use or political opposition are most likely to be defined as deviant. And yet they need not be intentionally deviant to be defined by others as a problem. Agents of social control, both institutional and informal, actively engage in the process of defining music as popular or not. We will continue some of these ideas in Chapter 6, where we will see how the definitions of (un)popular music are guided in different ways—through thinking or ideology, through formal social institutions, and through the relatively informal process of maintaining community.

5

RELIGION AND POPULAR MUSIC

Religion has long been one of the most important topics for sociological thinking, research, and writing. All of the major theorists who contributed to the emergence of sociology in the 19th century felt two ways about religion. First, religion is one of the most important institutions in society. It serves as a major source of meaning for people, and it reflects many of society's core attributes and values. Second, understanding religion helps us understand society in general, including its history, conflicts, and goals.

A common sociological definition of religion is "a social institution involving beliefs and practices based on a conception of the sacred" (Macionis 2003: 491). The key word here is *sacred*. The sacred, or sacred things, are not ordinarily visible or observable in everyday life. The French sociologist Emile Durkheim (1953: 62), often referred to as the father of consensus or structural-functionalist thinking in sociology, made the conceptual distinction between *profane* and *sacred* objects. Profane things are ordinary things, whereas sacred things are extraordinary and worthy of attention, respect, and awe. Religion serves to teach people the distinction between the sacred and profane, and the proper ways to deal with both.

The four major paradigms in sociology each approach the study of religion in tune with their major assumptions as to how society operates. Consensus theory focuses on the *integrative* function of society. Religion provides a basis for cooperation, a mechanism for controlling members, and a source of meaning for members to use in addressing problems in everyday life. Durkheim extended these ideas through his concept of the *totem*, which is a regular item in the world that is attributed special characteristics—even power—by the community. Following the writings of Karl Marx (1964: 27), conflict theory sees religion as all too often a powerful tool used by capitalists to control the subservient classes by controlling the values used by all (e.g., the "work ethic" that says that we should feel good simply working hard and being productive in society, regardless of whether we are paid a worthwhile wage). Symbolic interactionism very much follows the social constructionism logic: that religion is like any other social institution in that people assemble religious traditions, liturgies, theologies, and practices to create "the semblance of ultimate security and permanence" (Berger 1967: 36). And, of course, the postmodernist perspective is very interested in the way our evolving culture and the power of the mass media are blurring the distinction between the sacred and the profane. One of the best examples of this, as we will shortly see, is the way popular music can sometimes be equated with and be used as a form of sacred music.

One may not automatically think of religion and popular music as a topic of interest. Of course, musicologists and historians describe the intricacies of church music, and anthropologists study the ways different cultures generate different styles of religious music. Sociologists of everyday life focus on religion and popular music as two related, sometimes conflicting, but increasingly compatible, sources of meaning. In this chapter, we will explore five different ways popular music and religion relate in everyday life.

Popular Music Sometimes Critiques Religion

In 1995, "If God Was One of Us" was a very popular song that received much radio play. Joan Osbourne composed and performed the song. It is a very pleasant, singer-songwriter pop song. Although many critics consider it a "one hit wonder" (http://www.lyricsondemand.com/onehitwonders.html), the song elicited considerable discussion and even argument over whether it was sacrilegious (e.g., disrespectful to God) or merely a meaningless/vacuous pop song with the word "God" in it. Radio and television talk shows pitted religious folks against atheists.

If you listen to the song or read the lyrics, you will see that the song does not appear to say anything derogatory about God or organized religion. What it does, however, is violate Durkheim's notion of the *sacred*. Joan Osbourne's sin—pun intended—was to sing about God profanely as if he were an ordinary person and—well—not God. Many people took this as an insult to their faith. The profane portrayals of Jesus on musical productions such as *Jesus Christ, Superstar*, Madonna's "Like a Prayer," and R.E.M.'s "Losing My Religion" received the same strong reaction from Christian critics.

Popular Music Sometimes Appears to Threaten Religion

As mentioned in Chapter 2, conservative interest groups such as the Parents Music Resource Center (PMRC) took their concerns over heavy metal music all the way to the U.S. Congress. Although the parents' concerns included a wide range of issues, their action strategy was to categorize all of them under the rubric of health. Although others may not share the parents' primarily conservatively Christian moral concerns, who could not support concerns for the health and well-being of our youth? The list of heavy metal groups, songs performances, and album cover art perceived as posing threats to religion is very long. The attacks against Christianity specifically can be very explicit. One of the best catalogs of this work is the music video mentioned above, "Rock'n'Roll: A Search for God." The producer, Eric Holmberg, interprets the meaning of the artwork on numerous heavy metal album covers.

Popular Music Sometimes Supports Religion

Everyone has heard Irving Berlin's "God Bless America" performed at baseball games, Fourth of July celebrations, and other civic events—this song may be the ultimate pop song that supports religion. These songs are predictably linked with patriotism, and this format can be traced at least as far back as Kay Kyser's World War II anthem, "Praise the Lord and Pass the Ammunition." In the realm of country music, we have a number of songs like Lee Greenwood's "God Bless the USA."

We clearly see fewer and fewer popular songs that explicitly support religion. One of the main reasons for this is the increasing secularization of popular culture in general. In turn, there is even a movement within conservative Christian denominations, such as the Southern Baptist Convention, to remove patriotic songs from church services. The separation of Church and State that the Founding Fathers of the U.S.A. hoped for is still in process.

Popular Music Can be Spiritual Music

Nevertheless, the sacred has not been, and probably cannot be, totally removed from popular music. Beginning during the countercultural days of the late 1960s, we witness the emergence of popular music with sometimes distinctive and sometimes implicit spiritual content or effect. As a survivor of that period of our history, Joe Kotarba can attest to the fact that a number of hippies, space cowboys, earth mothers, freaks, draft dodgers, and erstwhile baby boomers—yes, dear students, I'm talking about your parents and, in some cases, grandparents!—rejected their parents' religious affiliations and embarked upon spiritual journeys to find meaningful truth about life and reality. The general feeling was that organized religion was not relevant to young people's lives and moral concerns. Furthermore, young people sometimes blamed organized religion for being co-conspirators in the oppression, discrimination, and hatred being discovered in Western societies.

Spiritual music from the 1960s onward took many forms. Following the dictates of everyday life sociology, young people found spirituality in a wide range of musical styles, whether intended or not. An acid (i.e., LSD) trip in the desert could well be perceived as a spiritual experience. Carlos Castaneda, an anthropologist at UCLA, wrote a series of incredibly popular books in the late 1960s and early 1970s that described in very elegant and mystical ways his apprenticeship with a Yaqui sorcerer in the Sonoran Desert—far out! Need we add that natural hallucinogenic substances, such as peyote, served as the medium for these psychedelic experiences? Spiritual experimentation was rampant, and few belief systems were out of bounds. Scientology, animism, Eastern meditation, Gnosticism, and philosophy were each fashionable at different times for the baby boomer generation.

The popular music performer who provided the soundtrack for these spiritual voyages included the Grateful Dead, Pink Floyd, and

Cream. Millions of young people discovered spiritual truth in the music of Bob Dylan, the Beatles, the Byrds, and Leonard Cohen. One of the major rock artists of the 1960s who has continued to provide spiritual experiences for his fans is Van Morrison (2004). Van began a very successful career as lead singer for the Them in Northern Ireland, and embarked on a solo career in 1968 with *Astral Weeks*, an album often listed as one of the best of all time (Rolling Stone 2010). This album, like much of Morrison's work, borrows from Celtic mysticism to create an aural, meditative experience. The songs are sufficiently suggestive, yet open-ended in interpretation, to provide an accessible vault of meanings and feelings for baby boomers in search of meanings and feelings.

Pop Music Can be Religious Music

Some religious songs can easily be classified as popular music. One of the best examples is the "Ave Maria," one of the most cherished songs in the Catholic tradition. There are several versions of this song, but it is essentially based upon the 15th-century prayer to Mary, the mother of Jesus ("Hail Mary"). As mentioned at the beginning of this text, Franz Schubert's classical version of the song is a staple at weddings, where a Catholic presence is desired. The Ave Maria continues to be "covered" by pop music performers. The most common of these can be found on albums dedicated to Christmas music. Barbra Streisand, Joan Baez, Josh Groban, Michael Bublé, Aaron Neville, Celine Dion, Stevie Wonder, and Luciano Pavarotti have all recorded the song for Christmas albums. International opera singer Mark Vincent and pop diva Beyoncé both recorded the song for debut albums.

An interesting contemporary trend is the composition of religious music specifically designed according to popular music styles. A case in point is "contemporary Christian music" (CCM). This style of pop music began in the 1960s with the advent of "Jesus Music" among hippies and others seeking an alternative to traditional Christian music. The movement eventually included just about all styles of popular music, ranging from heavy metal and alternative rock to hip-hop and folk/singer-songwriter (Romanowski 2001). Major artists include Amy Grant, Toby Mac, dc Talk, Steven Curtis Chapman, and

Michael W. Smith. The controversy among Christian observers is whether CCM is liturgical music or entertainment. This controversy extends to perhaps the most popular style of CCM, "Praise and Worship" music. Praise and worship music is a very lush, orchestrated, choral, soothing style of music that has gained popularity across Christian denominations, including many Catholic parishes in North America. The music can be quite meditative, if not hypnotic.

A Postmodern Case Study in Authenticity: John Michael Talbot

Much of our discussion of the melding of pop music and religion can be summarized in, and illustrated by, the life and career of John Michael Talbot, an American Roman Catholic singer-songwriter who is also the founder of a monastic community: the Brothers and Sisters of Charity (Talbot 1999). He is the largest-selling Catholic musical artist ever, with over four million albums sold. He has authored or co-authored 15 books. John Michael tours through the U.S. in support of his monastic community nestled in the beautiful Ozark Mountains in Arkansas.

Talbot's work and career illustrate a major issue in CCM—authenticity (Kotarba 2009)—which is closely related to the issue raised above. Is CCM liturgical music or entertainment? Both Catholic leadership and laypersons wrestle with this issue. In general, CCM artists are considered to be authentic if they perform music primarily as a ministry and as a method of worship. Potential critics are suspicious of CCM artists who appear to be ego-involved, lack humility, want to be stars, and/or are too anxious to cross over to a mainstream pop music audience. John Michael met this test according to his followers (fans?), however, because he leads a simple lifestyle and does not personally profit from his talent and dedication. In a very postmodern way, John Michael is able to integrate his Internet site, concert tours, and many followers into a pristine, humble, and monastic lifestyle that will never make the cover of *People* magazine. His persona is refreshing—and authentic—to those baby boomers who are a bit overtaken by mass culture, even of an ecclesiastic sort.

John Michael Talbot embarked upon a spiritual journey befitting baby boomer rock musicians (Kotarba 2013a). In the 1970s, he was a member of the popular country rock band Mason Proffit, which toured with such famous performers as the Byrds, Pink Floyd, and even the Grateful Dead. After performing at the Ozark Mountain Folk Fair in Eureka Springs, Arkansas in 1973, John Michael had an epiphany. He realized that drug, alcohol, and other lifestyle excesses on, behind, and in front of the stage were not all they were cracked up to be:

> "Suddenly," he recalls, "the rock star life seemed empty and sad. It wasn't at all what I wanted my life to stand for." It was a prophetic experience for the youngster that caused him to question his whole lifestyle as he began to ask, "Isn't there something more?" . . . Up to that point he had rubbed shoulders with the rock stars he admired and emulated. He shared stages and dressing rooms with them, which gave him an insider's view of the rock scene. After meeting some of his heroes and seeing how they really lived their lives, Talbot came to an inescapable conclusion. "There were some real tragic scenarios being played out," he says, "and it caused me to stop cold and do some serious thinking."
>
> (Baur 2011: n.p.)

John Michael left the band to seek a more spiritual lifestyle. For four years he explored Native American religions, Hinduism, Judaism, Buddhism, and Fundamentalism. He joined the Jesus Movement and examined all the Christian denominations. He concluded that Catholicism was the path for him.

John Michael felt impelled to use his particular talent to experience the ascetic. He believes that sacred music is sacramental and,

> from an arts perspective, both reflects and guides the faithful. That music, based on faith, can take the listener on a closer walk with God, actually taking them into the heart of the Lord. "It brings out the mysterious and speaks the unspeakable, bringing to light that which is beyond human reason. Furthermore," he says, "the role of music and prayer fulfills a prophetic function. Not that musicians are prophets," he notes, "but they do have an obligation to lead."
>
> (Baur 2011: n.p.)

John Michael embarked on a career that to date has produced over 40 musical recordings and four million album sales. In 1982, he was the recipient of the prestigious Dove Award for Worship Album of the Year, *Light Eternal*, with producer and long-time friend, Phil Perkins. Four years later, he became one of only nine artists to receive the President's Merit Award from the National Academy of Recording Arts and Sciences and, in 1988, he was named the number one Christian artist by *Billboard* magazine.

John Michael performs at 50 or so live concerts a year, largely at parish church venues around the country. In an interview with Joe Kotarba, he related that his audiences consisted of people who adhere to a range of religious and spiritual beliefs—Protestants, agnostics, Buddhists, Jews, and others—all with one particular need: "They love the music. For some, it serves as a pathway to find a way. For others who have found a way for themselves, the music helps make the journey along that path pleasant, meaningful, and relevant."

John Michael Talbot is an archetypical baby boomer: postmodern, yet traditional, yet experimental. He is able to navigate through what might appear to be numerous religious and spiritual contradictions without compromising his commitment to, and acceptance by, the formal Roman Catholic Church. For example, his music is very eclectic, integrating rock, folk, ecclesiastic, classical, chant, early church music, and the music of the medieval and Renaissance eras. He uses the funds generated by his music to support a monastic community that includes married as well as single people, the Brothers and Sisters of Charity, at Little Portion Hermitage. All commit to vows of poverty, chastity, and obedience. His ministry is open to all, but he has also shared his music with Pope John Paul II and Mother Teresa (Baur 2011). His ministry is timeless, yet the infrastructure is state-of-the art recording and Internet communications. The message is simple, the media is complex, yet the encouragement to followers is to engage in spiritual readings, vigils, fasting, and manual labor.

Conclusion

Christian music is not the only religious genre incorporating pop sensibilities. Matisyahu (or Happy Merchant) is a Jewish hip-hop artist who combines rap with beatboxing (i.e., a vocalized style of percussion), traditional vocal-jazz scat singing, Judaism's hazzan style of songful prayer, and a reggae beat. The explosion of interest in rap music among young people involved in the resistance movements in North Africa and the Middle East often has clear Islamic characteristics (Kotarba 2012).

The fact that popular music is permeating religious music should not be surprising. The history of religious and spiritual music clearly shows that religious music has always reflected local cultural norms and styles. In a consensus theory sense, religions need people. In an everyday life theory sense, people are attracted to music that fits their aesthetic values while providing practical meanings for everyday life's very changing problems and issues.

6

POLITICS AND POPULAR MUSIC

If a man were permitted to make all the ballads, he need not care who should make the laws of a nation.

—Andrew Fletcher 1997 (1703)

Within the field of popular music studies, the notion of "politics" typically denotes either political songs or protest music in the world of pop music. Also, it seems that when politics and music are explicitly mixed, a listener is in for either tunes that work as a "struggle against dominant institutions like the state and economic system" (Balliger 1999: 57) or for music that serves to support existing values, like official national anthems such as "God Bless America" or Quebec's patriotic hymn, "Gens du Pays." To limit a discussion of politics in music to these genres is, however, unwise. More insightfully, instead, we can say that music (popular and otherwise) has a political *structure* and *polity-forming capacity* of its own.

In the case of the contemporary popular music industry, this structure is generally understood as a cultural and political oligarchy—an arrangement of power in which a few social agents rule a mass of many. Pop music's oligarchy manifests itself through powerful commercial alliances among music production labels. These labels control the global market by promoting unlimited consumer access to musical genres and artists, but by restricting such access in actual practice. Such restriction is achieved via control of both production and distribution through the standardization of popular music sounds. Because of pop music's close relation with the rest of pop culture (movies, fashion, lifestyle, etc.), this oligarchy has the capacity to draw and even shape like-minded audiences characterized by similarities in outlooks, values, and taste. Popular music, in its capacity to draw and form communities, may then be said to be a social and political force.

Cultural and political oligarchies are important, but not the only means of framing politics and music. Politics enters music, and music enters politics, in numerous and often subtle ways. A sociological approach to music might find political values even in songs that have nothing to do with patriotism or protest. For example, even a harmlessly apolitical hook like "Na, na, na, na, na" sung by the bubbliest of bubbly pop stars may have a deep cultural and political significance. According to a major European theorist of culture, Theodor Adorno (Adorno and Hullot-Kentor 2006), the infantilization of pop songs is both a symptom and a cause of the formation of mass culture. A mass culture is one in which people's sense of taste has been standardized by a culture industry keen on preserving the political and economic status quo rather than in the elevation of artistic and political consciousness. If Adorno and his colleagues are right, then politics is everywhere in popular music—despite the fact that we are sometimes oblivious to the hidden political realities of musical production, distribution, or consumption. It should be interesting to uncover some of the more profound political meanings that music holds in everyday life. Following our customary approach of examining the mundane in order to appreciate the deep connection between music and society, in this chapter we examine the relationship between popular music and politics, polity, and community by taking into consideration the multiple meanings of "politics" in popular music studies. We begin by examining the practice of cardboard CD packaging as a way of posing alternatives to the political, economic, and aesthetic oligarchy of the music industry. We then analyze some subtle parallels between *American Idol* and presidential elections in the USA. We conclude with a consideration of the power that communities can wield against unpopular music by studying the case of the West Memphis Three. Through these examples, we want to get you thinking about the importance of three concepts—ideology, institutions, and community—in developing an understanding of how power operates in the social world.

Ideology

There are several different sociological understandings of the concept of ideology, yet the most basic definition simply views ideology as a set of ideas about something—by ideas, here we mean things such as values, beliefs, and ideals about social conduct. Within sociology and related disciplines, the concept of ideology is inevitably a social one, in the sense that ideologies are always systems of ideas about how society is and about how it should be. Moreover, ideologies are social in the sense that they are shared by groups of people. Of course, by suggesting that ideologies are shared, we are not implying that they are shared by everyone. As a matter of fact, ideologies and the groups who create and support them are often in conflict with one another. Yet, the point that more than one individual, somewhere, at some point in time, will share an ideology is a powerful one in and of itself, and an even more powerful one in light of its consequences.

When people share an ideology, they tend to forget that alternative ideologies exist and that these alternatives may be as plausible as their preferred view. What makes ideologies so powerful is that they have a tendency to legitimize behavior and to become reified. Take, for example, the idea (loaded with beliefs, values, assumptions, and so on) that classical music is "better"—that is, more refined, sophisticated, enlightened—than pop music. Ultimately there is no way of proving this to be an unchallengeable truth, yet the idea is strong enough to become so "real" in its consequences, so much a matter of fact, so "reified," that for the most part public schools all over the world abstain from teaching popular music courses. Some even formally condemn pop music as a negative influence and focus instead on instructing children to play "classical" instruments as part of their art curriculum. Here we can see how an ideology—the idea that classical music is inherently more valuable than popular music—legitimizes certain educational practices and delegitimizes others. The more an ideology becomes legitimized, the more it tends to be experienced as an incontrovertible truth and not as mere opinions, outlooks, or ideas. Indeed, the "fact" that classical music "does good things" to children, and the "fact" that rap or metal music "do bad things" to them, becomes a belief *reified*—that is, materialized—deeply enough that parents "caught" exposing their wee ones to 50 Cent or Slayer promptly need to account for their "irresponsible" behavior.

In general sociological terms, people in power have at least two means of maintaining their privileges: forceful means and symbolic means. Music is rarely used in forceful ways—though it has been used as such in the past. As examples: the FBI used popular hits to wear down Branch Davidians during the siege in Waco, Texas, in 1993; in Ontario, Canada, police once blared out "boy band" music to disperse a crowd of street protesters; and military police in Iraq and Guantanamo Bay have cycled hip-hop and death metal loudly and continuously to destroy prisoners psychologically. For the most part, though, music's power rests in its symbolic force, that is, as a medium for ideology.

According to many critical theorists, the ideology that is most often present in popular music is that of conservatism—the ideology supported by the alliance of commercial groups who hold the political and economic power within a capitalist society. For obvious reasons these groups have a keen interest in maintaining the status quo. The best way to maintain such a state of affairs is to sell people something they want to buy and at the same time something they want to believe in. Marxian and Italian sociologist Antonio Gramsci referred to this process as *hegemony*. Accordingly, music appreciation tends to work in hegemonic fashion by appeasing people and enticing them to accept and even support the status quo—whether they do this consciously or not. For example, due to its merry repetitiveness, catchy simplicity, and inoffensive superficiality, the consumption of pop music is believed to lead to the regression of the listener to childlike mental states—a regression which serves the purpose of distracting individuals away from realizing the depth of the social conditions that oppress them and others. (This is a critical/conflict interpretation of the addictive pop music song phenomenon we discussed in Chapter 1 on interaction.) This hegemonic function of music—that is, its complicit role in supporting the status quo—has been traditionally condemned by scholars, both in light of its political consequences and in light of the actual means used; that is, the texts, sounds, and performances that made such music so "bad."

In contrast, popular music that is "good" in itself and good in terms of its consequences for people is autonomous music; or, at least, so the critical theoretical argument goes. According to this counter-hegemonic ideology, autonomous, independent, genuine music is believed to be synonymous with authenticity—something which is highly valued (at least on the surface) by many people of character, and especially, and perhaps stereotypically, by artists. Autonomy and authenticity mean many different things, but they generally entail independence from shallow values—think fame, economic success, political collusion, and so on—that "corrupt" the ideal purity of musical expression (Vannini and Williams 2009). Autonomous and authentic music is often politically resistant, working as "cultural" alternatives to the lifestyles of the "mainstream." This type of music often falls into one of the following categories: protest against oppression or exploitation; aspiration toward a better and more just life; satire of those in power; philosophical reflection; commemoration of popular struggles; inspiration for collective movements; tribute to martyrs; expression of working-class solidarity; and critical social commentary. Regardless of the actual category that a musical performance, recording, or genre may fall into, autonomous and authentic music intends to solicit or arouse support for a movement or cause, create solidarity and cohesion, promote awareness or evoke solutions to social problems, or simply provide hope. In a sense, this authenticity position is itself elitist, at least in a political (if not aesthetic) sense.

Autonomy and authenticity sound like good values, but in actuality they are hardly achievable. A sociological understanding of autonomy leads us to find that music-making is for the most part dependent on strategic compromises and negotiation. As Howard Becker (1982) has shown, the production of art is a complex joint act between vast numbers of people with different, yet related, goals. Despite the myth of the lonely genius doing music on his or her own, like all social activities, music-making is a collective accomplishment. As we can see below in the case of Montreal-based production label Constellation Records, despite a strong ideology of autonomy and authenticity, certain negotiations and compromises with the system are inevitable.

Politics, Technology, and Indie Music

Any new technological medium of musical expression "changes the way in which we experience music" and poses "both constraints and opportunities in terms of the organization of production" (Shuker 2001: 51). The history of music in the Western hemisphere is marked by a series of shifts from oral and live performance to musical notation and then onward to recording and dissemination through a multitude of media. From a related perspective, music's history can be said to be one of the technological transitions from a context in which the human voice was the only technology of production to one in which the voice is accompanied by a variety of sonorous technologies. If we agree that singing is a technique of expression and that musical sound is a technique or medium of expression, we should agree that music itself is a form of technology.

Like music, politics is also a form of technology. To understand this claim, we ought to begin by understanding technology broadly as a general body of knowledge comprised of "how-to" specifications for action. Of course, a technology is not just a collection of tools and "how-to" specifications on how to operate those tools, but also a body of values specifying how tools should be used and for what purposes. Understood this way, the difference between politics and technology is tenuous and both politics and music are technologies of expression. Politics focuses on the expression of political value and the implementation of social ideas through political means, and music focuses on the expression of aesthetic value and orients itself to sound as the tool through which expressiveness can be achieved. In this section, we examine how technology and specific musical techniques acquire political importance and, more precisely, how different forms of technology contribute to the formation and maintenance of political boundaries between communities.

We begin in Montreal, Canada, where a relatively obscure music production company known as Constellation Records has made an interesting choice for the material with which all the CDs in their catalog are packaged: cardboard. Cardboard is a material that, once treated and adapted for the purpose of CD packaging can constitute an alternative to the plastic generally used for the manufacturing of CD jewel cases. But why do so, when plastic is obviously more time-efficient for labor, more durable, and cheaper? And how is this choice for cardboard sociologically significant? According to the masterminds of this strategy at Constellation:

> Mechanical reproduction, whether digital or analogue with regard to the music itself, whether at the local die-cutter or silk-screener with regard to packaging and printing, is accessible technology and allows for the duplication and dissemination of cultural work at the micro-level, even if the macroscopic potentials of the technology machine, with respect to art no less than labour practice or weaponry, are terrifying. It's all about maintaining a human scale. Fin-de-siècle capitalism both facilitates and threatens independent production, and the key for us is to utilize those technologies that capitalism itself has marginalized and dispersed in order to create cultural objects that are inherently critical of the system. To the extent this condemns us to pursuing quality at the expense of quantity, it is a fate to which we willingly submit.
>
> (Constellation Records n.d.)

Constellation's technological position is a political stance intended to separate it from the mainstream, a stance that expresses common values in "indie" music—a synonym for independent, that is, independent from economic, political, aesthetic, and technological pressures from the rest of the music industry and mainstream music and society. Indie music labels like Constellation attempt to build unique communities on the political philosophy of punk and post-punk in order to separate themselves from other musical communities and exercise resistance against pressures to conform.

It is not always easy to do so. While it is true that by choosing techniques and material like cardboard over conventional plastic Constellation artisans and artists tend to achieve a certain sense of difference—a distinct identity, if you will—it is also true that dealing with recycled cardboard packaging means involving complex networks of local artisans, craftsmen, and environmentally sensitive local business suppliers, as well as applying more intensive human labor such as cutting, folding, trimming, and drawing, which results in increasing costs and possibly lowering consumer demand. Yet, this also results in avoiding plastic and the environmental problems it embodies, and allowing "the sensibility of the music [to be] reflected in and reinforced by the tactility of the package that contains it" (Constellation Records n.d).

Constellation's alternative approach to technology does not end with cardboard. Take, for example, its politics of distribution. Far from representing a mere technical process of getting live or recorded sound from a point of origin to a destination, the process of distribution needs to take into consideration the geographic organization of retail stores and the clients that frequent these stores. After all, could you reject plastic and still feel good about shipping off your cardboard-packaged records to a suburban shopping mall? Rather than malls, Constellation, similarly to other indie labels, then mostly attempts to rely on a network of Mom-and-Pop stores across Canada and the United States, as well as low-budget-site Internet distribution and marketing via word-of-mouth and underground zine coverage. Obviously this keeps Constellation's profits to a minimum, but it also allows its artists to remain relatively free from the pressure of making marketable music.

Take, for example, its most famous band, Godspeed! You Black Emperor (GYBE). GYBE remain keen on touring small venues, playing on pitch-dark stages to avoid emphasizing their image more than their sound, refusing interviews with most media outlets, and obstinately refusing to compromise their aesthetic and political ideologies of resistance, no matter how obscure and controversial these can get. Through their music, instrumental sounds, and lyrics, GYBE and other Constellation bands are outspokenly critical of commodified and standardized musical and political expression typical of post-industrial neo-liberal society. For example, by privileging the production of an immediate and almost "live" sound (as "live" as recordings can get), Constellation condemn commodified duplication and mechanical reproduction. Furthermore, Constellation's music is openly political and at times their rhetoric is inflammatory.

In other instances Constellation's random noise adds to the cacophony of their politics. Take, for example, GYBE's recording *Yanqui U.X.O.* ("Yankee Unexploded Ordinance"), a wordless condemnation of

American military interventionism. The music alone, in its sheer symphonic violence of ups and downs resembling the rhythms of airplanes rising and bombs falling, does all the talking. Yet, at the periphery of the sound, on the very cardboard in which the disc is enveloped, GYBE's belligerent overtones are most audible. A folder depicting a hammer inexorably squelching the word "hope" written in relief in the midst of white flying chimeras reinforces the impression of muted silence imposed by the American bomber featured on the cover. The disc itself bears the inscription "Rockets fall on Rocket Fans"—an obvious indictment of turn-of-the-century U.S. foreign policy. "U.X.O.," GYBE adds, "is unexploded ordinance is landmines is duster bombs. All of it mixed by god's pee." The backside of the cover art blurs music and politics even more. There, a chart links Sony, AOL Time-Warner, Universal, and BMG to shared financial holdings in the military/weaponry industry: a controversial but certainly thought-provoking addition to the idea of the politico-industrial-military complex. GYBE's and Constellation's ideology is one that is deeply counter-hegemonic and built on values of autonomy and authenticity as resistance—a common yet vanishing strategy in the world of trademarked alternative rock (see Moore 2005). Let us now turn to a detailed discussion of the pop music institutions against which Constellation Records and indie music are defined.

Institution

The most obvious commonsensical meaning of the word "institution" is a mental asylum. Yet within sociology the word has several meanings, some of which are not readily apparent. Let us begin to explain the sociological significance of institution as if we were, indeed, referring to mental institutions and explore that concept from the angle of popular music. Imagine that you decide to start a new band featuring the absence of any obvious trace of melody. As if the oddness of your sound was not enough, you decide to add to your tracks extremely loud, distorted recordings of half a dozen trains operating their rusty brakes in the midst of a windstorm. Next, you decide that the band members ought to wear chicken uniforms both on and off stage. Finally, you write lyrics featuring nothing but Simglish words (the type of English featured on the video game The Sims) and as the band leader you proceed to scream those words through a megaphone while a back-up singer randomly barks the world "sailor" in a contrived Australian accent.

Now imagine that by sheer accident your manager books you for a Christmas show at an old folks' home. While you can probably manage to leave the stage and the scene without actually being institutionalized, chances are that most of the members would want to have you committed. But why would they? The answers to this question hold the key to a better understanding of the concept of institution. First, your audience deemed you offensive because your band does not resemble, in the terms of the style of your performance, the musical styles to which they are accustomed. People believe that customs are important because they represent long-standing ways of doing things. Likewise, institutions have a clear historical impetus. Second, your reception was poor because your audience believed you lack a social organization that supports what you do. The music industry as a whole is an example of such a social organization. Its support of custom is manifested through sales charts, awards, multi-year contracts, and so on. So, because in your audience's mind your band is not backed by such organizational support, you come across to them as lacking institutional approval and therefore you are worthy of condemnation. What we can say here is that these two components, institution as custom and institution as recognized social organization, are both important sociologically.

The formation and upholding of custom and social organization are political matters. Institutions, in other words, have a political force that is rooted in no small part in customs. Custom is no less a concern for music artists than anyone else. In fact, no matter how innovative and even revolutionary a form of art may be, it has to deal with institutional gatekeepers (Frith 1991) who enforce existing ways of doing things and existing criteria of what is good and bad. Art institutions are known by sociologists as "art worlds" (Becker 1982: x): "network[s] of people whose cooperative activity, organized via their joint knowledge of conventional means of doing things, produce[s] the kind of art world that art world is known for." While institutionalization makes life difficult for original expression—and unfortunately that is too bad for you and your chicken-uniform-donning band members—it allows for familiar and customary performances to register more easily with audiences. From all of this it follows that, despite its aura of originality, much art needs to be conventional to be successful. As we discuss below, the case of *American Idol* shows this phenomenon quite clearly; not only is the music featured on *American Idol* customary, but its very makeup draws from deep-rooted institutions of American society and from a vision of audiences/constituents as customers. To boot, the show itself, in its sheer duration and repeated exposure to emerging artists, is an exercise in creating "idols" as institutions.

American Idol: *Rock the Vote (But Not Too Loudly)!*

If you have never heard of the televised singing contest known as *American Idol* in the U.S., or *Canadian Idol* in Canada, *Australian Idol* in Australia, *Pop Idol* in the U.K., or any of the national *Idol* competitions featured in more than 15 countries around the world, you must live under a rock. The popularity of *American Idol* is the stuff of TV producers' dreams. Now more than a decade old, the Fox Network show has outlasted, outwitted, and outposted all other shows that have dared to challenge it—not only other reality shows, but even mega-TV events such as the Olympics, the NBA and NHL playoffs, the Grammy Awards, and the Academy Awards as well. Although its ratings have begun to slip since 2012 (relative to its own incredible past), *American Idol* remains, without exaggeration, the biggest musical phenomenon of the 21st century.

Despite the fact that featured songs change from country to country, the show is remarkably consistent in its format across the world. Generally, the contest begins with early auditions hosted in a country's major urban centers. Hopeful contestants sing off against tens of thousands of competitors by performing before a panel of judges, and, if they pass this preliminary round—either thanks to their good singing skills, comedic potential, or to the human interest of their personal biographies—they are invited to sing for a panel of celebrity judges. During these and later auditions the judges make further cuts until a final list of 12 contestants is selected for the final rounds of the show. Week after week the group loses one unlucky contestant until a winner is crowned the country's singing "Idol" in the season's finale. The process is not dissimilar to that through which the American president is chosen, although ironically much fewer American adults would prefer to be president than to be a pop star. In both cases, contestants engage in a series of meetings where their knowledge and skills are tested against one another. They are closely scrutinized, from their clothing choices to the words that come out of their mouths, the amount of confidence that is allegedly felt by the audience, and the overall authenticity that they express. Contestants subject themselves to public scrutiny of their private lives as well, although access to such information is highly controlled and scripted for strategic reasons. And, once elected, winners in both contests have a limited term, indicated by constitutional laws in the president's case and stipulated by the annual succession of winners in *Idol*.

How do American Idols describe their experiences being crowned, and what does winning mean to them? Questions about such experiences are common in American politics, no less so for the presidency. For instance, 2010 *American Idol* winner Scotty McCreery pronounced that becoming American Idol was "just such a humbling and a great experience" and admitted how, "never in my wildest dreams did I expect to make it as far as I did" (McCreery n.d.).Presidents invariably make similar comments, referring to "the most humbling part of my job" and about the long, hard road behind and ahead (Obama n.d.). Such discourse suggests an overarching set of norms or rules about how people in power ought to describe their experiences. One could argue that such discourse is purely informal and represents the autonomous experiences of individuals (as suggested with Constellation earlier), but we suggest that the similarities are the result of an institutional process through which certain types of answers are bound to emerge. Let us look further into this by considering how *American Idol*, like the American presidency, epitomizes a specific set of political values central to America's culture, with an emphasis on the Weberian concept of rationalization (see Ritzer 1993).

Max Weber argued that there were four different ideal types of rationality: value-oriented, traditional, affectual, and instrumental (Bendix 1978). Value-oriented rationality refers to conduct undertaken in light of ethical, aesthetic, religious, or other types of motives that are intrinsic to behavior and not goal-driven. Traditional rationality refers to conduct undertaken as a result of custom or habit. Affectual rationality refers to action undertaken to satisfy emotional needs, drives, and wishes. Finally, instrumental rationality refers to behavior enacted as means to an end, that is, as calculated pursuit. Weber believed that, in modern societies, there was a shift in people's behaviors from being supported by traditions and values to being motivated by rational, calculated concerns. Given the quotes above and what else we see going on in modern media culture today, it seems that the central characteristic of *American Idol* and the American electoral campaign is a combination of affectual and instrumental rationality. The two rationalities combine in the newly formed relationships among media producers, culture industries sponsors, and media users into something akin to what Henry Jenkins (2008) calls "affective economics."

To succeed in becoming and remaining powerful, modern politicians must balance a disinterested distance between themselves and the governed, on the one hand (look at how female politicians are regularly blasted for being too emotional to be "good" politicians), and, on the other, a connection with the common citizen (thus the myths of humbling experiences and hard work that allegedly sum up their successes). The architects of *American Idol* understand all this. On *American Idol*, musical vocation, talent, and hard work are the objects of constant lip service, but in the end the true strength of the show is not musical and aesthetic but instead political and bureaucratic. The contemporary music industry—an artistic counterpart of the modern state—exercises its quasi-monopoly on the public's musical knowledge by selecting candidates for musical leadership that can serve as a bridge between corporate sponsors and the social-economic, cultural, and emotional positions of viewers. The most talented are those who stand out only in some small way; otherwise, they are quite normal people who avoid taking risks or alienating themselves from the larger political/cultural climate of the show. Past winners of *American Idol* are epitomes of *McDonaldized* (Ritzer 1993) music: they represent efficient formulas calculated to ensure predictability and control in sound and sales. Mediocrity, in a McDonaldized economy, becomes a marketing stratagem. And, indeed, as the case goes in a McDonaldized market, there is little tolerance for deviations from the instrumental rational norm. This is the best way to maximize the size of the audience and thus the revenues generated from the show. Viewers must not only feel connected to the contestants, they must *want* to tune in again and again to see how the story unfolds. For their part, contestants themselves become media objects, presented publicly by the funding sponsors (e.g., Ford or Coca-Cola). It is much the same in presidential politics, with candidates struggling to maintain their own individuality in the maelstrom of party politics and private-interest lobbying.

American Idols are typically very explicit in what drew them to auditions—the potential future as a megastar and artist who is no longer bound by the reality of everyday life. American politicians express eerily similar reasons for contesting the presidency, though their reasons are masked behind concerns for the public good and the future of the country. Yet, in fact, becoming president does make one a type of megastar who is no longer bound to reality in the way other citizens are. Thus we arrive at the first of three important characteristics of rationality to be considered—freedom of access. Anyone in the U.S. may participate in the race to be president and to be American Idol, regardless of race, gender, class, or other ascribed social status (though in both cases age limitations exist). Freedom of access to both contests reveals a fundamental principle of American democracy: power and its structures are seemingly universally accessible, and anyone can become a leader by way of individual achievement. But herein lies also a pair of notable contradictions of the system. First, those from certain backgrounds or in possession of certain characteristics are more likely to win, and, second, the rewards promised to the wannabe Idol or wannabe president are not limited to gratefulness for their selfless dedication to the public good (whether aesthetic or moral) as the democratic principle should have it. Instead, the rewards include personal career advancement, fame, success, power, and wealth that often turn the strategies of achievement into an instrumental pursuit. In the case of the presidency, the elected contestant becomes the most powerful person in the world, whereas in *American Idol* the winner gets a record deal with a major label (the parent company of which also produces the show). Both get free cars and innumerable opportunities for enrichment as a celebrity for the rest of their lives.

Second, and obviously related to the above point, participation in the race to become either an American Idol or an American president is not only based on free access as a competitor, but also on free access as a voter. As Stahl (2004) has remarked, this is a crucial difference between, say, *American Idol* and other successful reality shows like *Big Brother* or *Survivor*. Whereas on the latter two shows contestants are kicked off weekly by members of the same cast, *American Idol* runners are voted off by "America." "America"—as contestants, judges, and Ryan Seacrest (the show's merry host) constantly refer to as their voting viewers—assumes a mystical aura in the show, almost as if she was a demigoddess with an enlightened musical mind and artistic taste of her own, but an authority coming not from tradition but populist acceptance. Anytime "America" is evoked—as in "The judges loved it, but will America love it as well?" or "Vote for me, America!"—she appears more and more real and yet more and more ethereal and goddess-like at the same time. Not unlike much religious practice, her divinity works by instilling fear in her apostles. Inevitably concerned with accidentally offending her, *Idol* and presidential contestants alike thus avoid taking chances with original material or with performances that deviate far from the canons of shared taste.

A third interesting political feature of the show, and the third parallel between *American Idol* and American presidential politics, has to do with the show's ideology of meritocracy. As Weber has explained, merit-centered ideologies have taken an especially strong hold in Protestant societies because merit is a manifestation of religious devotion and self-abnegation through faith and hard work. On *American Idol*, merit is determined by "America" through a process based on quasi-religious display of collective faith and will, but also through the exercise of forces more similar to the brutality of a modified social Darwinism than the grace of a musical demigoddess. In fact, year after year, the show begins with exposure of a few musical freaks to public humiliation. This is when the slow-witted, the out-of-shape, the weird, and the uncool get their 25 seconds of fame/shame. Something similar happens in presidential campaigns. Because anyone can run, it just so happens that the majority of those who do will embarrass themselves for lacking the characteristics desired by the masses, regardless of how far-sighted, original, or courageous they are.

After the early rounds give way to the more competitive stages, the show's ideology of merit takes on its most obvious and also most unbecoming features. Week after week, the contestants choose and perform familiar songs on stage, parroting the conventions of well-known performers, singing styles, and musical genres. Wannabe "American Idols" are never good enough (or at least they are not allowed) to write and perform their own songs and their cover-song choices are highly restricted by what the producers want "America" to hear, much like in presidential debates. The singers' merit, therefore, lies in the ability to be as "bland and derivative" (Stahl 2004: 217) as the most undemanding audiences may demand. After all, the audience of *American Idol* is the widest on TV, cross-cutting boundaries of age, class, gender, and race. The merit of the contestants, then, is connected to their ability to sing institutionalized music in an institutionalized fashion for an institutional medium. She or he who manages to offend the least number of people during the 40-plus number of marketing sessions—that is, a season's worth of *American Idol* episodes—becomes the best choice for an audience that is sufficiently comfortable with the ideologies and institutions they represent.

Qualities of potential for institutional fit aside, the winner's merit becomes synonymous with being the least objectionable. This is the same type of rhetoric that revolves around presidential campaigns; every cycle people discuss voting not for the best candidates, but rather for the ones that suck the least. The instrumental rationality that leads to belief in and support of the American political system turns back to the affectual and instrumental rationalities that help support it. The presidency and *Idol* are equally grounded in affective economics—the emotional underpinnings of decision making that tie consumer-citizens into political and economic institutions.

Community

While the previous section considered some links between music and politics as formal institutions, politics are practiced most often via communities—those informal social organizations that govern everyday life. "Community" shares its root with "communication," the process of exchanging information. Music is obviously a form of communication, but so is the discourse surrounding it. Any investigation of the political significance of music must therefore consider music and the culture surrounding it as communication. In this section we discuss how the formation of a polity—another word for political community— is grounded in discourse.

"Discourse" is the technical term referring to the whole of communicative exchanges taking place among people, as well as to discrete instances of communication. Ethnomethodologists, whose work is a form of everyday life sociology, refer to both the content of exchange and the form in which exchange takes place (e.g., Mehan and Wood 1975). Discourse is not only made of talk and words, but, more importantly for us, also symbolic vehicles like musical sounds, styles, and practices. Discourse is powerful. It has the potential to repress as much as it does to create or produce.

As we have seen, music can be viewed as a discursive force that "dumbs down" social groups, exerting power over what and how they consume. But music has the power to discursively form communities as well. A common example of communities formed around music is that of subcultures. The concepts of subculture and scene refer in similar ways to networks of people loosely affiliated around shared understandings, ways of communicating, and similar lifestyles. As we saw in Chapter 4, subcultural scenes include communities formed around musical genres. These have included jazz, punk, indie rock, extreme metal, riot grrrl rock, rap and hip-hop, goth, and straight edge, to name a few. Music communities emerge out of communicative exchanges, whether these happen at sanctioned events in dance clubs, on the radio or official band websites, or through informal channels that can be found in teens' bedrooms, at school, or online via blogs, chat forums, and social networking sites. The nature of these communities is often political in the traditional sense, as in the case of social protest music in the punk and riot grrrl subcultures, but not always. Fans of many different genres communicate their musical interests to others by chatting on MySpace or Facebook fan pages as a form of leisure and fun, with no obvious political intent.

By their very definition, communities have social boundaries. These boundaries are shaped in part through the shared interests and lifestyles of individuals. In the more traditional sense, they are also shaped by geography, as we see when we refer to a neighborhood or small town as a community. In many modern societies, especially those that control large geographical areas, small town communities are a basic fact of life. Even if you grew up claiming to be from a large metropolis like Atlanta or Chicago, you may very well have actually grown up in a nearby suburb with a small town, community feel. In such areas, communities can have a strong normative structure, meaning that members of the community are expected to more or less act similarly and share interests. Rural America is especially well known for conservative local communities where everyone is expected to dress similarly, go to football games on Friday nights, and to church on Sunday mornings. When subcultural music "infiltrates" such communities, and members start to express themselves in non-traditional ways, very real problems can emerge. The instance of Swing Kids in Nazi Germany in the 1930s that we discussed in Chapter 4 is a very good example of this, and you may want to return to it. Likewise, the following story of the "West Memphis Three" describes the power of discourse in shaping communities and their boundaries around musical tastes.

The West Memphis Three and the Limits of Community

On May 5, 1993, three 8-year-old boys went missing near a children's playground in West Memphis, Arkansas. The following day, police discovered the boys' submerged bodies in a wooded drainage creek nearby. The boys had been hog-tied, stripped, and beaten. Two were drowned in the creek, while the third exhibited signs of sexual mutilation. The tragedy was quickly (and rightly) defined as a threat to the community, not only because of the murders, but also because of the absence of any suspects and of any obvious motive.

The threat of unknown pedophilic killers fueled speculation as to who would do such a thing, but nearly a month later no suspects had been named. A local teenager named Damien Wayne Echols, however, had been questioned several times. Echols was an enigma in the community. He dyed his long hair jet black, often wore black clothes, and had expressed dissatisfaction with the overtly Christian culture that surrounded him. Amid public demand for headway in the case, news agencies started circulating stories that linked the murders to possible

Satanic rituals. A report on Jonesboro, Arkansas, KAIT evening news in early June stated that, "since the very beginning of the investigation, people all around West Memphis have come forward with stories of satanic cults" (Sinofsky 1996). Television coverage of Satanic activity among young people was not unique to the West Memphis case. Rather, Satanism had appeared in the previous decade as a "catch-all category for unacceptable behavior of youth ... [while] newspapers portrayed heavy metal music as a catalyst for Satanism" (Rowe and Cavender 1991: 271). The name "Damien Echols," who was known to be a fan of the then-subcultural heavy metal band Metallica, began circulating among community members as a likely perpetrator.

With only two pieces of fiber as potential physical evidence, Echols, along with Jason Baldwin and Jessie Misskelley, Jr., were charged with the crime in early June 1993 after Misskelley (whose IQ was 72) emerged from a 12-hour police interrogation. Allegations similar to those found in Rowe and Cavender's (1991) study were immediately leveled against the "West Memphis Three." Once the teens were identified as the alleged killers, public reaction was swift and presented regularly in local and regional news reports. Take the following TV news interview with Pam Hobbs, the mother of one of the murdered boys, as one example:

> Reporter: Do you feel like the people who did this were worship-ping, uh [interrupted]
> Hobbs: [interrupting] Satan? Yes I do.
> Reporter: Why?
> Hobbs: Just look at the freaks. I mean just look at 'em. They look like punks.
>
> (Sinofsky 1996)

First, note how the mother was able to finish the reporter's question for him, suggesting the extent to which the community was already abuzz with stories about Satanism. Second, notice how quickly she reduced the alleged killers' guilt to their style, a fact of which the West Memphis Three themselves were well aware. Speaking about his alleged involve-ment during an interview while in jail, Jason Baldwin, then 16 years old, said, "I can see where they might really think I was in a cult cuz I wear Metallica t-shirts and stuff like that" (Sinofsky 1996). Echols, two years older than Baldwin, pessimistically articulated the outcome of such stereotypification in a similar interview: "The public was getting real upset seeing the cops were incompetent . . . couldn't do their jobs, so they had to do something fast. We were really the obvious choice cuz we stood out from everybody else. So it worked out to their advantage" (Sinofsky 1996).

Prior moral panics about heavy metal and Satanism provided the cultural backdrop against which the West Memphis Three were labeled and then handled by the mass media and the public alike. Stereotypical images of subcultural behaviors floated freely within the mediasphere in the early 1990s. Music and religion in particular were key dimensions of these images. Many community leaders repeatedly defined the sinister tones found in 1980s heavy metal music as the soundtrack to youths' moral decay. As we noted in Chapter 4, there had been a variety of community-centered attacks against heavy metal music that often attempted to establish links between the music genre and Satanism. The PMRC functioned to provide a national resource for local communities in their fight against heavy metal and other "troublemaking" music cultures. This was so successful in no small part because the PMRC's leadership was comprised of prominent "Washington wives"— spouses of federal legislators who were stationed in Washington DC. From the nation's capital, the group was able to leverage political and mass media channels to spread the word to all of America (as one big community) that music was increasingly becoming a danger to children. Local polities around the nation developed their own stances toward the invasiveness of heavy metal, punk, and rap (among other genres) in their communities and acted accordingly. In many areas of the U.S., heavy metal was reduced to the "shocking" sounds and lyrics of the music and styles and behaviors of its producers and fans. Back at the West Memphis Three's trials, the prosecution's reliance on circumstantial evidence—no physical or eyewitness evidence was ever produced that could directly or definitively link any of the young men to the murders—did little to deter what Echols called the "New Salem" atmosphere in the community at the time. Like in Lowney's (1995) study of teenage Satanism in rural Georgia, the overtly conservative Christian community in West Memphis was quick to identify these young men as folk devils and to assume the worst from them based on their musical interests, stylistic choices, and lack of popular friends.

The music that is popular (or unpopular) among communities around the country is linked to deeply significant political processes. All three teens were convicted of murder; Echols was sentenced to death, while Baldwin and Misskelley were sentenced to life imprisonment. In the same stroke, the local community of West Memphis—and indeed the larger community across America—resignified its own cohesiveness and sameness through a discourse that labeled, marginalized, and condemned three young men for their unpopular musical interests and styles. Communal discourses such as these can be slow to change, and intimations of Satanism are not quickly forgotten in the community's memory. Through its rejection of unpopular music and its alleged links to evil, West Memphis reconstituted itself as a polity. All those who agreed with the verdict, the larger community of conservative Americans who supported the PMRC's values and actions in the previous decade, were active in the maintenance of a community that sometimes shows little tolerance for difference. Only in 2011, after more than 18 years in prison, were the West Memphis Three released from prison following new DNA evidence. Strengthened by what it sees as continual scapegoating by outsiders, the heavy metal community has for decades now been held together in part on a distrust of authority, whether it be in the form of law enforcement, organized religion or sports, or the education system.

Continuous public discourse against heavy metal music resulted in the formation of two dialectically related communities. The discourse against unpopular music becomes a kind of sacred ritual "that draws persons together in fellowship and commonality" (Carey 1992: 18). Forced to live among the larger wary, and even hateful, community of right-thinking people, fans of unpopular music also find themselves relying on one another for community. Among those who form a community based on shared interest and shared marginalization, listening to music can be a type of communal ritual (through acts of playing, dancing, or singing, for example) that binds people together. Publicly decrying music that goes against a community's dominant culture serves a similar function. The community's condemnation of the West Memphis Three based on little more than their music interests and style represents the discursive realization of:

> [a] symbolic order that operates to provide not information but confirmation, not to alter attitudes or change minds but to represent an underlying order of things, not to perform functions but to manifest an ongoing and fragile social process.
>
> (Carey 1992: 19)

Much like the comic example of the chicken-uniformed musicians at risk of being institutionalized earlier in this chapter, the West Memphis Three provide a very real instance of the extent to which musical preference is implicated in notions of polity and community.

Conclusion

The three contexts examined here—Constellation's politicized practices, *American Idol*'s instrumental rationality, and community reaction toward unpopular music—show how music works as a technology in the production of the polity. Music can be used to control, shape, form, and even oppress groups, thus working as an effective tool in social organization. At the same time, music can serve as a medium that connects and binds people, sometimes in support of the status quo (*American Idol*) and other times in critique of it (Constellation Records). As these examples have shown, politics and music are intertwined in multiple ways, often radically removed from the traditional connotation of "political music" as simply patriotic music or protest music.

7

GENDER, RACE, AND CLASS

For many sociologists the issue of social stratification lies at the very core of their research and theoretical concerns. Social stratification—the ordering of society into hierarchies of people in relation to the amount of broadly defined privileges they enjoy—is so important to sociologists because it holds the key to a better understanding, and consequently to the potential rectification, of social injustices. It is common for sociologists who lean toward rectifying social injustices to refer to stratification as "inequality." The term "stratification" has more neutral connotations than inequality, and usage of either sometimes reveals a particular sociologist's ideological preferences. Either way, the study of social stratification (or inequality) is also important to sociologists because it deals with at least three of the most important markers of social existence: gender, race, and class.

For the most part sociologists tend to study gender, race, and class as either causes or effects of social and cultural forces. Think about—even on the basis of anecdotal data that may be easily available to you—how variables like musical preferences, subcultural involvement, or concert attendance seem to be often related to gender, racial, or class categories. For example, we may very well observe and conclude (more or less systematically) that opera attendance is more typical among upper-class whites than others. Observations such as that are easy to make and difficult to refute. Yet, they often explain less than it seems. For instance, how do we explain the fact that people from other ethnic and class backgrounds enjoy going to the opera, too?

In this chapter we attempt to challenge the very ideas of gender, race, and class as conventionally understood. More precisely, we believe and argue that treating gender, race, and class as "given"—that is, as characteristics that can be easily assessed along a range of discrete variables much like one would do when answering a questionnaire for a survey—and studying them as causes and effects can only tell part of a story. We suggest instead that gender, race, and class ought to be studied as intersubjective accomplishments: meaningful things that people do together (see Garfinkel 1967; West and Zimmerman 2002). By taking this approach we obviously do not intend to deny that gender, race, and class are "real." It is obvious that they are real, as it should be apparent to anyone that visible forms of discrimination, stereotyping, and disadvantage are meted out on the basis of such characteristics. Nonetheless, we intend to show that these characteristics are not as immutable as most people think and that they *become* real through social processes. By exposing the social dynamics of these processes, we hope to show that the realities of gender, race, and class are contingent on social action, and thus amenable to change, to being otherwise.

Sociologists of everyday life argue that reality is the emergent outcome of processes of social interaction. Social realities are dependent on such factors as language and language use, history and collective memory-making, power, the social meanings of space, as well as material social forces. Social constructionists, in particular, believe that meaning—such as what it means to be a "man," to be "Asian," or to be "poor"—is achieved through the process of people communicating with one another in diverse situations. Such processes yield outcomes marked by *relatively* stable and *relatively* fixed agreed-upon meanings—that is, meanings open to interpretation and to change.

We begin the chapter with an extended look at the constructionist literature on doing gender. This topic is arguably the clearest for pedagogical purposes, and it constitutes much of the background for our later discussions in this chapter. Our first example consists of a look into the phenomenon of making, being, and becoming a female pop star. Through a brief analysis of media coverage of the personal life of Jessica Simpson, we show that it is in the realms of visual language and spoken discourse that the social identities of famous women in music are made.

The enormous attention that stars like Beyoncé, Lady Gaga, and Rihanna (but others could be mentioned) receive—especially in relation to their non-musical (e.g., gendered and sexual) lives—are examples of what historian and social theorist Michel Foucault (1990) called "confession," and thus reveal how gender and sex are subjects of discursive production, and thus of social interaction. Next we move to the world of contemporary mainstream hip-hop music. As our illustration goes to show, hip-hop fans and popular personas "do" race and class through an extremely delicate management of the impressions they convey about their personas. Yet, as we suggest, in doing so they expose the fragility of the very concepts of race and class as fixed categories and thus posit an ironic challenge to the idea of musical authenticity and self-expression based on immutable notions of race and class. We conclude this chapter with a look into the career and music of Canadian "pop punk princess" Avril Lavigne . . . Well, the expression isn't ours. Actually, we wonder precisely whether "pop punk princess" is a double oxymoron: can punk, a class-based musical expression, be popular among all classes, like a princess would be? By examining fan reviews of her debut CD, we reflect on audience reception of class performance.

Doing Gender

A central concern in sociology, and especially for everyday life sociologists, is people's talk (Garfinkel 1967). People talk in a variety of circumstances for a variety of reasons, and in the process of talking they often accomplish things. For example, sociolinguists have observed that certain forms of talk are not only representational (i.e., about things, or in reference to things), but also performative, or in other words creative, constitutive of the social realities indicated in that very same talk. This is what everyday life sociologists mean by *reflexivity* (Mehan and Wood 1975). Think, for example, of the consequences of saying "I do" at a wedding ceremony. By saying "I do," a marriage is all of a sudden created. A common type of talk is that of giving *accounts* (Mills 1941; Scott and Lyman 1975). People routinely engage in "descriptive accountings of states of affairs to one another," says Heritage (1984: 136–137). Indeed, human beings determine their own future lines of conduct knowing that their conduct is open to such commentary and criticism. In other words, before they are about to do something, people wonder what they are going to say if they are asked to account for what they did and why.

A common context in which people account for their actions is that of *confession*. During religious confessions, religious followers are asked to account for what they have done wrong, to ask for forgiveness, and to express remorse. Confession must be truthful and based on values of full disclosure and trust. Within the context of religious practice confession takes places on church grounds. Yet, within the greater context of social relations confession may take place elsewhere as well. Foucault (1990) found that confession—whether by religious followers or not—was so common that confession itself served as a model for many practices of disclosure. He further commented that certain types of actions—namely those dealing with the most private aspect of one's lives, like intimate relationships, sexual behavior, and sexual preferences—are especially subject to the demand for public disclosure and to being discussed ad nauseam.

Much like sex, gender, as West and Zimmerman (2002) have argued, is subject to extensive scrutiny, public talk, and stringent criteria of accountability. Gender and sex are indeed inextricable. Think, for example, of the rumor campaigns over the sexual orientation of *American Idol* runner-up Clay Aiken and 'N Sync's Lance Bass—followed by heated announcements and revelations to the press. As these cases would show if we examined them in detail, by accounting for one's gender and sexuality people reinforce and/or contribute to the changing of attitudes, beliefs, and behaviors. Indeed, we can say that gender is an interactional "doing," a reality subject to social definitions and negotiations, and a practice undertaken by individuals in the most routine interpersonal contexts of everyday life.

Garfinkel's (1967) classic analysis of gender is illustrative of these principles. He studied the life of Agnes, a male-to-female transsexual who had chosen to undergo sex reassignment at the age of 17. In his study, Garfinkel explained that Agnes had to re-educate herself to the gendered world in which she lived. Having lived as a male for the first 17 years of her life, and then gradually needing to adapt to her identity as a female, this meant having to learn the practical methods whose knowledge and application was necessary for passing as a fully competent "normal" woman. In other words, prior to and after her surgery, Agnes "needed to display herself as a woman" and she was "obliged to analyze and figure out how to act within socially structured circumstances and conceptions of femininity" (West and Zimmerman 2002: 43) that those who are classified as women since birth learn early in their life.

Agnes's experiences showed that gender is a form of work—a social production, if you will—that highlights "a complex of socially guided perceptual, interactional, and micropolitical activities" (West and Zimmerman 2002: 42) that results in the categorization of someone as a man or a woman. Gender, therefore, is a social accomplishment, something that is transparently practiced in the presence of others, and carried out according to the social norms existent within particular social situations. Gender, in sum, is an emergent feature of the categorization of social interaction, something that comes off a situation in light of people's conceptions of what is proper and on the basis of beliefs and routine activities expected of members of a sex category. A good example of this comes from what Suzanne Kessler and Wendy McKenna (1978) call the *gender attribution process*. These authors write about a child who, upon seeing the photograph of someone in a business suit, contends that the photographed person is "a man, because he has a pee-pee" (Kessler and McKenna 1978: 154). Obviously the child cannot see the presence of a penis, but he imputes it to the person on the basis of visual signs of known masculinity (the business attire). What this case goes to show is that gender is thus imputed, or attributed, to others on the basis of the surfaces (appearance, conduct, etc.) detectable in social interaction.

Understanding gender as something that people do allows us to conceptualize the interaction between a gendered audience and a gendered social actor as a *performance*. Because all musical expressions are based on performances, the field of popular music studies thus turns out to be a convenient one for the study of gender performance. Our precise interest in the following section is in how popular female musicians do gender in mediated situations and how mediated situations structure the gender performance of said musicians. We became interested in this after repeated observations that most media outlets seem to be less interested in musical sounds than they are in the mundane lives of musical celebrities. Take, for example, the likes of Jessica Simpson and her sister Ashlee, Britney Spears, Hilary Duff, or Jennifer Lopez, and try and reflect on when their names are mentioned. You will quickly conclude that their music seems to matter less and less and that, despite the limited coverage of their musical performances, everyone can promptly recognize the names of these celebrities, match names with their pictures, and even talk about these celebrities' sexual and relationship histories or their preferences when it comes to fashion, style, and travel. In these cases, music, it seems, takes a back seat to incessant mediated exposure to their everyday routines. In this process we can see a clear example of doing gender in the mediated situation.

We find that in the process of doing gender in the mediated situation female celebrities enact a unique type of femininity: the female pop star or prima donna—a construction similar to what Connell (1987) called emphasized femininity. In what follows we dissect some common characteristics of doing emphasized femininity in the mediated situation. Because of limited space we focus only on one celebrity, Jessica Simpson, but we believe that many of our arguments could be generalized to other popular personas.

Becoming a Prima Donna

The 1980s saw the start of a unique musical and cultural revolution as MTV began to bridge sound and image through the new medium of the music video (Kaplan 1987). Today, approximately three decades later, neither MTV, nor its "grown-up" music television counterpart (VH1) nor its Canadian cousin (Much Music) hardly shows music videos any more. Instead, today's MTV or Much Music viewer is greeted every day with endless gossip and talk, "reality shows," "interactive" television, alternative sports and freak shows, award shows, soaps, "college specials," and other non-musical productions defying easy categorization. A good recent example of this "reality turn" of MTV is represented by the reality/soap show *Newlyweds* with Nick Lachey and Jessica Simpson. On these highly mediated and scrupulously edited peeks into the ordinary lives of "hot" celebrities of the day, the stars live with cameras following their every (well, almost) move, showing them as they develop, maintain, and end relationships; debate the existential status of tuna fish in the context of a hurried lunch; and pretty themselves up for even more public appearances.

MTV is not alone in this trend, and for once it may even have failed at being the first to set it. Gossip and celebrity magazines have been around for a long time, yet what seems different about recent televised iterations of this genre is that (a) in their numerous public appearances celebrities themselves seem to care less and less about the "official" reasons (like their artistic performances) that made them celebrities in the first place; and (b) celebrities and media seem to depend more and more on one another. Thus entertainment media have all but relinquished their public role as critics, and celebrities have without reservation given more and more of their private lives to the intrusive eye of the popular media. The interaction of these two trends makes for an interesting social situation, which allows us to study how media and female pop music celebrities interact with one another, and how, out of their interaction, there emerge (among other things) unique gender categories. Examples of these situations abound, so let us take a look at one, and reflect on its sociological relevance in the context of our discussion on gender.

The daughter of a Baptist minister in Texas, Jessica Simpson's early attempts to join the music biz included performances with church choirs and on Christian music tours in the U.S.A. Her entry into the pantheon of pop culture dates as far back as 1999, with the release of her album *Sweet Kisses*—featuring the platinum-selling single "I Wanna Love You Forever." Despite a slow start, the album went on to sell about three million copies. Two years later, Jessica Simpson released her second album, *Irresistible*, which proved to be irresistible "only" for about 750,000 consumers. But little did it matter at that point, because Jessica had already secured herself a stable position in the eyes of the media with her reality show *Newlyweds*, chronicling the trials and tribulations of married life with heart-throb husband Nick Lachey, then lead singer of aptly named stud boy band 98 Degrees. The popularity of the show was in large part due to her "Southern ingenuity," manifested through a series of much-talked-about hooplas, including her famous chicken of the sea mix-up (her confusion over whether she was eating chicken or tuna), her apparent belief that buffalo wings are made of buffalo meat, and her awkward congratulatory remark to U.S. Secretary of the Interior Gale Norton ("You've done a nice job decorating the White House!"). Following the popularity of her show, there came a third studio album, a Christmas album, major movie parts, product endorsements, talk show appearances, reality spinoffs, and a constant presence on award shows.

Whereas Jessica Simpson's singing career has continued with ups and downs, her career as a celebrity has been truly remarkable. Her claims of premarital virginity—and her subsequent hypersexualized lingerie-clad appearances for *Maxim*—have raised the eyebrows of skeptics, traditionalists, and voyeurs. Also her "dumb blonde" image has been the subject of controversy; both the film critic Roger Ebert, and *Rolling Stone* writer Rob Sheffield have questioned whether her personality is real or staged for the camera. Magazine covers have also been busy with the never-ending tale of her divorce from Lachey and her subsequent high-profile dates, as well as with carefully staged photo ops of her charity work (a charity group providing reconstructing surgery for children with facial deformities), promotion of her dessert and beauty products line, as well as scrutiny of her waxing and waning body weight. Popularity contests (albeit seemingly friendly) with sister Ashlee have also contributed to raising both of their profiles. So, what is sociologically interesting about Jessica Simpson's ways?

Contemporary sociologists argue that there are innumerable ways of doing gender, and therefore, rather than "masculinity" or "femininity," we should speak of multiple *masculinities* and *femininities*. Speaking of masculinities and femininities allows us to reflect on the different performances of gender enacted in everyday life and on the different scripts available for performing gender. Instead of thinking about the sex roles of a man and a woman, therefore, we could think of gender role models available to all. Take, for example, in the context of popular music, famous women like Alanis Morissette, Bette Midler, Shania Twain, Erykah Badu, Björk, and Bikini Kill's singer Kathleen Hanna. These women embody completely different notions of what it means to be "a woman." Of course, something similar could be said for men—compare the variation across the gender styles of Clay Aiken, Jon Bon Jovi, Frank Sinatra, Nelly, Enrique Iglesias, Garth Brooks, and Tommy Lee (obviously, different "actors" and different ways of acting out gender scripts, right?). The lesson that we learn here is that there are no feminine women and masculine men or unfeminine women and unmasculine women. There simply are different ways of being feminine and masculine, of being woman and being man, and being both, or neither, or some of both.

Despite the fact that there are multiple scripts available for performing one's gender, it seems that popular entertainment media (both in their magazine and television forms) are most intrigued with *very few* particular ways of doing femininity. We refer to one of these gender categories as "postmodern prima donna." What is a prima donna?

During the modern era the prima donna was the "first lady" of Italian opera, the leading female singer of an opera company. Legend has it that these prima donnas were affected by the "diva complex" in that their success led them to become superficial, materialistic, vain, unpredictable, irritable, unreasonable, egotistical, obsessed with their own fame, and narcissistic. Today's (postmodern) prima donnas are seemingly a bit different, judging, of course, from the public personas they display. While they maintain some of the characteristics of their earlier and modern counterparts, they also tend to resemble what Connell (1987) has called emphasized femininity and to embrace some of the traits that some theorists have found to be common in our contemporary, postmodern culture. Emphasized femininity rediscovers traditional (read: conservative) ways of being a woman in a retro fashion. This way of doing femininity entails "compliance, nurturance, and empathy" (Connell 1987: 187–188) and is linked with the traditional realms of the home and the bedroom. Emphasized femininity scripts demand that a woman be at peace with accommodating the desires of men and that she draw much of her sense of worth from being popular among them.

Yet, contemporary emphasized femininity also draws from more contemporary scripts. A contemporary prima donna blurs diverse traits by borrowing from an earlier style and recycling it in the context of the times, marked by a culture of endless superficial appearances and mediated imagery. Today's postmodern prima donnas, then, are a unique mix of "diva" and "girl next door," of princess and pauper, of cosmopolitan jetsetter and wholesome small town girl, of hypersexualized seductress and virgin. This formula for performing gender is often applied today by several pop music stars (e.g., Britney Spears, Hilary Duff . . .) and by the media outlets that broadcast their performances. Being a postmodern prima donna is therefore both about celebrities acting this way to be easily recognized and about media framing their public personas in this fashion to feed audiences' expectations. Being a postmodern prima donna is a complex mediated act of gender construction.

Acting like a prima donna entails, for example, regular acts of public confession to the media. Celebrity confessions are incredibly extensive these days. Anyone with media access can easily find what Jessica likes to eat, how she likes to decorate the table, that she is in the midst of considering adoptions, and that she has had fantasies about Brad Pitt, and more. Her private life, because of her continuous confessions, is constantly public and neither she nor her publicists seem to mind.

In confessing with regularity and depth, prima donnas like Jessica Simpson blur the distance between private and public spaces. The concepts of *private and public spheres,* often used by sociologists, help us understand prima donnas' performance of gender a bit better. Traditionally, sociologists explain, men's domain has been in the public sphere—for example, in the work of paid employment, politics, and so forth. Women's activities and identities, instead, have been for the most part focused around the home, where "labor of love" activities such as child-rearing, relationship maintenance, and housework are meant to take place. Of course, these boundaries have become blurred over time, yet sociologists find with great regularity examples of women being pulled back (or pushing themselves back) in the private sphere. For example, when musicians become famous, most mass media continuously attempt to uncover their "private" lives, thus incidentally confining them again to the private sphere of child-rearing, homemaking, and relationships. Jessica Simpson's own reality shows—staged in the context of her home—function in this sense as a return to the private sphere. Besides the mentioned reality show, public attention to Simpson constantly focuses on her dating adventures, struggles with divorce, with her body shape, and family life. Her own presentation of self in the context of children's charity work, adoption plans, and promotion of both beauty and food products also continues to emphasize her emphasized femininity. To boot, her small town ingenuity and naivety, traditional moral values, and emotional ups and downs mark her emphasized femininity as a particularly histrionic one, punctually combined with her image as a demure yet glamorous, successful, vain, hypersexualized diva.

Confession, according to Foucault (1990), does not uncover a preexisting reality, but instead makes one anew. Thus, in being a consistent player in public discourse—in other words, in constantly generating talk about their private lives—postmodern prima donnas like Jessica Simpson can never logically lament "unfair media representation." The media are hardly *re-presenting* these women, since barely any trace of their livelihood *outside* of the media's eye seems to exist. Rather than media representation of a pre-existing reality, then, this is a case of actual social *construction of meaning* in the mediated situation. Therefore, as West and Zimmerman (2002: 42) explain, their prima donna persona is best understood as a "situated doing, carried out in the virtual or real presence of others . . . as both an outcome and a rationale" for their actions.

Being and becoming a prima donna demands careful efforts. Agnes, whom you will recall was studied by Garfinkel (1967), did everything she could to pass for a "normal woman." Prima donnas like Jessica Simpson need to do everything they can to pass for diva-like "emphasized" women—star-like women who do what some others only wish they could do, including being beautiful and glamorous, talented, popular, successful, famous, graceful, and enjoying romance, yet all of it mixed with a certain grounding in conservative ideals like selflessness, sacrifice, ingenuity, innocence, willingness to stick it out during hardship, etc. Acting like a prima donna is—to borrow again from Garfinkel's (1967: 129) analysis of Agnes—attempting to be "120 per cent female," that is, managing to conduct herself appropriately in the most mundane occasions in order to be accountable as "normal" as the girl next door (with the same wishes, hopes, fears, misfortunes, limitations, etc.) and yet as "special" as the downtown girl (with the ability to make dreams and hopes come true, fearless, famed, and free, and yet at times nostalgically longing for a simpler lifestyle).

The Male Prima Donna: Justin Bieber

In all fairness, we should note the parallel phenomenon of male artists facing strong gender expectations. The case in point—Justin Bieber, who is *the* major Canadian pop megastar. If we observe the development of his career as pop singer, we can easily and readily see how his "growing up" is displayed—through creative artist management—in terms of commonsensical images of emerging masculinity. When Bieber first gained popularity, there was an attempt to link his persona with hip-hop culture, for example, when Justin grabbed his crotch during the dance scenes in the very popular music video for "Baby." Next in line was the acquisition of a girlfriend in 2009, as every normal young teenage boy should have, in the person of Selena Gomez. Next was the movement into a bit "tougher" identity more fitting of an older teenaged boy on the verge of adulthood. Do you remember the photo of Bieber on the cover of *Rolling Stone* magazine in February 2011 wearing a sleeveless, tank top T-shirt sometimes referred to as a "wife beater"? Most recently, in August 2012 Bieber again featured on the cover of *Rolling Stone*, appearing very much as the adult, next coming of James Dean. Our point is that, although we may argue that the gender expectations for women are somewhat more severe and telling, cultural hegemony in no way excuses men from stereotypic gender identity work.

In conclusion, the media—as important social agents in our post-modern times—play an obvious role in setting the parameters of what constitutes normal and expected gendered behavior, for women much more stringently than for men. Doing gender in the mediated situation is therefore as much about "doing" gender as it is about "being done" by available gender categories and preferred media casts. The activity of doing gender in the mediated situation is thus hardly free from restrictions. It is hardly possible for someone to plan in advance what types of gender performances one will engage in for the next five or ten years and then freely execute that plan. Even trendsetters like Madonna and, more recently, Lady Gaga, who have wished to play by their own rules, have often collided with insurmountable walls of expectations. Chipping away at that wall, if one wishes to build new roles, is, however, an act that shows both courage and promise.

Doing Race: Performing the "Wigger"

Despite the fact that it has now been in use for about 10 years, the term "wigger"—or the accent-inflected spelling "wigga"—is absent from most English-language dictionaries. Yet, ask any 10- to 18-year-old in North America to give you a definition and chances are that you will hear a similar answer: "a wigger is a white man or woman who acts like a black man or woman." The Internet-based encyclopedia Wikipedia (n.d.) similarly defines a "wigger" as a "white person who emulates mannerisms, language, and fashions associated with African-American culture, particularly hip hop in the United States or the Grime/Garage scene in Britain." The term is a slang expression combining "w"—the initial of "white" or "wannabe" and "–igger" from the highly derogatory word "nigger." Similar combinations are known among youths, such as "migger" and "chigger"—respectively indicating a Mexican and/or a Muslim and/or a Middle Eastern, and a Chinese man or woman, heavily involved in the hip-hop scene, and obviously "acting black." While all of these words are likely to offend some, leave others perplexed or neutral, and even evoke a sense of pride among those who embrace the label, the recent success of characters like Ali G—impersonated by British comedian Sacha Baron Cohen—clearly testifies to the fact that wiggers have become more highly visible than ever in popular culture and the media and that a sociological understanding of this phenomenon is badly needed.

From a historical perspective, there is nothing new about the phenomenon of people from different ethnic backgrounds adopting the subculture of people from other ethnic backgrounds. For example, white people have mimicked black people's music-centered subcultural behaviors and taste throughout the 20th century. In the 1920s and 1930s, the white Negroes; in the 1930s and 1940s, the Zoot Suiters and later hipsters; in the 1950s, the beatniks; and in the 1960s and 1970s, the mods—all have been believed to be imitating the mannerisms and fashion of black Americans or black Britons of the times. Various scholars might remark that these and similar phenomena constitute examples of *cultural appropriation*: attempts by one person or group belonging to one culture or subculture to co-opt a style that originated among people of a different culture or subculture. Cultural appropriation, or *co-optation*, has been subject to a great deal of condemnation in popular culture studies. Most scholars and observers agree that co-optation is a reflection of the commercialization of culture, the commodification of style and identity, and the disrespect that some social agents pay toward values such as originality, individuality, and unique style. But, whereas cultural appropriation arguments are generally very useful for understanding "why" co-optation occurs, in this chapter we are more interested in explaining "how" such phenomena occur, especially at the level of mundane practice.

Following our analysis of the persona of Jessica Simpson in light of her gender performance, in what follows we extend our constructionist performative argument to the case of race. From this perspective we view wiggers as social agents engaged in the presentation of self and identity in everyday life. Studying wiggers highlights how race is performed through impression management, and how appearances of the racialized self may be successful (that is, convincing) or unsuccessful on the basis of both categorizations by audiences of their performances and on the basis of the very qualities of those performances. To assist us in this endeavor we draw upon the *dramaturgy* of Erving Goffman (1959). Goffman's dramaturgic study of everyday life employs a view of social interaction as drama. From this perspective individual and collective expression is understood as carefully—albeit at times involuntarily—managed self-expressive action and impression-making.

Studying the dramaturgic performance of a "wigger" identity is an exercise in observing the effectiveness of a role performance. When a role is performed well, the person who performs it will be accorded respect and admiration. When a role is not performed well, the actor may be subject to ridicule and stigma. It is important to highlight what this type of study can achieve. By interpreting this approach incorrectly, one could end up suggesting that race is nothing but a form of empty play and that therefore anyone may freely *choose* the racial or ethnic category to which one wishes to belong and, upon acting the part right, successfully gain that social identity. Such an interpretation would be nonsense. Ethnic categories are often created on the basis of racialized appearances, and for all one may "do" on an interaction stage one's claims will still be subject to scrutiny and categorization by scrupulous audiences. Yet, this is precisely the point we wish to emphasize: race is meaningful only insofar as people direct their attention to it as a significant symbol, and thus engage in the interpretation of its meanings on the basis of role performances. The potential of the constructionist approach in the realm of studies of race is in fact its aptness at discovering how racial appearances and role performances come to *pass* and thus become institutionalized and taken for granted.

Let us begin with a close observation of what "wiggers" may do. A popular humorous website on "wiggers" (wiggaz.com) provides us with a nice insight into the typical behavior and appearance of a wigger: a "wigga" must be fly, must listen to rap/hip-hop, and must dress in "wigger gear." This handy definition holds the key to the "wigger's" presentation of self as it highlights its three central dimensions: character, taste, and appearance. Let us examine these in order.

A wigger's character, as we learned, must be "fly." The online "Urban Dictionary"—extremely useful for all slang expressions—succinctly defines "fly" as cool and in style. Coolness, as conceptualized by dramaturgist sociologists Lyman and Scott (1970: 145) refers "to the capacity to execute physical acts, including conversation, in a concerted, smooth, self-controlled fashion in risky situations, or to maintain affective detachment during the course of encounters involving considerable emotion." Being cool, therefore, is about "keeping one's cool" in situations where poise may be under pressure. Lyman and Scott (1970: 145–146) assert that losing one's cool holds physical risk (as in getting beat up), financial risk, and social risk. Social risks are of particular interest here, as they may arise just about any time people interact with one another.

The most common social risk "wiggers" may perceive is that of being exposed to others for what they "really are" and thus ridiculed for alleged lack of originality or authenticity. Yet, and this is important, "wiggers" are not *automatically* reprimanded in all social interactions by all people; indeed there are situations in which an individual performing a "wigger" persona and claiming a "wigger" identity may be accepted by others. Such acceptance reveals an interesting phenomenon, especially when it occurs in the context of interracial relationships. When an actor's claim to a particular subcultural identity closely tied to ethnic markers is accepted, *ethnic identity* is "made." This goes to show that ethnic social identity is based on both performance (what the actor does) and categorization (the audience's response). When, as in the case of "wiggers," an actor's visible racial traits (i.e., skin color) do not correspond to the racial traits typical of the ethnic identity into which he or she wants to be categorized, and, despite this claim, he or she is still successful, we can say that ethnicity itself is being "done" in open disregard of the obtrusive markers of race.

A pair of examples ought to simplify this considerably. Let us examine first Eminem and later Fergie. Eminem—born Marshall Mathers—is a thirtysomething white rapper from Detroit whose enormous success as a rapper and hip-hopper has undoubtedly been facilitated by his coolness—some might suggest—in an art world dominated by African-American performers. Eminem's coolness (again, for at least some of his audiences) comes from the aplomb with which he has handled numerous scandalous situations in which he has been involved. Whether he has been accused of misogyny, homophobia, hatred for the U.S. President or for other rappers, Eminem has always parlayed accusations into claims of his authenticity as a straight-talking, driven, tough-skinned, self-made-from-the-'hood rapper. His coolness has allowed him to expand his audience by crossing racial, age, class, and gender boundaries. Furthermore, his coolness of character has highlighted his singing abilities and musical skills. His talent for alliteration, assonance, and his ability to change both tone of voice and rhythm with ease, even within the same tune, have garnered him levels of credibility unprecedented for white rappers. As Lyman and Scott (1970: 151) remarked, "tests of coolness" such as "highly stylized dialogue of insult" (traditionally, rap *is* a form of dialogue) and self-aggrandizement require the effective mobilization and control of material and symbolic objects and forces.

The second normative characteristic of a "wigger" is that he or she listens to hip-hop or rap. This is an essential component of the social identity of the "wigger." Hip-hop and rap are the two most popular musical expressions of black youths today. From a dramaturgical perspective, hip-hop music functions as a "prop" supporting the staging of the "wigger" persona. Remember that, for Goffman, presentation of the self is understood from a theatrical metaphor: individuals wear masks to project a particular image to an audience. In doing so on stage—that is, in front of others—they follow scripts, manipulate the setting where they stage their performances, and within their role they perform what is expected of them by their audiences; that is, they act out a line to protect their front. Hip-hop music works as a prop in the sense that it enables the performer to convey a convincing expression of self. Listening is a private activity, but private listening does not have much potential for conveying social meanings. Listening to music is then turned into a prop for a social performance whereby the listener becomes an actor publicly staging his or her performances before an audience. "Wiggers"' public acts of listening, as conspicuous displays of their taste, take well-known forms: walking on public sidewalks while carrying "ghetto blasters," wearing oversized headphones that only in part muffle loud music sound, driving low-rider or "pimp" automobiles turned into bass cars, and more.

Listening publicly to rap clearly demonstrates subcultural involvement and identity, but it does not do so as clearly as *performing* music. "Wiggers," much like rappers, will then often turn everyday conversation settings into improvised rap sessions and rhyme contests. Doing so, the point goes, constitutes a way through which claims to ethnic social identities can be successfully achieved. In other words, music in this case turns into an instrumental tool utilized by people to manage impressions, manipulate realities, and achieve their social aims. Doing race in "the 'wigger' way" thus primarily entails a set of staging techniques and props whose meanings are socially variable, rather than fixed racial traits.

Being in style is a necessary component of this process. Style entails aspects of consuming behavior. Style is a form of conspicuous consumption of taste and a strategy for the performance of identity, but it is also a racialized performance that does not only refer to clothing and body adornment but to an entire ensemble of signs that works by staging and sustaining the difference of social actors from others. Try, for instance, to compare the style (not the fashion sense, but the signing style) of Jessica Simpson with that of Black Eyed Peas singer Fergie.

In her album *Sweet Kisses*, Jessica Simpson sings of virginity and related gender performance in terms of "I have a gift for you, something that I've held on to . . ." In contrast, take the more aggressive, urban, overtly seductive, and in-charge "street-like" style of Fergie. Consider, for example, the song "My Humps" off the Black Eyed Peas' album *Monkey Business*. Addressing Will.i.am, who inquires what she intends on doing with all that junk that she seemingly has inside her trunk, she responds, "I'ma get, get, get, get, you drunk, / Get you love drunk off my hump." By borrowing from hip-hop imagery and iconic behaviors, by using African-American slang, and by directly engaging a black man, Will.i.am, on stage, Fergie performs a style of racialized femininity typical, *arguably*, of *some* young urban African-American women and crosses racial boundaries, perhaps—in the eyes of some—attempting to pass as a black persona. Or does she? As an audience member you have an important say in all of this, because race, like gender, is a performance.

Doing Class: Is Avril Lavigne Punk?

We conclude our reflection on race, class, and gender with an analysis of the class-based performance of Canadian rocker Avril Lavigne, who reached stardom in the spring of 2002, when she made her debut with the incredibly successful CD *Let Go*. In addition to her catchy "pop-punk" hooks, Avril caught the world of pop music by storm with what at the time seemed like an anti-Britney Spears formula of skateboarder looks, street attitude, and dark appeal. *Let Go*, and especially her single "Complicated," reached the top of the *Billboard* charts, gained nominations for Best Pop New Artist and Best Pop Female Artist at the 2002 *Billboard* Music Awards, received five Grammy nominations, and won the Best Song, Best CD, Best Female Artist, and Best Homework Song at the 2002 Radio Disney Music Awards, as well as the MTV Video Music Award for best new artist in a video. *Let Go* also went platinum on July 12, 2002, breaking the record for short-time increases in sales and radio spins. At the time of writing, the album had sold over 15 million copies worldwide. Media appearances, endorsements, endless play of her videos, and celebrity gossip have now made Avril Lavigne one of the more successful female singers of the last decade. Her persona, especially at the time of her debut, is our object of interest here.

In examining Avril Lavigne, like we have done with Jessica Simpson, Eminem, and Fergie, we are not concerned with her self or personal identity. Instead we are interested in her public persona—in other words, with her public image and with the discourses surrounding her mediated presentation of self. By studying her self-presentation through the mass media as a complex and multifaceted performance, and by focusing on how she "does" class, we are interested in questioning how she stages her front before her audiences through the management of her style, physical appearance, life story, career, her status as a celebrity, her song lyrics, and even more. So far in this chapter we have examined elements of performance of race and gender without giving too much consideration to how audiences interpret performances. Whereas in the case of Fergie we left it up to you to discuss the contours of her performance, now we take it upon ourselves to observe how fans of Avril Lavigne, as well as non-fans, deconstruct the credibility of her self-presentation. Our data consist of reviews of *Let Go* voluntarily submitted to various websites by Internet users. Using a socio-semiotic frame of analysis, we focus on how audiences interpret the authenticity of Avril Lavigne's performance of class.

As an analytical tool we can divide audiences' readings of her CD and her persona into two broad categories: the category of *hegemonic readings* and that of *counter-hegemonic readings*. The former category includes readings *preferred* by a performer. For example, when teachers deliver a lecture in a classroom, they hope that their students will buy into their argument without challenging them too much. A politician will have the same attitude toward a speech; a parent, toward a lesson imparted to his or her children; and so forth. Hegemonic readings of Avril Lavigne's performances reveal that what she intended to communicate went over well with some fans:

> Hey, I wish people would stop saying such bad stuff about Avril! So she's a punk. So? Get over it! That's how she likes to express herself. Not everyone likes to be the same as everyone else.
> Yeah she's punky and I hope she puts more songs out. If you like

Avril, then get the CD! I am hooked on it! Get it! You will be satisfied with your purchase. She wrote all her songs AND plays her own music. She is so good! You all really need to try this CD out. I am so glad I did!

Punk music is the soundtrack of autonomy, independence, and rebellion. These traits are often associated with the ideal of authenticity. Authenticity is not only a moral and aesthetic value, but also something that must be concretely performed, something that must be "done." When audiences believe in the sincerity of a performer and in the originality and authenticity of musical expression, a performer—regardless of how actually sincere he or she may be—has managed to convey his or her front and preferred persona well. Avril's persona, at least at the time of her debut, revolved critically around stories told about her start in the musical world. Avril rebelliously dropped out of high school when she was 16 to follow her dream of becoming a singer. Her independence from social constraints continued to mark her biography and career: Avril was believed to be uncompromising on how her records were to be produced, what her image was, and what she wanted her lyrics to communicate. Compared to the likes of Christina Aguilera, Mandy Moore, and Britney Spears, her audiences found her to be low maintenance, unpretentious and down to earth, and unaffected by her celebrity status. Her looks seemingly embodied this. Avril (and her fans) were often seen wearing work shirts and rebelliously loose neck ties—a true punk uniform of sorts, a sign which expresses at once affiliation with working-class fashion and condemnation of middle- and executive- or debutante-class respectability.

However, what works with some audiences does not work with others. Counter-hegemonic readings of Avril Lavigne's persona point to her insincerity and manufactured authenticity. These readings can be called *oppositional*. Particularly jarring to some audiences are her inconsistencies—definitive give-aways of what seems like an attempt to commodify authenticity. As music critic Jessica Zietz (n.d.) notes: "Let me go draw a big skull and crossbones on my arm so that I can be punk too. Please. Avril Lavigne just seems fake, plain and simple."

Punk is first and foremost a class movement and ideology. Its roots are to be found in working-class youth and in their alienation from a political and economic system that—these youth feel—commodifies all individual expressions (Hebdige 1979). Punk is also an aesthetic ideology of sorts. Its raw sound is virtue made out of necessity: studio production, good instruments, and music lessons are expensive, unaffordable, and thus deemed undesirable. Punk is therefore rough, all but pretty, gritty, and uninterested in pretentiousness. For some audiences, therefore, "to call her punk is to tarnish the images of actual punk artists and their contributions to music as a whole. Please, people, stop listening to this CD, stop wearing socks on your arms, get some real music" (Zietz n.d.).

By pointing out attempts at the commodification of punk, these writers resist the co-optation of class and a class-based aesthetics and ideology. What these examples go to show is that impression management does not always work. Despite how well a person may play a role, certain audiences will at times remain skeptical and challenge the sincerity and authenticity of performances. This does not take away from the notion that class is something that is performed, however. In fact, and interestingly enough, in publicly rejecting the sincerity and credibility of Avril Lavigne's performance, these Internet users reassert the significance of performing class in certain ways and not in others. Furthermore, in doing so they too perform class, don't they?

Conclusion

What we have attempted to demonstrate in this chapter is that gender, race, and class are not fixed categories. In certain situations in social interaction, these important markers of individual existence may look and feel as if they are unchangeable, but to think of them as unchangeable does little for a critical sociological cause keen on the eradication of social injustice based on ascribed social status and qualities. If we take gender, race, and class as performances—that is, as something that people do—we enable ourselves to think in alternative ways and to reflect on how things could be otherwise. Conceptualizing gender, race, and class as performatives further allows us to reflect on social interaction, rather than on biology, as the site where social realities are created, communicated, and interpreted.

8

TECHNOLOGY

I [Bryce] am in my living room on a Sunday morning strumming my beautifully built but slightly out-of-tune classical guitar. The fluctuating humidity, including extreme dryness here, means rarely staying in tune. I recently purchased an electronic chromatic tuner that clips onto the headstock of the guitar and uses a small sensor to detect string vibrations and assist with tuning. Calibrated to 440 Hz, it is small and powered by one AAA battery; it makes keeping my guitar in tune a breeze. Its size also makes it easy to lose under couch cushions, in the pockets of guitar cases, or, in one instance, sitting where I left it on top of the thermostat in my living room. And, today, I have no clue where it is hiding. As I resign my unproductive search for it, but not for a song free of sour notes, I remember a great iPhone app [mobile web application] I purchased: the chromatic tuner app! A couple of years ago I bought a Boss chromatic tuner for approximately $100. I spent somewhere in the neighborhood of $5 for the same functionality, but as a part of my cell phone and not some bulky foot pedal. The approximate size of a tuning fork, but far more versatile, my cell phone is my go-to back-up. I reach for my phone, tap on the screen until I arrive at the tuner app, and proceed to remedy the slightly sour B and D strings that tend to go flat on my beautifully built and now perfectly in tune classical guitar.

There is a misleading tendency in popular culture to think of all technology as digital technology or in similarly contemporary or futuristic terms. When we say that technology, for example, has dramatically transformed the music industry, we reference digital technologies like

SoundCloud, iTunes, and (once) Napster. However, as Paul Theberge (1997) and others (Chanan 1995; Jones 1992; Merrill 2009; Sterne 2003) have written, the current climate of the music industry was in part made possible by previous developments in non-digital audio technologies, such as the evolution of analog tape. Timothy Taylor (2001), for example, points out that, as far as digitization and music is concerned, the gramophone was to music storage and retrieval in the past what iTunes is today. Bryce Merrill's research (2009) on the technological evolution of home recording technologies connects today's recording technologies like ProTools, GarageBand, and even the Sony *American Idol* Extreme Music Creator Software, to the previous innovations of Thomas Edison, Nazi scientists, and guitar guru Les Paul. Indeed, the rise of the amateur home recordists, on whom National Public Radio's Rick Karr recently ran a six-part feature, owes its lineage largely to the Japanese conglomerate TEAC and their development of the TASCAM 141 Portastudio home recording station. While digital music technologies surely usurped the place of previous technologies as engines of change for the music in society in the mid-1980s—notably, as home recording in the mid-1980s was the introduction of digital audio tape (DAT)—we can only understand technology (and thus society) if we remain aware of both the influence of the past on the present and the way we conceptualize technology.

This conflation of digital technologies with all technologies is understandable, of course, as contemporary social life in Western societies is a digital one. A quick scan around Bryce Merrill's house reveals the digital clock on his oven, HD television and Wii game console, two laptop computers, and cell phone in his immediate presence. And he likely falls on the "Luddite" side of those who welcome all technologies into their lives. Many of you reading this book are likely far more plugged in than he is! Certainly "technology" is a big part of our contemporary lives, but the problem for social scientists is one of conceptual clarity. By *conceptual clarity*, we mean that terms like "technology" must have a clear definition and be used according to these definitions. In this chapter, we explore some of the ways social scientists conceptualize technology as much more than just the next big app.

Let's go back to the opening epigraph on Bryce and his options for tuning his guitar. Were you asked to point out the "technologies" in this story, which ones would you identify? The headstock tuner? The Boss chromatic tuner? Certainly Bryce's iPhone and the tuning app would make your list. But would his guitar also be included as a technology? From web-based recording interfaces like beatlab.com to the dreaded plastic recorders most of us were forced to play in elementary school, social scientists would argue that all musical instruments are technologies—they are instruments of human action. A guitar is a thing made by people to do something that people want to do. In Bryce's case, sit around and avoid working on his house by playing the guitar!

In this chapter, we approach technology by considering its physical, symbolic, interactive, and influential dimensions. We present technologies as material components of a culture, but also as objects that are given meaning by people and that exert an influence over the meanings we make. Traditional social studies of technology have referred to the physical and symbolic elements of technology as "material" and "non-material" culture. These concepts are discussed here, but we use the term "technoculture" to explain the complex interconnections between technology as things, symbols, and practices. Our interest, ultimately, is in the ways that social life—from bike riding to memory-making and Christmas shopping—is formatively influenced by technology. We conclude by recognizing a few of the new frontiers for music, technology, and society studies.

Technology as Material and Symbolic Culture

Social scientists generally understand a technology to be a tool for social action. In this general definition, there are three important components. First, technologies are objects. Technologies are tools. Personal stereos and noise-cancelling headphones, in-ear monitors and boom stands, electric guitars and voice synthesizers such as the Vocoder or the "auto-tune" processor (ubiquitous in popular music these days—think Cher's "Believe" or anything by T-Pain): all are technologies of popular music. They are instruments for consuming and producing popular music. Technologies are also instruments for action; in this case, the actions these technologies enable are the production and consumption of music. I recently used the app Instagram to take a picture of the Brooklyn band Battles performing at a music festival in Denver and instantly shared it with friends around the world. Simultaneously, Battles projected a video of Kazu Makino of the band Blonde Redhead onto a 20-foot screen on stage where her electronically synced vocals accompanied the band's live performance. Next to me, a festival-goer folded her program into a fan and tried to cool off as the temperature broke 100 degrees. These technologies enabled the many actions associated with attending a summer music festival. And this is the last, but critical part of our definition: technologies enable social action. Whether it's mega festivals like Tennessee's Bonnaroo, the Vans Warped Tour, or Rock the Bells, or smaller local festivals, attending summer music festivals is a part of American culture. It is something that we do together and can only do together because of technology. Sometimes "technological acts" contribute more directly to essential human needs, such as making a fan out of paper so that we avoid heatstroke. Other times, our technological actions contribute less to basic survival instincts and more to our desires to participate in a shared culture. It is a culturally sanctioned practice to act as one's own paparazzo, and so we willingly use our phones to send pictures of ourselves to others. In this way, a technological object enables a technological act that is reasonable in a given cultural context. Therefore, when we speak of technologies, we are referring to things that enable actions that occur in and because of culturally specific contexts.

Material culture is the term that most social scientists use when defining technology as tools. The word "material" obviously refers to the physical properties of technology, while the second part, "culture," indicates that a technology is a part of a larger cultural system of social beliefs and practices. Ethnomusicologists, for example, have put a great deal of time into studying the historical and cultural origins of musical instruments, such as the banjo. They argue that banjos, for example, are artifacts of several different cultures and that banjos as physical objects tell stories about the people and cultures that created and played them. *Symbolic culture*, the fraternal twin of the material culture concept, is the term used to describe the meanings people give to technologies. When we just mentioned the banjo, it's likely some image entered your mind— perhaps it was of a folksy gent in overalls gently plucking a tune. For Bryce, the banjo is almost always symbolically associated with the infamous "Dueling Banjos" scene in the movie *Deliverance*. Strangely, the banjo also reminds him of Broken Social Scene's "Anthems for a 17-Year-Old Girl," a song that he can only guess has no material connection whatsoever to Burt Reynolds! The idea here is that technologies, like all things, have both physical and symbolic dimensions. They are meaningful and, as we have previously learned, meanings are inherently changeable and dynamic, which makes studying the symbolic dimensions of technology quite challenging.

Violins, pianos, Moog synthesizers, and Roland 808 drum machines that produced so many famous hip-hop beats—these are all technologies for making music. But what about analog voice transcription machines, cell phones, or even humming fluorescent lights? Carey Sargent (2010) has written about a particular genre of music, Experimental Improv and Noise (EIN), where noise musicians use just about anything but traditional musical instruments (or anything intended to be a musical instrument) to make noise "music." During her research on EIN music scenes, Sargent was surprised by an EIN musician setting up to perform a set with an electric guitar. She had observed previous performances that were notably devoid of traditional instruments such as guitars. Instead, the EIN performers she regularly observed hung hacked cell phones from ceilings to project noises and programmed computer voice synthesizers to contribute odd phrases and commands throughout the "songs," such as one performance where a computer interjected, "Stop! My leg is hurting!" (Sargent 2010: 192). As the performer with the guitar prepared to perform, Sargent asked about the guitar and was schooled by an EIN enthusiast that the performer would not be using the guitar like a guitar, but "more like an oscillator." In other words, the guitar was going to be used in an instrumental fashion, but not in the way it is expected to be or regularly used. Sargent's research reinforces the important consideration of technology as both objects that can be used and meanings that can be changed. She has demonstrated that the material and symbolic dimensions of technology are inextricably linked, and they are so during technological acts.

Technology as Cultural Practice (AKA Technoculture)

While the term "symbolic culture" is often used to address how people meaningfully interact with technology, it falls short in capturing the connection of the non-material to the material. Focusing only on the material dimensions of technology can lead us to overly deterministic views of technology—the technology-will-save-or-destroy-the-world varieties are most common. Focusing solely on the symbolic dimensions of technology, as social scientists are prone to do, can lead to a radical ignorance of the material world and the influence it exerts on our meanings and actions. Instead, the term *technoculture* is one that explains more suitably how people meaningfully interact with techno-logical things. Phillip Vannini (2009) uses the term as an appropriate replacement for the binary of material/symbolic culture as it relates to technology. Technoculture, he argues, can be understood "as an emergent process consisting of the interaction between human actors and nonhuman actors—all acting with their strategies and techniques, endowed with material properties" (Vannini 2009: 4). What this term does is capture the importance of the interaction between people and things and identify their mutually agentic roles.

The Playing for Change (PFC) Foundation is an organization that coalesced on the heels of a remarkable technological and musical accomplishment. Originally, PFC was a multimedia project that used mobile recording and communication technologies to record one version of a song performed by musicians throughout the world. Songs like "Stand by Me" were performed and recorded by musicians in New Orleans, Barcelona, Johannesburg, and other locations, and the PFC producers edited these performances together into one. The videos of the performances went viral, as the both musically and technologically compelling project garnered international audiences and support. How can we use the term "technoculture" or "technocultural" to explain PFC? Certainly evident is the importance of material technologies to PFC. Without the many and evolving technologies the producers employed to capture and combine the performances—to say nothing of those they used to fly around the world—PFC could not have happened. By using technology to combine, even virtually, the different performers, we could also argue that PFC represents a kind of technological interaction, not just between actors and technologies, but between actors and other actors. Lastly, and a point that cannot be understated, PFC makes sense as a technocultural act because it reflects our current cultural practice of using the Internet to connect socially, including connecting over music. Thinking of PFC as a technocultural act allows us to give priority to technology as practical things, but also as things that are sensible in social contexts.

Two additional concepts help us to understand technocultures: technics and techniques (Lemonnier 1993; Merrill 2010; Vannini 2009). The first, which may be used synonymously with material culture, is "technic." A technic refers to a physical technology and its material properties. Many different technics were employed in the production of PFC, as their website explains:

> As technology [technics] changed, our power demands were downsized from golf car batteries to car batteries, and finally to laptops. Similarly the quality with which we were able to film and document the project was gradually upgraded from a variety of formats—each the best we could attain at a time—finally to full HD.
>
> (Playing for Change n.d.)

It is critical for social scientists to think in material terms about technocultures as changes in technics often enable (or disable) changes in technological practices, or what can be referred to as "techniques." The term "technique" is shorthand for actions that we take with technology. Putting on romantic mood music for a dinner for two is a technique for engineering a social interaction. The producers of PFC loftily suggest that using various recording technologies to produce each song constitutes a technique for "unifying people through music." One point of studying technocultural happenings like PFC is to understand how technics and techniques may or may not affect individuals and societies—it is an unanswered question whether PFC harmonized the world, but we do know at least that they unified a for-profit entity around their work. That is, we know that there are consequences to their technological work, but these consequences are ripe for exploration.

Christopher Tilley has written about the concept of "objectification," which has implications for a social understanding of technology. Objectification refers to an idea that "through making things," Tilly writes, "people make themselves in the process" (2001: 260). This notion of objectification or the ways that people use technology to create themselves is critical to understanding the place of technology in society as a force for shaping individuals and societies. And that is the real hook for social scientists.

Technology as Social Force

Technology is of interest to social scientists because it is, and has always been, omnipresent in social life. We live in a world of things and many of these things are technologies that are used to navigate our worlds. Michael Bull's (2000) research on personal stereo use is an excellent example of how portable music technologies shape the ways people inhabit, make sense of, and negotiate with others' public spaces. Writing about the emergence of personal stereo technologies—famously, the Sony Walkman, but the iPod would be its commercial contemporary—Bull wants to understand, among other things, how mobile music listening might influence public interaction and how it might also shape the multi-sensory experiences of public places. Bull presents in his research findings accounts of people using personal stereos to modulate emotional and cognitive states. That is, the people he studied intentionally listened to music in order to align their feelings and thoughts depending on the situation. Bryce Merrill rides his bike home after work up a short but very steep hill; after a long day, he is rarely in the mood to climb that hill. One of his tricks to motivate himself to ride, as also employed by the people Bull studied, is to listen to music on his ride home that will, with any luck, transform his dread into something more Rocky-like—heroic and anthemic, rather than a soundtrack to his existing loathing of that climb. The National's "Mr. November" is a bombastic anthem that often does the trick. (If Obama can use it to get elected, Bryce surely can use it to ride home from work.) Bryce also identifies with the people in Bull's research who use personal stereos to block potential social interactions. Bull argues that personal stereos as a technology can be used to create a sense, both within individuals and those they interact with, of privacy in public—Bryce feels certain he is not the first person to put on a set of headphones just to avoid talking to the person sitting next to him on the airplane who seems like they haven't talked to another human being in decades. Bull suggests that personal stereos create "an invisible shell for the user within which the boundaries of both cognitive and physical space become reformulated" (2000: 31). Music delivered through a technology enables (or disables) certain social interactions to ensure their success. Could we survive without mobile music? Certainly. But listening to music in public is a technological practice that is significant within our culture; for many, personal stereos are as important to mobility as most other technologies.

Michael Bull's research is part of a recent resurgence in music studies to consider the ways in which music influences societies. Led by sociologist Tia DeNora (2000, 2003), this scholarship has attempted to conceptualize the ways that music may exert an influence over selves and societies. We say this is a resurgence in this approach because the social studies of music were once dominated by this perspective, influenced primarily by Theodor Adorno's theories of music. Adorno is important to DeNora because he developed a distinctively sociological approach to studying the power of music. A member of the Frankfurt School of social theory, Adorno looked to culture and consciousness to explain the failures of the Enlightenment and, more importantly, for the reason why Marx's predicted revolution and triumph of the working class never materialized. What he found, his theory goes, is that music has acted as a mechanism for shaping forms of consciousness preferred by dominant classes. He argued that music composed, performed, and distributed by dominant classes enslaves audiences to dominant ways of thinking and being. In Adorno's words, actual structures of music reinforced the reality of dominant ideologies (structures of society). Peter Martin (2006) summarizes Adorno's outlook by suggesting that consumption of modern music by the working class served to further alienate them from true consciousness. Adorno's approach has been repeatedly challenged for being overly deterministic and, quite frankly, snobby—Bryce suspects musicians like Against Me!, Talib Kweli, and others might take exception to being accused of writing music to be oppressed by. However, Adorno's work is important to DeNora because she uses his work to think about the power of music through a social lens, instead of the quasi-scientific or religious perspectives that often produce crank theories like the Mozart effect. And, like Michael Bull, DeNora views technology (or, as appropriate here, "technoculture") as an empirical starting point for studying music's force.

Tia DeNora's formative work has been to understand how music gets into social life. She suggests music creates conditions for action, including a range of physical, intrapersonal, and interpersonal responses. Often focusing her research on music listening practices, DeNora explores music's transformational effects that manifest in the intersection of music as form (sound) and music as practice (listening). She offers the humorous example of a wine store playing German music when it needs to sell German wine or French music when wine from France needs moving off the shelves. DeNora also draws on more serious examples of mentally, socially, and physically challenged individuals interacting successfully while playing music with a therapist. Acting musically in concert with others, DeNora argues, provides otherwise challenged individuals opportunities to collaborate with others and gain a sense of self-control and control over others and their environment. Playing music in a music therapy session can be conceptualized as a technology of self-production or, to put it more simply, music is a "technology of self" (2000: 46). She writes that people use music as a resource for their "ongoing constitution of themselves and their social psychological, physiological and emotional states" (2000: 47). Individuals use music to regulate their inner lives, but they do so within social contexts and, such as the case with Michael Bull's personal stereo listeners, in response to and as a means of adapting to their surroundings. For DeNora, listening to or performing music are viewed as technologically enabled actions that produce results, such as the ability to interact successfully with others, or, in some cases, to aid in how we actually think of ourselves and others.

Combining DeNora's call to study the influence of music on social life with an interest in technology and music, Bryce Merrill has written elsewhere (2009, 2010) about home music recording as a "technology of memory." The term conceptualizes a musical practice such as home music recording as a way that people interact with technologies to create memories and, therefore, to create their own identities and the identities of others. Home recordists, mostly amateurs in his research, write and record music in order to engage in a number of acts of self-construction. Drawing on data from these recordists, Merrill identifies four types of technologically enabled music memory work: composing, cataloging, revisiting, and revising. Each category reflects a way that a person uses technology to write and record music in a way that influences their memory and sense of self. Composing songs encourages the transformation of personal experiences into recorded songs, using a blend of songwriting and technology to create a mnemonic record of experience. Cataloging songs previously recorded and composed is another process of sorting experience and meaning, where digital storage technologies (from compact discs to MP3s) aid in the compartmentalization of self. Revisiting and revising are related technologies of memory, wherein the content of memories embedded in song can be reconstructed as the circumstances of the recordist's life change. For example, one participant in Merrill's research talked about a song he originally recorded after a painful breakup. He confessed that this song was pathetically (his words) sad and distraught and, in light of his current happy relationship, he rewrote the song to make it less depressing. Critically, he used the editing functionality on his home recording gear to manipulate the song according to his current emotional and social standing. To put it differently, he revised the song and thus his remembrance of the original inspiration in light of his present situation. He used technology to revise his recording, memory, and self.

Rob Sheffield's (2007) *Love is a Mix Tape* similarly (and heartbreakingly) portrays the musical memory work that goes into making mixes for—and about—our loved ones. He makes mixes on cassettes in part to memorialize his wife, who died young from a pulmonary embolism. The title of his book adeptly exemplifies what we mean by "technoculture." The technics and techniques illustrated here are the cassette tapes (technics) he fills with songs by Pavement and Big Star, and the obsessive and laborious and poetic work (technique) that goes into making the perfect mix tape. What is also clear in his book is the notion that love is a culturally specific thing, or at least the expression of it is. Love is, for Sheffield, a technocultural thing.

Music as a Commercial Technology

If we understand music as a means to an end, such as the creation of memories and selves, we can conceptualize *music itself* as a technology. Again, we are using the term "technology" to mean more than just a technic. Music as a technology refers to a way of doing things with things. Music can be sold as a commodity with little or no apparent regard to the aesthetic ideal of originality or genuine artistic self-expression. It can be a technology for commerce.

Music is not the only technology used to communicate information or to change the definition of a situation in everyday life. As Arlie Hochschild (1983) found in her classic study of flight attendants, public displays of emotions are also used as technologies to maximize customer satisfaction and therefore economic goals. Hochschild called this *emotional labor*. Certain forms of music are also used as emotional techniques. Think, for example, of the music (generally soft rock or New Age) piped into dentists' offices or massage parlors, or the soothing New Age sounds played upon airplane landing and takeoff on long flights. The point here, in sum, is that *music as a public form of emotional expression* may play, and often does play, a role in defining a social situation as economically profitable for the social agents that choose to adopt it in such instrumental fashion. When this occurs, we may say that music becomes a commercial—and in certain cases corporate—technology.

As companies increasingly realize the potential of using music as commercial technology, music comes to play an increasingly greater role in what Hochschild (1983) would call the *commercialization of human feelings*—this concept refers to the buying and selling of emotions in the way that we have examined earlier in relation to teen pop lyrics (see Chapter 1). Also, music begins to play a more important role in the solidification of social structures and public order. This use of music as instrumental means is not new. Think, for example, of how nations have used hymns to cement collective allegiance to patriotic ideals and collective causes. Yet, what is truly unique about the use of music in this fashion in post-industrial society is its pliability in rendering almost any social context one in which consumption of commercial goods and services can and should take place.

Take Christmas music. While there is no doubt that there are some people out there who really loathe Christmas music, the sociologically interesting social function of Christmas music is to put people in a "holiday mood." Imagine yourself driving in suburban weekend traffic on a snowy or stormy day scoring as many special deals as possible on your holiday gift-shopping list. As your emotions are overwhelmed by thoughts of piling up credit card bills, things you'd rather do on a Saturday afternoon instead of looking for an elusive parking spot, and the ever-growing number of people in your extended family and circle of friends to buy for . . . Bam! Here comes Frank Sinatra's unmistakable voice singing on the radio "Have yourself a merry little Christmas," and for at least three minutes and thirty seconds you actually do get the feel that this is indeed a special time of the year.

Holiday music is a big business. A search of the phrase "holiday music" on Amazon.com returns over 385,000 results, including *A Very She and Him Christmas* and *A Feast of Songs: Holiday Music from the Middle Ages*. Some of the more popular Christmas recordings include albums by jazzy Canadian Diana Krall, and *American Idol* runner-up Clay Aiken. The second-best-selling album in the U.S. in 2011 was Canadian Michael Bublé's *Christmas*, and the eighth-best-selling album of the year was Canadian Justin Bieber's *Under the Mistletoe* (*Billboard* n.d.). It seems that just about every mainstream group or solo performer these days has a holiday album out on the market, including (in a revealing parodying demonstration of the case we are making) the irreverent *South Park*'s own "Mr. Hankey"—an animated and often high-on-drugs poo donning a Christmas hat and brightly colored scarf singing renditions and remixes of such classics(?) as "Merry Fucking Christmas," "Dead, Dead, Dead," and "Christmas Time in Hell."

The insistence of Christmas albums on carols, folk songs, and other jingles and tunes that have been in the public domain for decades and decades goes to show how consumerist culture is slowly replacing traditionally gratis musical performances, like singing on the street (now most carolers are hired by public or private groups) or family chorus-singing. Radio has adapted to this logic, too, as several of the soft-rock-oriented stations now feature all-day-long Christmas music around that magical time of the year. While not music-related, the phenomenon of the media market replacing "authentic" objects with commodities is also exemplified by those television channels which during the holiday season broadcast 24/7 burning, crackling logs (supposedly intended to be played in the living-room background, as a substitute for the fireplace, rather than as a form of reality TV on pyromania). The point here, in sum, is that a "mood" is now for sale.

Music works as a commercial technology in other ways. Again, Amazon.com (which, despite appearances, we guarantee is *not* sponsoring this chapter) features in its catalog such functional music as wedding, self-help, nostalgia, exercise, and sports music. For example, the wedding music category includes compilations of "ethnic" favorites such as "The Italian Wedding" and "The Celtic Wedding," as well as songs exclusively written to be played during certain moments of the wedding ritual (like "A Song for My Daughter on Her Wedding Day," meant to be played for the father and bride dance during the wedding reception). The self-help category (and please: read this list slowly and try to imagine what these actually sound like!) includes music for healing, meditation, inner peace, sleep, relaxation, self-hypnosis, accelerated learning, weight loss, self-esteem enhancement, achieving success, attracting prosperity, breaking addiction, and, incredibly enough, even more.

These examples show that, when music is produced, distributed, and consumed to satisfy goals other than appreciation of its aesthetic qualities, its instrumental functions work as commercial technologies marketed and sold to change definitions of social situations and in order to reproduce, imitate, or alter individual feelings and collective emotional dispositions. Music as commercial technology is increasingly typical of a post-industrial society in which individuals exist as consumers and in which rituals are almost exclusively mediated by market relations.

Conclusion

Popular music has been a fruitful avenue of study for technology and society researchers, in no small part because both music and popular culture (and thus popular music) are inherently technological. At music's core are the instruments, be they physical or virtual, needed to produce music or, in the case of popular music, to mass-produce it. Technologies of music consumption are also deeply a part of the experience of popular music in society. As Simon Frith (2002) has noted, technologies of music consumption have proliferated sounds such that, in his assessment, music has become noise, and silence a rare and valuable commodity. In this chapter, we have taken technology to mean both a noun and a verb: a thing and a practice. Our interest has been in identifying technology as things that occupy nearly every square inch of social life—advances in nanotechnology might cause us to reflect that every square millimeter will be occupied by technology soon—and to demonstrate that such omnipresence necessitates the interest of those trying to understand society. But we have avoided a fetishistic approach to technology, where the wonder of things obscures the wondrous ways people give meaning to and derive meaning from things. Satellite radio technology is certainly fascinating in its own right, but, for social scientists, it is equally compelling to think of how classical music streamed from XM Radio can be used to keep homeless individuals from loitering in front of stores and restaurants in an outdoor mall. The technology presents music, but it takes people—homeless, business owners, patrons—to make sense of it. And this technologically enabled use of music reveals a technocultural phenomenon, where within a given culture music is understood to be an effective and at least legally sanctioned deterrent for an undesirable activity.

We led off this chapter by downplaying digital technologies in an effort to reset the way we think of technologies from a social scientific viewpoint, one in which "digital" is an important qualifier of technics, techniques, and technocultures, but there are many other important qualifiers, too. Let's conclude by reversing our position and putting a greater emphasis on the digital. Social scientists are currently grappling with researching and explaining rapidly emerging digital technologies around which new technocultures are formed. Economists and others (Florida 2002; Healy 2002), for example, are trying to understand the nature of transforming global and local economies fueled by advances in information technology often referred to as "creative economies." These are knowledge-based (rather than manufacturing-based) economies,

9

GLOBALIZATION AND
SOCIAL CHANGE

The sociological study of globalization and social change can take multiple shapes. Sociologists study economic and political world systems, the emergence of a global risk society, the dynamics of colonization and cultural imperialism, and the growing environmental interconnectedness of the globe, to mention only a few of the approaches to the general topic. In keeping with our attention on popular music, in this chapter we focus on the globalization of music and the social changes it brings about in everyday life experiences. Rather than discuss globalization or social change in terms of abstract political, economic, and cultural transactions among multinational entities, we will focus on the processes through which these concepts are made meaningful to people at a micro, interactional level. To begin clarifying what we mean by globalization and social change, let us introduce an example that will serve to illustrate our focus and perspective.

Several years ago, Phillip Vannini was enjoying a vacation in the Nepali Himalayas, away from the stresses of graduate school and from the modern comforts of the Western world. In the sweltering heat and noise of Kathmandu, he and his girlfriend decided to abandon the city and embark on a three-week trek through the Annapurna mountain range, which sits across the northern side of Nepal, bordering Tibet, and is not too far from the more famous trekking area surrounding Mount Everest. Compared to the latter, they felt that Annapurna was much more off-the-beaten track and promised to give a more authentic look into the lives of rural and mountainous peoples of the Himalayas.

The journey, by a series of local buses, took them through narrow, winding roads, remote villages, and landslide-swept grounds. When after 10 hours they reached the physical end of the unpaved road, they unloaded, tightened their climbing boots' laces, saddled themselves with their backpacks, and ventured off on the mountain trail with their local Nepali guide, Uttar. Along the way, they sought occasional refuge in small tea houses—guesthouses open for both travelers and the numerous local porters transporting goods of all kinds on their own backs and shoulders up the steep, rocky, narrow mountainous trail. If you have never traveled through this neck of the woods, imagine a physical context in which most of the modern conveniences generally found in accommodations are absent. The toilet of their guesthouse was a latrine-style outhouse. No telephones, no television sets, no radios were available in their room or in the house. Running water was also unavailable. Electricity worked on and off, but mostly off, especially when needed on. In short, it was paradise for adventure-seekers.

Stopping at a tea house deep in the mountains one day, Phillip dropped his backpack and sat down, groaning from the long and exhausting day of trekking. As Uttar scooted into the kitchen to find either the hosts or some ready-made tea left behind for them, Phillip's wife asked for their camera.

"I just put it away in the backpack," Phillip replied. "There's no way I'm getting up again."

"Then just turn around for now, and look what's behind your back," his girlfriend said. "I know you'll want to take a picture later."

Curious, he turned around and came face to face with the American corporate music machine, complete with tattoos, teased hair, and glossy lips—it was a Guns N' Roses poster.

Music is everywhere (and quite possibly Guns N' Roses are too). Arguably the most effective global medium of communication, music is a universal language that people can immediately relate to and share. Music, as a form of culture, travels. On its travels it transits through and stops in places far away from its origin, changing lives and in turn itself. This is, in a way, what we mean when we talk about globalization: a process whereby cultural symbols and objects move away, with consequential outcomes, from the contexts in which they originated—sometimes intentionally and other times regardless or even in spite of geographic and political boundaries or distance. Throughout this process, both cultural expressions and human members of cultures change. With globalization, new worlds emerge. A Chinese farmer may become a butt-rock fan after listening to a forgotten mix tape featuring songs from Guns N' Roses. A Polish teenager may use the rebel yell of American rock'n'roll to resist Catholic or Socialist ideologies. And an American draft-dodger expatriate may get back in touch with his hippie youth by listening to Tibetan chants while taking a yoga class in his new home town in Western Canada.

Globalization refers to a dynamic that is inherent to culture: movement. By examining the movement of music across contexts and traditions, this chapter raises issues about hybridity and social change, the nature of the global and the local, and the "global generalized Other" in relation to whom many musical (and non-musical) identities are shaped. We begin with an overview of the idea of cultural globalization and then focus on two studies that exemplify the global currents on which music and people flow. The first study examines changes in young people's relations to popular music in Central and Eastern Europe, especially surrounding the demise of state socialism in 1989. The major theme we discuss is the way the major political and economic changes that have taken place in that region over the past 25 years or so are accompanied by the concurrent Westernization and fragmentation of popular music experiences. The second case study begins with a conversation between an ethnographer and a global nomad and then expands to consider the larger global milieu within which the genres of world music and electronic dance music exist and change. What we want to emphasize in that case is how people's identities are created at the intersection of global movement, digitalization, and reflexivity. In discussing these two cases, we demonstrate the pervasiveness of globalizing forces of social change as well as the role music plays in them.

Music, Culture, and Globalization

One reason why seeing that Guns N' Roses poster in Nepal upset Phillip Vannini so much—besides the fact that he never liked Axl and his buddies—was because he felt that its presence corrupted the cultural authenticity of the idyllic Himalayan mountain setting. Seeing traces of Western "civilization" was not what he had bargained for. He wanted to see a society suspended somewhere between the Middle Ages and the turn of the 20th century; he wanted pure foreignness in its exotic allure; he wanted Tibetan chants and the echo of prayer bells, not images of hair metal. He wanted, in other words, to be in contact with the "Other" in its authentic, genuine, unmediated, unadulterated identity. Yet, this was pure selfishness on his part. That identity was one that he had given this "Other." It was a myth; a fruit of his Western imagination and romantic attitude. To believe in the authenticity of some foreign land or people or experience, unaffected by larger cultural patterns, was to forget that everything is in the process of constant social change and of imagination in the first place.

This is only one way of talking about globalization; there are certainly others. One rather narrow definition of this phenomenon would see it as the commodification and colonization of the globe by the hand of transnational corporations and their international governmental supporters and alliances, such as NAFTA, GATT, and so on. According to this view, the West—and for the most part North America and Europe, but increasingly also Japan and Australia—is the perpetrator of global cultural genocide. This is not a bloody crime, but a subtle one based on the endless seduction of Coca-Cola, Big Macs, shiny new cars, and Guns N' Roses too, all put together and wrapped in Christmas gift paper. Proponents of this perspective view globalization as an instance of cultural and economic imperialism: a symbolic and material colonization that works unidirectionally from the stronger to the weaker, destroying all resistance in its path. Other scholars have put forth more comprehensive understandings of globalization, seeing it not as synonymous with uniformity, but instead with creolization (Hannerz 1987), indigenization (Robertson 1992), and hybridization (Canclini 1995). All of these processes point not to a unidirectional movement of culture from center to periphery, but to a complex network of influences that crisscross the globe and turn it into a heightened version of what it has always been: a large and diverse, but deeply interconnected and forever changing place. Such a view supports the idea that continuous exchanges among people in terms of communication, economy, language, politics, religion, and other social and cultural processes give globalization its character.

British sociologist Anthony Giddens has advanced one of the clearest conceptualizations of globalization. While admitting that the world has always been interconnected, Giddens (2000) demonstrates that the increasing speed at which international economic, political, technological, and cultural transactions take place has decentered people's beliefs that their society/culture is at the center of the world and resulted in the diffusion of diversity and an emphasis on the relative (albeit hybrid) power of many local cultures and identities. This results in, among other things, Guns N' Roses fans emerging among the Nepalese. To stress the significance of a multi-directional and multi-dimensional view of globalization, let us examine the movement of music and culture from the West to the East, and then vice versa.

Popular Music and Social Change: A Look at Central and Eastern Europe

The changes taking place in Central and Eastern European societies from the late 1980s through the present have been broad and complex. Beginning with Poland, the former satellites and client states of the Soviet Union have all experienced various degrees of democratization and capitalization. Many people living in Central and Eastern Europe have worked feverishly to catch up with the West in economic, cultural, and political terms (supported heavily by Western companies and polities). The contemporary culture of the West, which they are alleged to covet and which Frederick Jameson (1991) and many other observers have referred to as postmodernism, is most notably marked by a shift in the economy from production to consumption, the disappearance of the distinction between high and popular art, and the near hegemony of the mass media and the popular culture industries. Music is a key dimension of this frenzied social, political, and cultural activity, and the people of Central and Eastern Europe have experienced rapid changes in the types and functions of music available to them (e.g., Szemere 2001).

The history of popular music in Central and Eastern Europe is marked by a long and rich love affair between young people and rock'n'roll music (Kan and Hayes 1994). Ryback (1990) and other observers have cited the significance of rock music beginning in the 1950s and continuing throughout the Soviet era. Its popularity has not waned since the fall of the Berlin Wall, although other genres like dance and alternative music have increased alongside rock music as being significant in people's lives. Every country has had its share of local artists performing music ranging from punk and heavy metal to rap and techno. Rock in particular was very popular among Central and Eastern European youths, with most preferring Western-style rock to any other musical genre (Sasinska-Klas 1993). Today one might simply assume that this is because of the power of Western culture industries to cross geographic boundaries with ease, but it was popular during the Soviet era more because of "its relation to the formation of both individual and collective 'counteridentities' within the context of social industrial society" (Cushman 1995: 89). Over the last quarter-century, rap, rave, and other genres have functioned in similar ways (see Bennett 2001).

Popular music plays a complicated yet critical role in times of social change, as "it helps to construct the nation state while at the same time being constructed by it" (Lipsitz 1994: 138). Accordingly, rock music has served as a political medium during the cyclical episodes of economic and political unrest that marked Central and Eastern Europe's history under communism, especially as an instrument of protest. Rock music did not protest *directly* against authorities, but "instead, it was focused upon broad, 'existential' or 'all-human' universal issues in a post-hippie style" (Pekacz 1992: 205). On the one hand, many people wanted to experience Western culture, whether music or otherwise, and thus Western music became a problem for socialist states to deal with. The Russian and other governments dealt with young people's desire for Western popular music first in terms of a "victims of Western influence" epidemic. Later, after largely accepting the popularity of rock music, those in authority sought to limit access to its "worst excesses" (Pilkington 1994: 106). On the other hand, and alongside the imposition of stricter controls of populations in the 1980s, socialist governments used rock music to co-opt potentially revolutionary feelings among youths by injecting rock lyrics and icons with pro-socialist ideologies. Yet, if there is one truism about globalization, it is that its effects are relatively inevitable. Despite attempts by government leaders and other moral entrepreneurs, rock, punk, heavy resulted in an explosion of the amount, quality, and diversity of popular music available to young people. The emergence of Western-style, mall-like music stores in all major cities brought CDs into the marketplace. Major record companies like Sony and Warner Music are distributing not only CDs and MP3 downloads, but investing in local talent for eventual global marketing as well. Consequently, the styles of popular music available to young people have expanded in at least three ways. First, they now have instant access to all the popular music via the global digital market. The traditional time lag between popularity in primary versus secondary markets has virtually disappeared. Central and Eastern Europeans no longer have to rely on Voice of America to broadcast popular American music, nor do they have to rely on poor-quality bootleg cassette tape recordings. Second, local artists have the tools (culturally and technologically) to create new local forms of music derived from the global music sphere. For example, one can easily find Polish gangsta rap, Russian "boy bands," and Serbian thrash metal. Third, these artists renegotiate the form, content, and style of incoming music in ways that often retain links to more traditional music. Cabaret music, performed in melancholy or torch style by a singer accompanied by piano or some other very simple instrumentation, was traditionally very popular in Poland, for example, and has remained so, as seen in the performances of Anna Maria Jopek and others. There are other indicators of globalizing processes of popular music. The market for teen music magazines, largely from Germany, exploded in the 1990s as entrepreneurs began publishing local-language versions of them. Bands and artists from around the world now regularly tour the region, while local bands also tour Western Europe and elsewhere. Before 1990, such opportunities were very rare because of the weak prospects of economic success for such ventures, even in cases where bands or artists were allowed to cross borders in the first place. Now, the European summer months are filled with festivals from Zagreb to Budapest to St. Petersburg, and middle-class kids, flush with cash, are able and willing to travel to see their favorite acts.

It is not only the middle class that benefits from economic change. During visits to Poland in 1992 and 2000, Joe Kotarba talked to teens who were already experiencing both the high expectations associated with democratization and, to a more modest degree, the early economic rewards of capitalization. The important point is that their musical experiences had become very diverse.

The Center in Wrocław was an afternoon and weekend place for teens to visit when they were not in school. These teens came from working-class families in rural areas in the Silesian or southwestern section of Poland and were sent to Wrocław to attend high school. They lived either in dormitories or with host families. Since they lived away from their own families, they were often lonely and emotionally "uneasy," as one young man put it, and used popular music as a source of comfort during times of loneliness. The boys at the Center preferred Western heavy metal music such as Queensrÿche and AC/DC. They related to this music because it fit homologically with their own focal concerns, such as family strife and economic hardship, conflict with teachers, problems with drugs, and so forth. Like their American counterparts, Polish headbangers listened to speed metal music, such as Slayer and Metallica, as a way of relieving everyday life stress. The working-class girls at the Center tended toward dance music, especially female artists such as Madonna and Destiny's Child. They not only appreciated songs about love and relationships, but they paid close attention to the fashion and style trends highlighted by these stars.

When Joe Kotarba talked to these teens about their favorite songs, they generally indicated a preference for songs about relationships, parents, adults, morality, and personal problems, regardless of the genre or style of music to which the kids were committed. The Polish rock song cited most frequently as the kids' favorite was "For Ann," by the group Kult, which they indicated is a song about boyfriends and girlfriends. Another favorite song was "Autobiography," mentioned above, which the kids said was about the complexity of growing up. One 16-year-old boy had been living in a high-school dormitory for three months. He indicated that the song functioned almost like a good friend for him: "I like the song because I have the same kinds of dreams. My life is like the song . . . It warns against certain things in life. It helps me get over melancholy feelings." Interestingly, this boy's interpretation of the theme of "Autobiography" was very different from Kan and Hayes's (1994) political interpretation of the same song, as cited above.

One of the very powerful features of popular music, in this case heavy metal music, was the open horizon of meaning in its songs. The intensive use of metaphoric imagery allowed listeners to interpret the song and apply the feelings of the music to their personal needs in everyday life. In the movement toward capitalism, these personal needs supplanted political needs, and thus, in at least one respect, Polish teens and American teens were becoming more alike through their music consumption (Kotarba 1994a).

By 2000, working-class teens' tastes in music had changed, much like they had in North America. Interest in heavy metal music in general had become limited to two themes. First, the teenage boys Kotarba talked with in Katowice now enjoyed "death metal" music, a style of heavy metal music spiced with lyrics drawn from the imagery of horror films. Such extreme metal was somewhat available to Polish kids in the late 1980s, but its widespread availability by 2000 reflected the effects of globalization. Like their counterparts in the West, working-class boys in Poland were most excited about rap music and rock integrated with rap (e.g., Linkin Park). The meaning of rap music had changed considerably since 1992. Then, the kids he talked with from all backgrounds were fascinated by rap music, including Ice Cube, Ice-T, Public Enemy, and Sister Souljah. The working-class boys were especially drawn to rap because of its rhythmic power at high volume, but also because of its apparent function as a window to ever-intriguing American issues such as race and ethnic relations. Drawing on knowledge that bridged metal and rap genres, they were familiar with the political controversy over the Ice-T song "Cop Killer." They were very anxious to talk to Kotarba about the Rodney King affair in Los Angeles. A common interpretation of the Polish news media coverage of these phenomena was that the United States is racked by racial violence, and that rap music is the distinct voice of politically disenfranchised and militant African-American youth.

The working-class boys Kotarba talked with in 2000 appreciated rap more for its lifestyle dimensions and its increasing compatibility with rock music. They all spoke well of recent Polish attempts at rap music. A universal favorite was Kazik, who was also the lead singer for the most popular band in Poland, Kult. His rap songs talked about very current political issues in Poland. For example, one song repeated the line "Lech, where are my ten million zloty?" in reference to former President Walesa's unfulfilled campaign promise to give all Polish citizens the equivalent of $667 once he was elected.

Both boys and girls from the working class showed great interest in a major element of social class cultural conflict in Poland—"disco polo," a very simple, if not primitive, form of disco music unique to the Polish media. There were television programs in Poland devoted to hours of broadcasting disco polo videos. To an American observer, disco polo music videos would come across as almost a parody of American youth culture. The lyrics were almost childlike, but contained a bit of sexual overtone. The music videos were basically about having fun, typically involving groups of young people, either partying at the beach, riding around in convertibles, or dancing at discos. The kids Kotarba talked to noted the globalizing characteristics of disco polo. For example, a 19-year-old girl who regularly patronized a popular disco in Kraków with her friends noted: "I like disco polo because it's fun. We like to dance and disco polo is fun to dance to ... The videos show us how young people in America have fun. They're lucky: lots of beaches to party on. We don't have beaches like that here in Poland." Working-class teens in Poland still depended primarily on radio and television for their music and their views of the West. In line with studies of other Central and Eastern European youths, these findings suggest that taste and experience with popular music among teens from the former "Second World" has evolved as their lives were impacted by globalization. Young people from all backgrounds voiced familiarity with pop music from Germany, techno dance music from Denmark, and death/black metal from the Baltic. Although they were not limited to American music as their primary source of Western teen culture, they still desired and admired American popular culture in general. In a then-timely New York Times (1994: 31) article, a list of the most popular American movies, television programs, and pop musical artists was compiled. The most popular American musical artists in Poland were Whitney Houston, Aerosmith, R.E.M., and Guns N' Roses—representing a fairly diverse group of styles (although all from the U.S.).

The major finding of this study was the convergence of Polish and American views on what it meant culturally to be young. This convergence can be summarized in terms of the concept of "teenager." Sociologically, "teenager" does not refer to a person, but to a status or a social identity. Hine (1999) described the history and complexity of this idea in great detail. Although the movement toward conceptualizing young people as adolescents and warehousing them in high schools can be traced at least as far back as the Great Depression, the term "teenager" gained currency after World War II and referred to the period in life between childhood and adulthood marked by high levels of leisure time (Frith 1981). Widespread affluence following World War II enabled middle- and working-class families alike to survive on the parents' income, freeing adolescents from economic responsibilities. Adolescents populated high schools during the day and spent their allowances on consumer objects in the evenings and on the weekends. Young people had the opportunity to give much of their time and attention to dating, fun, and other youthful concerns. The marketing of music to teenagers addressed these concerns with Top 40 radio, 45 rpm records, sock hops, and fan clubs. Political issues did not become much of a concern to young people before the Vietnam War.

Young people in other parts of the world are experiencing cultural change similar to postwar Western teens, yet they are not likely to recreate and relive the relatively naive world of American youths in the 1950s—global cultural flows guarantee that. As capitalism has gained global momentum and market economies have taken hold, more young people experience increased leisure time. Identities based upon consumption and fun are simultaneously merging with those based upon the political need to deal with oppressive governments, the lack of available work, and other hardships in everyday life. This is a two-way process to be clear. Just as Central and Eastern European kids may be seen as experiencing increased social and cultural opportunities compared to 25 years ago, the deep (and growing deeper) economic troubles in North America and Western Europe are imprinting today's youths with fear of the future. Young people from around the world are increasingly aware of what they share with each other—a complex world that requires limited expectations and practical approaches to life. Their complex experiences of popular music reflect these social changes.

World Music Flows

As we mentioned earlier in this chapter, globalization is a multi-directional process. It is not merely about Western culture being spread outward, but about the evaporation of distinctions like "East" and "West" as the world continually shrinks with the spread of information and communication technologies.

Phillip Vannini lives on Vancouver Island, on the West Coast of British Columbia, Canada. Vancouver Island is surrounded by an archipelago of small islands up and down its eastern side, with populations ranging from 30 to 5,000. By way of ethnographic investigation he has been studying the everyday life rituals and culture of these islands for quite some time now. One of the characteristics of these islands' culture is that of a hypersensitivity to the importance of movement. Many islanders, it seems, are constantly on the move, either because they need to catch the ferry to go to school, work, or to the supermarket, or doctor's office, or because they need to, or wish to, travel farther away. The ferries that connect these islands—as the only mode of transportation on and off—are very interesting portals of their movement (Vannini 2012). The following excerpt from Phillip Vannini's field notes tells of a unique cultural expression he observed, and more precisely an element of a unique musical scene, moving through one of these ferries:

> August 2007: I have been wondering for some time now what this guy looked like in person. His picture—posted on any key bulletin board around, from the ferry's to the grocery store's—is one of a kind: smacking of a hybrid-like aura like nothing I've seen before. The Sandokan-style moustache and beard, the Jesus hairstyle, the loose Indian-style satin dress, the Yoga leg-crossover, the made-in-Kathmandu incense burning in the background that I could almost smell just by looking at the photo. And yet he looks like any ole yippie from West Vancouver who traded in his blue chip stocks for a lot of flights to Thailand and Bangalore. A few days ago, on a

different trip, I wrote down somewhere in my notes an insight into what he does: he does the world. Under the aegis of aural meditation, sonorous relaxation, and soundscape-production what he does is no different from what any minor rock band on a world tour does: he is a small-scale global merchant of culture. He's on the ferry today. Even he has to take the ferry to come over to the island. I'd better go over and talk to him. I'm curious to see what he's all about.

"How's it going, man?"—I open up.

"Beautiful sky, isn't it?"—he replies.

"I heard about your upcoming performance. Sorry I won't be able to make it on that day."

"Are you into the many musical styles of the world?"

"Only when they are into me."

We both laugh at my stupid joke. We begin to talk. He is a world music connoisseur, though he wouldn't say it like that. He's a healer, a mystic, and a student of the enchanting powers of polyharmonic music. He put it like that. His "show"—forgive the shorthand—is about involving his audience into a collective state of higher awareness of the senses of olfaction and hearing, as well as the sixth and seventh senses. By awakening people through his own fusion music, and his favorite world music tunes as well, he leads them into transporting their selves out of their bodies into a collective state of ecstatic, harmonious being. He's on a "tour" of the Gulf Islands of the Strait of Georgia. Not too far from where he tells me he was born: North Vancouver. I was close.

"A lot of people come to these shows?"—I inquire.

"Given the low number of souls who live on these small islands, yes. In relative terms this area is incredibly into different musical styles and diverse spiritual experiences."

I know the answer to the next question, but I want to hear it from him: "Why is that?"

"Well, a lot of people who live around here are global nomads. Many are draft dodgers from the U.S., from the hippie era, you know? A lot of them are continental Europeans who left the old continent in search of a closer connection with land and waterscape. Some are older Canadians who want to slow down their life's pace. And just about all of them are global travelers by lifestyle, very in tune with the possibility that their lifestyle is not the only lifestyle in the world, you know?"

Do we ever? Vannini lives around here. He fits boxes number two and four in the list. So, what's a nice African drumbeat doing in a cold and rainy place like this, one might wonder? What is the truthfulness of a Hindu-style aural meditation experience when it's rigidly scheduled from 5:30 to 6:45 p.m. at the community center, right after the kids' kayak lesson and right before the only Sushi takeout place on the island closes for the night? And what is the authenticity of a soundscape that fuses the rhythms of cultures as separate as Sufi, Tuva, Tibet, and Sumatra? Those are good questions. Yet, the most obvious answer, one that points to the phoniness of all of this, would entirely miss the point.

That's what Vannini's new "friend" has done (though he doesn't assume to know all the details). He is part of a group that calls themselves, as does D'Andrea (2007), "global nomads"—mostly white men and women who use music alongside a host of other cultural phenomena as part of a project of countercultural identity work. Some of them get heavily into techno music, while others are more eclectic in their tastes. What they share is an interest in non-Western "world music"— music that is created and played by indigenous musicians, and which remains closely related to the music of the regions of their origin (Nidel 2004). They see music as a key component of freeing the mind and body from the many problems associated with everyday life in modern times, such as stress, anger and violence, physical and mental illness.

Global nomads are contradictory in nature, supporting the sociological argument that they represent globalization in terms of hybridization. On the one hand, their embrace of "Eastern" philosophies and lifestyles signifies a rejection of or wish to minimize contact with the modern urban (Western) societies from whence they come and the culture industries that are their lifeblood. Yet, on the other hand, they are often people who have the educational, economic, social, and cultural capital necessary to spend a good deal of their time traveling or otherwise avoiding "normal life." In such a role, they are actually quite enmeshed in the process of globalization as they carry bits of culture to various parts of the world, bringing their white, Western culture to the Mediterranean or South Asia (or wherever) and then exchanging some of that culture for bits of clothing, music, relaxation techniques, and so on, which they then bring back to sell (maybe on islands off the western coast of Canada) to sustain their nomadic lifestyles. This way of viewing the man on the ferry paints him in an unfavorable light—a white guy trying to perform the role of an Indian guru. More broadly, this is one of the reasons why world music as a genre is seen by some as inauthentic. World music—that pastiche of sounds from every corner of the globe (often in compilation CDs that feature nameless artists and tracks titled only after cliché descriptions of the effect they intend to evoke in the listener) that is found in a special section of your favorite music store—is but an invention of the global culture industries. It shelves together musical expressions alien to one another and alien to their audiences, simply for the purpose of seducing potential buyers into a safe aural exploration of the globe. Think of it as a musical zoo, which one visits much like one would visit an animal zoo: by experiencing decontextualized realities with no relation to one another or to the place where they have been forcefully assembled.

This view has some historical evidence on its side. The expression "world music" dates back to 1987, when record company executives met in London to examine ways of marketing popular music from many part of the world to British audiences. "World music" became a catch-all expression, a marketing ploy also imitated in German-speaking (*Weltbeat*) and French markets (*musique mondiale*). In 1991, *Billboard* devised a chart of its own for world music, and a Grammy category was formed. From there on, the commercialization of world music can be seen as a textbook exercise in the social construction of meaning. As Pacini-Hernandez (1993: 50) has noted, world music is "a marketing term describing the products of musical cross-fertilisation between the north—the US and Western Europe—and south—primarily Africa and the Caribbean basin ... established specifically to cultivate and nurture the appetites of First World listeners for exotic new sounds from the Third World." Similarly critical is Erlmann (1996: 474), who notes that the term world music "displays a peculiar, self-congratulatory pathos: a mesmerizing formula for a new business venture, a kind of shorthand figure for a new—albeit fragmented—global economic reality with alluring commercial prospects." Those who argue for the inauthenticity of world music point to the forceful appropriation enacted by the West. Consuming distant musical styles, this argument goes, demands that distal musical performers and performances be packaged as premodern, natural, exotic, and raw. The forced convergence of these sounds not only results in their commodification, but also in their displacement, fetishization, and marginalization. It is no accident that the marketing of world music also involves the marketing of New Age practices that promise new experiences for Western bodies: from transcendence to meditation, from somatic exploration to unchoreographed dance and movement, together with the self-help books and merchandise that accompany these adventures in alternative shopping. Indeed, as the critical argument insightfully goes, the world of African souls and Asian healers is one closer to the bodily, animal element, and more distant from the typically white and European rational mind and thus appealing to the fetishizing gaze of the latter (Gilroy 1993).

It is difficult for many to reconcile the contradictions of the hybridized culture surrounding world music. How can one actively engage with the sounds of exotic foreign societies in order to find some authentic sense of self that is, it is argued, buried by the great weight of global social processes? And yet a simple dismissal of world music is problematic as well, because to do so signifies a failure to understand it as a phenomenon that is based not only on production and consumption, but on everyday life experiences of human beings. The communal rituals of peace and harmony led by white gurus, as well as the drug-saturated techno trance parties held in places like Ibiza, depict "a rare density of multinational and expressive elements gathering at the margins of a [society. These marginal spaces] appear as a node of transnational flows of exoticized peoples, practices and imaginaries whose circulation and hybridization across remote locations suggests a globalized phenomenon" (D'Andrea 2007: 2–3). Rather than reduce them to facile wannabes, the global nomads may instead be seen as countercultural agents of social change. Using global networks to their advantage, they seek out similar others with whom they may form close emotional bonds and then collectively seek out alternative options for living in postmodern societies. This is a characteristic of globalization: "the emergence of reflexive and fundamentalist forms of social organization and identity" (2007: 11).

Music is, as previously stated, a key part of this process. Forms of techno music such as trance, jungle, and bhangra combine indigenous music with digital sounds, melding "authentic" world music with entrancing beats that create the ritual atmosphere necessary for reflexivity and cultivation of the self. World music, driven by soothing sounds rather than pumping bass beats, also serves important functions for global nomads. So, let us go back to the production, distribution, and consumption of the fusion-driven soundscapes that are prepared for the aural meditation of island-dwelling Western Canadians and others seeking a more authentic sense of self through New Age and other postmodern spiritual scenes. Is there a trick being played on them, or is it an opportunity for them to connect authentically with a new musical experience? As a few of these islanders say, the opportunity to live their life in the place and community of their choice and engage in the lifestyle they prefer to practice is a deeply mean-ingful one. Music, as well as other visual and performance arts, plays an important role in their lives and communities . . . and so does respect for other cultures and the environment in which they live. These are people who are aware of the hybrid character of their small island societies. For many of them, connecting to the sounds of Punjabi or Nepali folk song brings them back to the times when in their young adulthood they danced as hippies in Haight-Ashbury in San Francisco or on Freak Street in downtown Kathmandu. For others, meditation and relaxation with the sounds of the island of Sumatra is a natural choice when the relaxing sounds and sights of their own small island life surround them daily. For others, understanding the melancholic melodies of diasporic sounds comes easy when they, too, are the sons and daughters of diaspora and expatriation. In sum, the possibility that a musical expression may be authentically experienced is there despite the distance that sometimes separates them from the music's origin.

Musical hybridity is an increasingly common feature in the global-ized 21st century. The movement of migrants, refugees, expatriates, nomads, and diasporic people, and the consequent movement of their cultural rituals and expressions alongside with them, as well as the increased flows of culture due to the more advanced communication technologies now available, have contributed to changing meanings of time and space, and thus to the formation of a heterophonic global musical scene in which traditional mainstream music genres are more and more often found lacking when trying to describe the music being listened to. Music, thanks to the potential for fluid cross-cultural communication that its sonorous qualities offer, opens up spaces where personal and cultural experiences may occur even when its production and distribution dynamics are enacted by large-scale multinational configurations.

Conclusion

Moments in time and space—trips to Poland and to Nepal, a conversation during a ferry ride home—provide us with micro-level views of globalization and social change. Of course, globalization is partly about macro-level interactions among nations and multinational corporations, but it is also embodied in personal experiences. We are surrounded by opportunities to reflect on the effects of music and other global media as we move about our everyday lives. Driving in the car listening to songs from the past, sampling music from around the world on the Internet, dancing in a foreign club while on vacation, and talking to others about our musical tastes are all examples that represent globalization. As our examples have shown, in the case of popular music globalization manifests itself through myriad styles and performances, of localities, identities, and outlooks on life. What the study of popular music—perhaps better than any other sociological topic—can contribute to a sociological understanding of globalization is a fresh perspective on the deep interconnections of movements of media cultures, technologies, ideas, and people. Musical scenes, arguably more than anything else, force us to play and listen locally and interact globally. In conclusion, what we have attempted to show is that globalization, as Robertson has remarked, is "a very long, uneven and complicated process" (1992: 10).

In this chapter we have discussed globalization and social change as unavoidable aspects of contemporary life. We examined both concepts from a perspective that puts a premium on the processes and everyday experience. Globalization is not synonymous with standardization, with imperialism, or with the colonization of the globe by the West. Rather, globalization can be better understood as a mixing of the global and the local—a phenomenon sometimes called glocalization—which renews the importance of locality at the expense of sameness and universality while positing the local as the true intersecting node of global flows. Globalization has to do with transformations of societies, cultures, and people that were previously thought of as bounded to narrowly defined geographic communities into hybrid networks of ideas, symbols, discourses, and practices. This new global order is one based on disjunctions (Appadurai 1996), and one that "is becoming increasingly decentered—not under the control of any group of nations, and still less of the large corporations" (Giddens 2000: 34). Importantly, the role that music plays in the processes of globalization and social change can be seen to occur in people's everyday experiences.

REFERENCES

Adorno, Theodor. 1949. *The Philosophy of Modern Music*. New York: Seabury Press.

Adorno, Theodor and Robert Hullot-Kentor. 2006. *Philosophy of New Music*. Minneapolis: University of Minnesota Press.

Appadurai, Arjun. 1996. *Modernity at Large: Cultural Dimensions of Globalization*. Minneapolis: University of Minnesota Press.

Balliger, Robin. 1999. "Politics." In Bruce Horner and Thomas Swiss (eds.), *Key Terms in Popular Music and Culture*, pp. 54–63. New York: Blackwell.

Banfield, William C. 2010. *Cultural Codes: Makings of a Black Music Philosophy*. Lanham, MD: Scarecrow Press.

Barnes, Ken. 1988. "Top 40 Radio: A Fragment of the Imagination." In S. Frith (ed.), *Facing the Music*, pp. 8–50. New York: Pantheon.

Baudrillard, Jean. 1983. *Simulations*. New York: Simeotext.

Baur, Bernard. 2011. John Michael Talbot: Biography. http://www.johnmichaeltalbot.com/biography.php.

Becker, Howard. 1986. *Doing Things Together: Selected Papers*. Evanston, IL: Northwestern University Press.

Becker, Howard. 1982. *Art Worlds*. Berkeley: University of California Press.

Becker, Howard. 1963. *Outsiders*. New York: Free Press.

Bendix, Reinhard. 1978. *Max Weber: An Intellectual Portrait*. Berkeley: University of California Press.

Benjamin, Walter. 1969. *Illuminations*. New York: Schocken.

Bennett, Andy. 2001. *Cultures of Popular Music*. Buckingham, UK: Open University Press.

Bennett, Andy and Richard A. Peterson. 2004. *Music Scenes*. Nashville, TN: Vanderbilt University Press.

Berendt, Joachim E. 1982. *The Jazz Book: From Ragtime to Fusion and Beyond*, trans. H. Bredigkeit and B. Bredigkeit with Dan Morgenstern. Brooklyn, NY: Lawrence Hill Books.

Berger, Peter. 1967. *The Sacred Canopy: Elements of a Sociological Theory of Religion*. Garden City, NY: Doubleday.

Billboard. n.d. "Adele Rules 2011 with Top Selling Album and Song." January 4, 2012. Retrieved September 10, 2012 from http://www.billboard.com/#/news/adele-rules-2011-with-top-selling-album-1005784152.story.

Bloom, Allan. 1987. *The Closing of the American Mind*. New York: Simon and Schuster.

Blumer, Herbert. 1969. *Symbolic Interactionism: Perspective and Method*. Englewood Cliffs, NJ: Prentice-Hall.

Braunstein, Peter. 1999. "Disco." *American Heritage Magazine*, 50(7). Available online at http://www.americanheritage.com/content/november-1999.

Bull, Michael. 2000. *Sounding out the City: Personal Stereos and the Management of Everyday Life*. Oxford and New York: Berg.

Burgess, Ernest W. 1926. "The Family as a Unit of Interacting Personalities." *Family*, 7: 3–9.

Canclini, Nestor Garcia. 1995. *Hybrid Cultures: Strategies for Entering and Leaving Modernity*. Minneapolis: University of Minnesota Press.

Carey, James W. 1992. *Communication as Culture*. New York: Routledge.

Chanan, Michael. 1995. *Repeated Takes: A Short History of Recording and Its Effects on Music*. New York: Verso.

Clair, Jeffrey, David Karp, and William Yoels. 1993. *Experiencing the Life Cycle*. Springfield, IL: Charles Thomas.

Clarke, John, Stuart Hall, Tony Jefferson, and Brian Roberts. 1976. "Subcultures, Cultures, and Class." In Stuart Hall and Tony Jefferson (eds.), *Resistance through Rituals*, pp. 9–74. London: Routledge.

Cohen, Stanley. 2002 [1972]. *Folk Devils and Moral Panics*, 3rd edn. London: Routledge.

Coleman, James S. 1961. *The Adolescent Society*. Glencoe, IL: The Free Press.

Condry, Ian. 1999. "The Social Production of Difference: Imitation and Authenticity in Japanese Rap Music." In Heide Fehrenbach and Uta G. Poiger (eds.), *Transactions, Transgressions, Transformations: American Culture in Western Europe and Japan*, pp. 166–184. Providence, RI: Berghahn.

Connell, R. W. 1987. *Masculinities*. Berkeley: University of California Press.

Constellation Records. n.d. Retrieved September 16, 2012 from http://web.archive.org/web/20060112192254/http://www.cstrecords.com/html/manifesto.html.

Copes, Heith and J. Patrick Williams. 2007. "Techniques of Affirmation: Deviant Behavior, Moral Commitment, and Subcultural Identity." *Deviant Behavior*, 28(3): 247–272.

Copes, Heith, Andy Hochstetler, and J. Patrick Williams. 2008. "'We Weren't Like No Regular Dope Fiends': Negotiating Hustler and Crackhead Identities." *Social Problems*, 55(2): 254–270.

Cummings, Sue. 1994. " 'Welcome to the Machine': The Techno Music Revolution Comes to Your Town." *Rolling Stone*, April 7: 15–16.

Cushman, Thomas. 1995. *Notes from the Underground: Rock Music Counterculture in Russia*. Albany: State University of New York Press.

D'Andrea, Anthony. 2007. *Global Nomads: Techno and New Age as Transnational Countercultures in Ibiza and Goa*. London: Routledge.

Davis, Joanna. 2006. "Growing up Punk: Negotiating Ageing Identity in a Local Music Scene." *Symbolic Interaction*, 29: 63–69.

DeNora. Tia. 2003. *After Adorno: Rethinking Music Sociology*. Cambridge: Cambridge University Press.

DeNora, Tia. 2000. *Music in Everyday Life*. Cambridge: Cambridge University Press.

Dimaggio, Paul and Toqir Mukhtar. 2004. "Arts Participation as Cultural Capital in the United States, 1982–2002: Signs of Decline?" *Poetics*, 32: 169–194.

Douglas, Jack D. 1984. "The Emergence, Security, and Growth of the Sense of Self." In Joseph A. Kotarba and Andrea Fontana (eds.), *The Existential Self and Society*, pp. 69–99. Chicago, IL: University of Chicago Press.

Douglas, Jack D. 1976. *Investigative Social Research: Individual and Team Field Research*. Beverly Hills, CA: Sage.

Durkheim, Emile. 1953. *Sociology and Philosophy*. New York: Free Press.

Erlmann, V. 1996. "The Aesthetics of the Global Imagination: Reflections on World Music in the 1990s." *Public Culture*, 8: 467–487.

Ferris, Kerry and Jill Stein. 2011. *The Real World: An Introduction to Sociology*, 3rd edn. New York: W. W. Norton.

Fine, Gary A. 1979. "Small Groups and Culture Creation: The Idioculture of Little League Baseball Teams." *American Sociological Review*, 44: 733–745.

Fletcher, Andrew. 1997 [1703]. *Conversation Concerning a Right Regulation of Governments for the Common Good of Mankind*. New York: Columbia University Press.

Florida, Richard. 2002. *The Rise of the Creative Class*. New York: Basic Books.

Foucault, Michel. 1990. *The History of Sexuality: An Introduction*. New York: Vintage.

Friedlander, P. 1996. *Rock'n'Roll*. Boulder, CO: Westview Press.

Frith, Simon. 2002. "Music and Everyday Life." *Critical Quarterly*, 44: 35–48.

Frith, Simon. 1991. "Anglo-America and Its Discontents." *Cultural Studies*, 5: 261–273.

Frith, Simon. 1981. *Sound Effects*. New York: Pantheon.

Fuller, Richard and Richard Myers. 1940. "The Natural History of a Social Problem." *American Sociological Review*, 6: 320–329.

Furstenberg, Frank. 1991. *Divided Families*. Cambridge, MA: Harvard University Press.

Garfinkel, Harold. 1967. *Studies in Ethnomethodology*. Englewood Cliffs, NJ: Prentice-Hall.

Gecas, Viktor. 1981. "Contexts of Socialization." In Morris Rosenberg and Ralph H. Turner (eds.), *Social Psychology: Sociological Perspectives*, pp. 165–199. New York: Basic Books.

Giddens, Anthony. 2000. *Runaway World*. New York: Routledge.

Giddens, Anthony. 1991. *Modernity and Self-Identity: Self and Society in Late-Modern Age*. New York: Polity Press.

Gilroy, Paul. 1993. *The Black Atlantic: Modernity and Double Consciousness*. Cambridge, MA: Harvard University Press.

Goffman, Erving. 1959. *The Presentation of Self in Everyday Life*. Garden City, NY: Doubleday.

Green, Andy. 2012. "Carly Rae Jepsen: 'I Want to Do Justin Bieber Proud.'" *Rolling Stone*, June 1.

Grossberg, Lawrence. 1992a. "Rock'n'Roll in Search of an Audience." In James Lull (ed.), *Popular Music and Communication*, pp. 152–175. Newbury Park, CA: Sage.

Grossberg, Lawrence. 1992b. *We Gotta Get Out of This Place*. New York: Routledge.

Gruenwald, David A. 2003. "Foundations of Place: A Multidisciplinary Framework for Place-Conscious Education." *American Educational Research Journal*, 40(3): 619–654.

Hall, Stuart. 1968. *The Hippies: An American "Moment."* Birmingham: Center for Contemporary Cultural Studies, University of Birmingham.

Hall, Stuart and Tony Jefferson. 1977. *Resistance Through Rituals, Youth Subcultures in Post-War Britain*. London: Hutchinson.

Hannerz, Ulf. 1987. "The World in Creolization." *Africa*, 57: 546–559.

Healy, Kieran. 2002. "What's New for Culture in the New Economy?" *Journal of Arts Management, Law, and Society*, 32(2): 86–103.

Hebdige, Dick. 1979. *Subculture: The Meaning of Style*. New York: Methuen.

Heritage, John. 1984. *Garfinkel and Ethnomethodology*. Cambridge: Polity.

Hill, Trent. 1992. "The Enemy Within: Censorship in Rock Music in the 1950s." In Anthony deCurtis (ed.), *Present Tense: Rock & Roll and Culture*, pp. 39–71. Durham, NC: Duke University Press.

Hine, Thomas. 1999. "The Rise and Decline of the Teenager." *American Heritage* (September): 71–82.

Hochschild, Arlie. 1983. *The Managed Heart*. Berkeley: University of California Press.

Holstein, James and Jaber Gubrium. 2003. "The Life Course." In Larry Reynolds and Nancy Herman-Kinney (eds.), *Handbook of Symbolic Interactionism*, pp. 835–856. Walnut Creek, CA: Alta Mira.

Huq, Rupa. 2006. *Beyond Subculture: Pop, Youth and Identity in a Postcolonial World*. London: Routledge.

Irwin, John. 1977. *Scenes*. Beverly Hills, CA: Sage.

Jameson, Frederic. 1991. *Postmodernism: Or, the Cultural Logic of Late Capitalism*. Durham, NC: Duke University Press.

Jenkins, Henry. 2008. *Convergence Culture*. New York: New York University Press.

Jones, LeRoi. 1963. *Blues People*. New York: Morrow.

Jones, Steve. 1992. *Rock Formation: Music, Technology, and Mass Communication*. Newbury Park, CA: Sage.

Kan, Alex and Nick Hayes. 1994. "Big Beat in Poland." In Sabrina Petra Ramet (ed.), *Rocking the State*, pp. 41–53. Boulder, CO: Westview Press.

Kaplan, E. Anne. 1987. *Rocking around the Clock*. New York: Routledge.

Kessler, Suzanne and Wendy McKenna. 1978. *Gender: An Ethnomethodological Approach*. New York: Wiley.

Klönne, Arno. 1995. *Jugend im Dritten Reich: Die Hitler-Jugend und ihre Gegner; Dokumente und Analysen*. Düsseldorf: Diedrichs.

Kotarba, Joseph A. 2013a. *Baby Boomer Rock'n'Roll Fans: The Music Never Ends*. New York: Scarecrow Press.

Kotarba, Joseph A. 2013b. "Towards a Sociological Model of the Pop Music Song." Paper presented at the annual meeting of the American Sociological Association, New York, August.

Kotarba, Joseph A. 2012. "Taking Chances in Everyday Life: Studying Culture Across Continents." In Andrea Salvini, Joseph A. Kotarba, and Bryce Merrill (eds.), *The Present and Future of Symbolic Interactionism*. Milan, Italy: Franco Angeli.

Kotarba, Joseph A. 2010. "The Impact of Popular Music on Symbolic Interaction: An Introduction." *Studies in Symbolic Interaction*, 35: 3–4.

Kotarba, Joseph A. 2009. " 'I'm just a Rock'n'roll Fan': Popular Music as a Meaning Resource for Aging." *Civitas*, 9(1): 118–132.

Kotarba, Joseph A. 2002a. "Rock'n'Roll Music as a Timepiece." *Symbolic Interaction*, 25: 397–404.

Kotarba, Joseph A. 2002b. "Baby Boomer Rock'n'Roll Fans and the Becoming of Self." In Joseph A. Kotarba and John M. Johnson (eds.), *Postmodern Existential Sociology*, pp. 103–126. Walnut Hills, CA: Alta Mira.

Kotarba, Joseph A. 1998. "The Commodification and Decommodification of Rock Music: Rock en Español and Rock Music in Poland." Paper presented at the annual meeting of the SSSI Couch-Stone Symposium, February 21, Houston, TX.

Kotarba, Joseph A. 1997. "Reading the Male Experience of Rock Music: Four Songs about Women." *Cultural Studies*, 2: 265–277.

Kotarba, Joseph A. 1994a. "The Postmodernization of Rock Music: The Case of Metallica." In Jonathan Epstein (ed.), *Adolescents and Their Music*, pp. 141–163. New York: Garland.

Kotarba, Joseph A. 1994b. "The Positive Functions of Rock'n'Roll Music." In Joel Best (ed.), *Troubling Children*, pp. 155–170. New York: Aldine.

Kotarba, Joseph A. 1993. "The Rave Scene in Houston, Texas: An Ethnographic Analysis." Presented at the annual meeting of the American Sociological Association, Miami, FL, August.

Kotarba, Joseph A. 1991. "Postmodernism, Ethnography and Culture." *Studies in Symbolic Interaction*, 12: 45–52.

Kotarba, Joseph A. 1987. "Adolescents and Rock'n'Roll." *Youth and Society*, 18: 323–325.

Kotarba, Joseph A. 1984. "A Synthesis: The Existential Self in Society." In A. Kotarba and A. Fontana (eds.), *The Existential Self in Society*, pp. 222–231. Chicago, IL: University of Chicago Press.

Kotarba, Joseph A. and John M. Johnson (eds.). 2002. *Postmodern Existential Sociology*. Walnut Hills, CA: Alta Mira.

Kotarba, Joseph A. and Phillip Vannini (eds.). 2006. Special issue of *Symbolic Interaction*, 26(1, Winter) on "Popular Music and Everyday Life."

Kotarba, Joseph A., Jennifer L. Fackler, and Kathryn M. Nowotny. (2009) "An Ethnography of Emerging Latino Music Scenes." *Symbolic Interaction*, 32(4): 310–333.

Leary, Timothy. 1983. *Flashback*. New York: Tarcher Books.

Lemonnier, Pierre. 1993. "Introduction." In *Technological Choices: Transformations in Material Cultures since the Neolithic*, pp. 1–35. New York: Routledge.

Levine, David. 1991. "Good Business, Bad Messages." *American Health*, May 10: 16.

Lewis, George. 1983. "The Meaning's In The Music And The Music's In Me: Popular Music As Symbolic Communication." *Theory, Culture and Society*, 1 (January): 133–141.

Light, Alan. 1992. "About a Salary or Reality: Rap's Recurrent Conflict." In Anthony DeCurtis (ed.), *Present Tense: Rock'n'Roll and Culture*, pp. 219–234. Durham, NC: Duke University Press.

Lipsitz, George. 1994. *Dangerous Crossroads*. London: Verso Press.

Lloyd, Richard. 2006. *Neo-Bohemia: Art and Commerce in the Post-Industrial City*. New York: Routledge.

Lowney, Kathleen S. 1995. "Teenage Satanism as Oppositional Youth Subculture." *Journal of Contemporary Ethnography*, 23(4, January): 453–484.

Lyman, Stanford and Marvin Scott. 1970. *A Sociology of the Absurd*. New York: Meredith.

McCreery, Scotty. n.d. "*American Idol's* Scotty McCreery OK! Interview." Retrieved August 22, 2012 from http://www.youtube.com/watch?v=SDKK21VX14k.

McLeod, Kembrew. 1999. "Authenticity Within Hip-Hop and Other Cultures Threatened with Assimilation." *Journal of Communication*, 49(4): 134–150.

McRobbie, A. 1978. "Working Class Girls and the Culture of Femininity." In CCCS Women's Study Group (eds.), *Women Take Issue*, pp. 34–54. London: Women's Study Group.

Macionis, John J. 2003. *Society: The Basics*. New York: Pearson.

Martin, Linda and Kerry Segrave. 1988. *Anti-Rock: The Opposition to Rock'n'Roll*. Hamden, CT: Da Capo Press.

Martin, Peter J. 2006. *Music and the Sociological Gaze: Art Worlds and Cultural Production*. Manchester: Manchester University Press.

Marx, Karl. 1964. *Economic and Philosophic Manuscripts of 1844*. New York: International Publishers.

Mead, George Herbert. 1934. *Mind, Self, and Society*. Chicago, IL: University of Chicago Press.

Mehan, Hugh and Houston Wood. 1975. *The Reality of Ethnomethodology*. New York: John Wiley.

Merleau-Ponty, M. 1962. *Phenomenology of Perception*. London: Routledge and Kegan Paul.

Merrill, Bryce. 2010. "Music to Remember Me By: Technologies of Memory in Home Music Recording." *Symbolic Interaction*, Summer, 33(3).

Merrill, Bryce. 2009. "Making It, not *Making It*: Creating Music in Everyday Life." In Phillip Vannini (ed.), *Material Culture and Technology in Everyday Life: Ethnographic Approaches*, pp. 193–209. New York: Peter Lang Publishing.

Middleton, Richard. 1990. *Studying Popular Music*. Philadelphia, PA: Open University Press.

Mills, C. Wright. 1959. *The Sociological Imagination*. New York: Oxford University Press.

Mills, C. Wright. 1941. "Situated Actions and Vocabularies of Motive." *American Sociological Review*, 5: 904–913.

Minor Threat. 1981. "Straight Edge." *Minor Threat* [EP]. Washington, DC: Dischord Records.

Mitchell, Tony (ed.). 2001. *Global Noise: Rap and Hip-Hop Outside the USA*. Middletown, CT: Wesleyan University Press.

Mogelonsky, Marcia. 1996. "The Rocky Road to Adulthood." *American Demographics*, 18 (May) 26–29.

Moore, Ryan. 2005. "Alternative to What? Subcultural Capital and the Commercialization of a Music Scene." *Deviant Behavior*, 26: 229–252.

Morrison, Van (2004). *Can You Feel The Silence? Van Morrison: A New Biography*. London, and Chicago, IL: Viking-Penguin and Chicago Review Press.

New York Times. 1994. "The Most Popular Lists." *New York Times*, (November 13), 31.

Nidel, Richard (2004). *World Music: The Basics*. London: Routledge.

Nowotny, Kastryn M., Jennifer L. Fackler, Gianncarlo Muschi, Carol Vargas, Lindsey Wilson, and Joseph A. Kotarba. 2010. "Established Latino Music Scenes: Sense of Place and the Challenge of Authenticity." *Studies in Symbolic Interaction*, 35: 29–50.

Obama, Barack. n.d. "The President and First Lady Announce the 2012 Launch of Veterans and Military Families for Obama." Retrieved May 17, 2012 from http://www.youtube.com/watch?v=whFecU62SyE.

Pacini-Hernandez, Deborah. 1993. "Spanish Caribbean Perspectives on World Beat." *The World of Music* (Berlin), 35: 48–69.

Pareles, Jon. 1988. "Heavy Metal, Weighty Words." *New York Times Magazine*, July 10: 26–27.

Parsons, Talcott. 1949. *Essays in Sociological Theory, Pure and Applied*. Glencoe, IL: The Free Press.

Pekacz, Joseph. 1992. "On Some Dilemmas of Polish Post-Communist Rock Music in Eastern Europe." *Popular Music*, 11(2): 205–208.

Peterson, Richard A. and Andy Bennett. 2004. *Music Scenes*. Nashville, TN: Vanderbilt University Press.

Pilkington, Hilary. 1994. *Russia's Youth and Its Culture: A Nation's Constructors and Constructed*. London: Routledge.

Playing for Change. n.d. Retrieved September 16, 2012 from playingforchange.org.

Psathas, George. 1973. *Phenomenological Sociology: Issues and Applications*. New York: Wiley.

Riesman, David 1950. *The Lonely Crowd*. New Haven, CT: Yale University Press.

Ritzer, George, 2011. *Sociological Theory*, 8th edn. New York: McGraw-Hill.

Ritzer, George. 1993. *The McDonaldization of Society*. New York: Pine Forge Press.

Robertson, Roland. 1992. *Globalization: Social Theory and Global Culture*. London: Sage.

Rolling Stone. 2010. "500 Greatest Albums of All Time." Retrieved July 1, 2010 from rollingstone.com.

Romanowski, William D. 2001. *Eyes Wide Open: Looking for God in Popular Culture*. Grand Rapids, MI: Brazos Press.

Rose, Tricia. 1994. *Black Noise: Rap Music and Black Culture in Contemporary America*. Middletown, CT: Wesleyan University Press.

Rosenbaum, Jill L. and Lorraine Prinsky. 1991. "The Presumption of Influence: Recent Responses to Popular Music Subcultures." *Crime and Delinquency*, 37(4): 528–535.

Ross, H. (Dir.). 1984. *Footloose*. Paramount Pictures.

Rowe, Laurel and Gray Cavender. 1991. "Caldrons Bubble, Satan's Trouble, but Witches Are Okay: Media Constructions of Satanism and Witchcraft." In James T. Richardson, Joel Best, and David G. Bromley (eds.), *The Satanism Scare*, pp. 263–275. New York: Aldine de Gruyter.

Ryback, Timothy W. 1990. *Rock Around the Block: A History of Rock Music in Eastern Europe and the Soviet Union*. New York: Oxford University Press.

Sandstrom, Kent L., Daniel D. Martin, and Gary Alan Fine. 2006. *Symbols, Selves, and Social Reality*, 2nd edn. Los Angeles, CA: Roxbury.

Sargent, Carey. 2010. "Noise in Action: The Sonic (De)Construction of Art Worlds." *Studies in Symbolic Interaction*, 35(1): 179–200.

Sartre, Jean-Paul. 1945. *The Age of Reason*. Paris: Gallimard.

Sasinska-Klas, Teresa (ed.). 1993. *Beyond Solidarnosc: Essays on Poland's Past and Present.* Guelph, Ontario: Guelph University Press.

Scott, Marvin B. and Stanford Lyman. 1975. "Accounts." In Dennis Brissett and Charles Edgley (eds.), *Life as Theater: A Dramaturgical Sourcebook,* pp. 171–191. Chicago, IL: Aldine.

Seay, D. and M. Neely. 1986. *Stairway to Heaven.* New York: Ballantine.

Shank, Barry. 1994. *Dissonant Identities: The Rock'n'Roll Scene in Austin, Texas.* Boston, MA: Wesleyan University Press.

Sheffield, Rob. 2007. *Love is a Mix Tape: Life and Loss, One Song at a Time.* New York: Three Rivers Press.

Shuker, Roy. 2001. *Popular Music: The Key Concepts.* New York: Routledge.

Sinofsky, Bruce. 1996. Documentary film. *Paradise Lost: The Child Murders at Robin Hood Hills.* New York: New Video Group.

Small, Adam and Peter Stuart. 1982. *Another State of Mind* [film]. Los Angeles, CA: Better Youth Organization.

Sokolowski, Robert. 2000. *Introduction to Phenomenology.* Cambridge: Cambridge University Press.

Stahl, Matthew Wheelock. 2004. "A Moment Like This: *American Idol* and Narratives of Meritocracy." In Christopher Washburne and Maiken Derno (eds.), *Bad Music: The Music We Love to Hate,* pp. 212–233. New York: Routledge.

Sterne, Jonathan. 2003. *The Audible Past: Cultural Origins of Sound Reproduction.* Durham, NC: Duke University Press.

Szemere, Anna. 2001. *Up From the Underground: The Cutlure of Rock Music in Postsocialist Hungary.* University Park, PA: Pennsylvania State University Press.

Talbot, John Michael. 1999. *The Music of Creation.* Collegeville, MN: Liturgical Press.

Taylor, Timothy. 2001. *Strange Sounds: Music, Technology, and Culture.* New York: Routledge.

Theberge, Paul. 1997. *Any Sound You Can Imagine: Making Music/Consuming Technology.* Hanover, NE: Wesleyan University Press.

Tilly, Christopher. 2001. "Ethnography and Material Culture." In Paul Atkinson, A. Coffey, S. Delamonnt, J. Lofland, and L. Lofland (eds.), *Handbook of Ethnography,* pp. 258–272. Thousand Oaks, CA: Sage.

Vannini, Phillip. 2012. *Ferry Tales: An Ethnography of Mobility, Place, and Time on Canada's West Coast.* New York: Routledge.

Vannini, Phillip (ed.). 2009. *Material Culture and Technology in Everyday Life.* New York: Peter Lang Publishing.

Vannini, Phillip. 2008. "Social Semiotics." In Michael H. Jacobsen (ed.), *Sociology of the Unnoticed: An Introduction to the Sociologies of Everyday Life.* London: Palgrave Macmillan.

Vannini, Phillip and J. Patrick Williams (eds.). 2009. *Authenticity in Self, Culture and Society.* Aldershot, UK: Ashgate.

Wallace, Claire and Raimund Alt. 2001. "Youth Cultures under Authoritarian Regimes: The Case of the Swings against the Nazis." *Youth and Society,* 32(3): 275–302.

Walser, Robert. 1993. *Running with the Devil: Power, Gender and Madness in Heavy Metal Music.* Middletown, CT: Wesleyan University Press.

Weinstein, Deena. 1991. *Heavy Metal: A Cultural Sociology.* New York: Lexington.

West, Candace and Don Zimmerman. 2002. "Doing Gender." In Stevi Jackson and Sue Scott (eds.), *Gender: A Sociological Reader,* pp. 42–47. New York: Routledge.

Wikipedia contributors. n.d. "Wigger." Retrieved August 10, 2004 from *Wikipedia, The Free Encyclopedia,* http://en.wikipedia.org/wiki/Wigger.

Williams, J. Patrick. 2011. *Subcultural Theory: Traditions and Methods.* Cambridge: Polity Press.

Williams, J. Patrick. 2010. "Music, Symbolic Interaction, and Study Abroad." *Studies in Symbolic Interaction,* 35(1): 223–240.

Williams, J. Patrick. 2009. "The Multidimensionality of Resistance in Youth-Subcultural Studies." *Resistance Studies*, 2(1): 20–33.

Williams, J. Patrick. 2006. "Authentic Identities: Straightedge Subculture, Music, and the Internet." *Journal of Contemporary Ethnography*, 35(2): 173–200.

Williams, J. Patrick and Heith Copes. 2005. "'How Edge Are You?' Constructing Authentic Identities and Subcultural Boundaries in a Straightedge Internet Forum." *Symbolic Interaction*, 28(1): 67–89.

Williams, Wendy M. 1998. "Do Parents Matter?" *Chronicle of Higher Education*, 45 (December 11): B6–B7.

Willis, Paul E. 1978. *Profane Culture*. London: Routledge and Kegan Paul.

Wilson, Stan Le Roy. 1989. *Mass Media/Mass Culture*. New York: Random House.

Yalom, Irvin. 1978. *Existential Psychotherapy*. New York: Basic Books.

Zietz, Jessica. n.d. "Avril Lavigne: Rising Star or Rising Asshole?" Retrieved September 23, 2012 from http://avrilsucks.tripod.com/al/id9.html.

Zurcher, Louis. 1977. *The Mutable Self*. Beverly Hills, CA: Sage.

INDEX

'Our song'

The 4 "Big Songs" (A) — was there a 5th?

Is Music a (B) social problem? — find example, was it?

(C) Oppositional youth movement! P87 (create a line of questions)

— Saddest song
— Angry Song
— funny song
— Best Love song

identity

(D) Music-based hedonism

→ Have them choose genres? (offer a list)